Rick Stein's
Fruits of the Sea

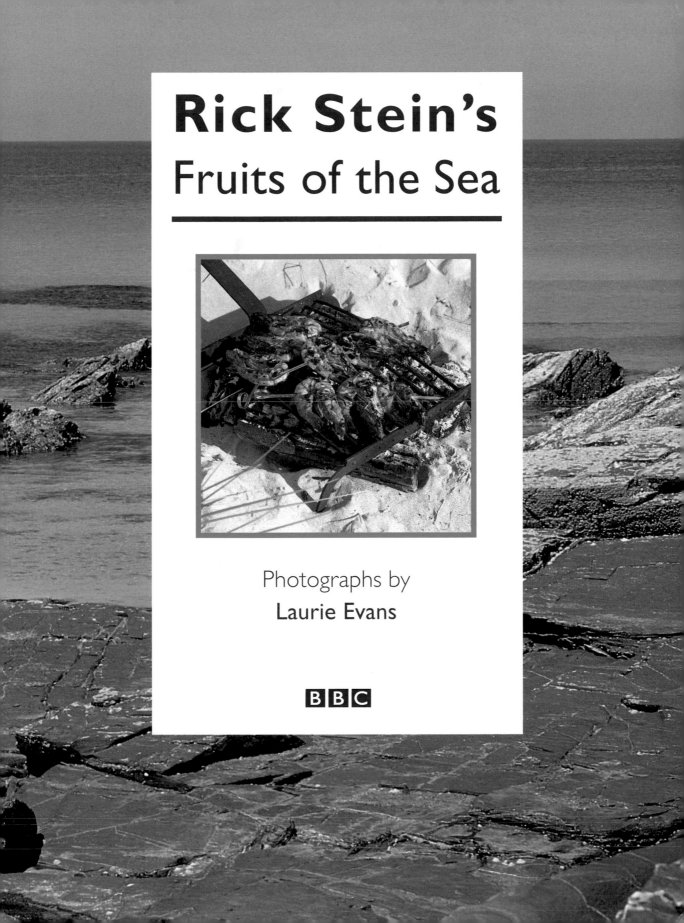

Rick Stein's
Fruits of the Sea

Photographs by
Laurie Evans

BBC

For my wife Jill and my boys
Edward, Jack and Charles

This book was published to accompany the television series *Rick Stein's
Fruits of the Sea* which was first broadcast in January 1997. The series
was produced for BBC Television by Denham Productions and directed by
David Pritchard.

Published by BBC Books, an imprint of BBC Worldwide Ltd.
Woodlands, 80 Wood Lane, London W12 0TT

First published 1997; reprinted 1997 (five times)
Copyright © Richard Stein 1997
First published in paperback in 1998; reprinted 1998 1999 (twice), 2001 (twice)
First published with this cover 2002; reprinted 2002
The moral right of Rick Stein to be identified as the author of this work has been asserted

Photographs by Laurie Evans, copyright © BBC Worldwide Ltd. 1997
Illustrations by Julie Whatley, copyright © BBC Worldwide Ltd. 1997

ISBN 0 563 38762 9 (hardback)
ISBN 0 563 38457 3 (paperback)

Designed by Isobel Gillan
Home Economist: Debbie Major
Styling by Lesley Richardson

The poem, *Ratatouille,* on page 154 from *St Kilda's Parliament* by Douglas Dunn,
reprinted by permission of Faber and Faber Ltd.
Recipe for *Cremets de Saumur with Fresh Raspberries* on page 209 taken from
French Provencial Cooking by Elizabeth David, courtesy of Michael Joseph.
Recipe for *Stir-fried Salt and Pepper Prawns* on page 56 taken from
The Classic Chinese Cookbook by Yan-kit So, courtesy of Papermac.

Photograph on page 1: *Moroccan Fish Tagine* (see p.30)
Photograph on page 3: *Tandoori Prawns* (see p.64)

Printed and bound in Great Britain by Butler and Tanner Ltd, Frome and London
Colour separations by Radstock Reproductions Ltd, Midsomer Norton
Jacket printed by Lawrence Allen Ltd, Weston-super-Mare
Cover printed by Belmont Press Ltd. Northampton

Acknowledgements Special thanks to Debbie Major for testing all the recipes, typing most of them out and generally being a great person to talk about food with. But also all those long-suffering chefs at *The Seafood Restaurant*, particularly Paul Ripley and David Pope who had to stop what they were doing to provide us with fish, vegetables and fruit for all the recipes. Thanks, yet again, to Heather Holden-Brown, Anna Ottewill, Pippa Middleton, Isobel Gillan and Frank Phillips at BBC Books for their serious professionalism and, again, sorry about the deadlines everyone! I'd also like to thank Laurie Evans who came down and took all the wonderful photographs in this book and put me through an extremely busy but fun two weeks all around Padstow.

Lastly, thanks to David Pritchard, the best director of cookery programmes in the business, and the rest of the crew, Julian, Tom, Maggie, Johnny and Phil, for being such fun to work with, even when we were bickering about things like those simple dishes, remember! And last, but not least, that small modest dog, Chalky, who somehow doesn't realize he's famous.

Author's Note Seven recipes in this book have been repeated from my first book *Taste of the Sea*. This is because I have demonstrated them in the new series *Fruits of the Sea*.

CONTENTS

INTRODUCTION

'I wonder if you'd mind signing this book for my husband? He's gone out to the car at the moment and I know he'd be too embarrassed to ask you himself.'

'Of course,' I said. 'But why didn't he want to ask me?'

'Well,' she said, 'he'd never cooked anything before I bought him your book [*Taste of the Sea*] but he saw your TV series and everything you cooked on the series he wanted to try himself, so I bought the book for him and he's never looked back.'

'Gosh,' I said. 'You couldn't have said anything more complimentary if you'd really thought about it.'

Her husband came back and I quickly signed his book and gave it to him.

'I hear you're quite interested in cooking,' I said.

'Well, yes, sort of,' he said shyly, almost looking the other way, obviously not wanting to make a fuss.

'Your wife says you quite liked the TV series.'

'I did actually,' he said, now becoming a little more animated. 'I really did, I thought it was wonderful. I thought you cooked dishes that I would like to eat and you didn't make it all seem too difficult or too technical.'

Then, even more enthusiastically, he began talking about how his love of fish had grown out of watching the series, and how he'd been given the book by his wife and had cooked well over half the recipes, and that he would never have believed that fish could taste so good.

After that, I felt I had to write another book. In fact, when I wrote my last book, *Taste of the Sea*, I got rather over-enthusiastic and had to cut fifty recipes out of it. So, I wanted to write a second book to incorporate those fifty recipes and lots of other dishes that I've always wanted to get down on paper, particularly lots of easy dishes designed to persuade harassed people living in the twentieth century to cook fish. I've written this book and blow me if I haven't had to cut out another fifty recipes.

Stir-fried Salt and Pepper Prawns (see p.56).

I wanted to have a whole chapter about spicy fish. Actually, initially I wanted to write a whole book about fish with spice to include the exotic delights of prawn masala, Sichuan squid, seafood laksa, tom yam gung, a Thai fish stew (tasted in Australia, of all places, which was served a bit like bouillabaisse but blew the top of my head off), a deep-fried whole fish with chopped chilli and garlic that I once had at Hua Hin in Thailand, some hot little Moroccan fish dishes with charmoula, and those wonderful fish tacos you get in the Baja California in Mexico. I certainly could have made a whole book out of my fascination with this area of fish cookery. But then, last time I was in Australia, I showed *Taste of the Sea* to some people who said how nostalgic it made them feel for good old Northern European butter sauces, and I realised that to include a variety of recipes to cater for all tastes is probably a good thing after all.

I also wanted to include a selection of fish dishes from colder climates with warming, comforting buttery sauces, braised and baked dishes, the sort of food that makes you think of convivial eating on winter nights, perhaps in a rented house near a wind-swept, foam-splattered beach in Cornwall.

I then thought of a section on what I love to call hand-held food – all those parcels, pasties, tacos and turnovers particularly well suited to cooking with fish. How lacking in joy are pasties served with a knife and fork; they're for fishermen and miners, and for sailors to take a satisfying bite between splicing the mainsail.

Then I thought of a section where I wouldn't make any bones about the fact that the recipes were hard to do, required a good deal of work in the kitchen but where the results would be elegant and deft and would impress and delight friends at a special dinner.

To balance this, I then put together a selection of light lunch dishes which would double up as simple first courses for a more elaborate evening meal and, last but not least, I included an area of cooking that is very dear to me but which I've never been able to put in a book before – puddings. Why not finish the book with a dozen or so of my favourite desserts, the sort of things that are so well loved at my restaurant? With both of my previous books, quite a few people have expressed their disappointment that they didn't include any of those wonderful sweet dishes, so, at last, here they are.

One of the criticisms of my first TV series, which I made in 1995, was that I used seafood of a quality very few people could get hold of. Therefore, in spite of the fact that the recipes were simple, they remained rather impracticable, rather exclusive. I appreciate the problem but I feel I must still use the best ingredients and encourage you to do so. At the risk of sounding flippant, I could hardly imagine introducing a recipe on television with, 'This dish is ideal for making with stale cod.'

Don't think, incidentally, that curry is the answer either. What is that old saying about silk purses and sows' ears? But while I'm on the subject, the recipe on p.185 for *Deep-Fried Shredded Fish with Chilli, Prawns and Coriander* just might fit the bill for not perfect, top quality or well-flavoured fish. Fishmongers do not always offer the best-quality fish and it's not usually their fault but rather the lack of brisk turnover in their shops. The more I can interest you in the quality, the more fish will get sold, the more demanding customers will become and we'll all benefit.

For this book, wherever possible, I bought fish at shops that most of us use – supermarkets and fishmongers – and I also made sure that the majority of the recipes use fish that are easily obtained. Having said that, however, I still like to include the occasional recipe using something quite special like *Spiny Lobster with Vanilla Sauce* on p.140 or *Salad of Chargrilled Garfish with Fennel Seeds* on p.93.

A further criticism of my last book was that many of the recipes are too complicated for ordinary cooks. I'd like to think this isn't really true, but nevertheless I've taken note and included a whole chapter of dishes that are quick and simple to prepare. And I've tried to simplify all the recipes in this book as much as possible by suggesting, for example, that you use ready-made pasta and puff pastry, or knock up mayonnaise and hollandaise in a liquidizer. But, just to keep the serious cooks happy, I've also slipped in the long way round as well.

About twenty years ago, in the early days at my restaurant, I went through a bit of a crisis of confidence about what I was doing cooking in a small kitchen in a small fishing port miles from anywhere. We weren't very busy then and were only just making ends meet. Few people seemed particularly interested in eating fish. My wife, Jill, and I seriously considered moving back to Oxfordshire where I originally came from. We thought we'd carry on selling mostly fish dishes but some meat dishes too and make a living in a place where people really took an interest in food. I used to play rugby with the Cornish comedian Jethro and I asked him why he didn't come to the restaurant at all.

'I don't like fish,' he said.
'Look, Jethro, we sell meat too,' I retorted.
'It'd still taste of fish.'

Well, I stuck it out. I suppose I always felt that there was something special and worth shouting about in freshly landed fish, simply cooked, and so it seems to have turned out.

I'll have to have another word with that Jethro.

PREPARING FISH

I'm really pleased to be able to include some proper step-by-step photographs showing you how to prepare raw fish. I've always felt that filleting, gutting and scaling are much more straightforward operations than most people think, and I hope these simple steps will allay any fears you might have about these processes. The bold type refers to the actions in the photos. Don't forget that there are always plenty of trimmings left over that can be turned into wonderful stocks, particularly the shells from the prawns (see p.18).

Cleaning Round Fish

1. Trim the fish by snipping off the fins with kitchen scissors. **Working over several sheets of newspaper or under cold running water, remove the scales by scraping the fish from tail to head with a blunt, thick-bladed knife or a fish scaler.** With some very delicate-skinned fish, such as sardines, pilchards and small herrings, you can simply rub off the scales with your thumb.

2. To remove the guts, slit open the belly from the anal fin (two-thirds of the way down the fish from the head) up towards the head. **Pull out most of the guts with your hand,** cut away any pieces of the entrails left behind and then wash out the cavity with plenty of cold water.

3. To remove the gills, **pull open the gill flaps and cut them away from the two places where they join the fish, at the back of the head and under the mouth.**

Filleting Large Round Fish
(such as sea bass and salmon)

1. Lay the fish on a chopping board and **cut closely around the head in a V-shape** so that you don't lose too much of the fillet.

2. Lay the fish with its back towards you. **Cut along the length of the back, keeping the blade of the knife above the horizontal back bones.**

3. Starting at the head, cut the fillet away from the bones, keeping the blade as close to them as you can. Once you have released some of the fillet, **lift it up with your fingers to make it easier to see where you are cutting.** When you near the rib bones which surround the intestines, if they are thick enough, cut as close to them as you can (with hake, for example); if very fine, cut through them and then remove the bones from the fillet with tweezers afterwards.

Turn the fish over and repeat on the other side.

Filleting Small Round Fish
(such as small sea bass, mackerel, herring and trout)

1. Lay the fish on a chopping board with its back towards you. **Cut around the back of the head, through the flesh of the fillet down to the backbone.**

2. Turn the knife towards the tail and, beginning just behind the head, carefully start to cut the fillet away from the bones, down towards the belly.

3. Once you have loosened enough flesh to enable you to get the whole blade of the knife underneath the fillet, **rest a hand on top of the fish and cut away the fillet in one clean sweep right down to the tail, keeping the blade close to the bones as you do so.** Remove any small bones left in the fillet with a pair of tweezers.

Turn the fish over and repeat on the other side.

Cleaning Flat Fish

1. To remove the guts, locate the gut cavity by pressing on the white side of the fish just below the head until you find an area that is much softer. Make a small incision across this area (if you wish to remove any roe at this stage, make a slightly longer incision) and pull out the guts (and roe if you wish) with your little finger. Trim the fish by snipping off the fins with kitchen scissors.

Dover sole and brill are the only flat fish that need cleaning. **If you do need to scale them, follow the method for round fish on p. 11.**

Filleting Flat Fish

1. You will get 4 fillets from one flat fish. Lay the fish on a chopping board and cut around the back of the head and across the tail. **Then cut through the skin down the centre of the fish, very slightly to one side of the raised backbone, working from the head down to the tail.**

2. Starting where the backbone meets the head, slide the blade of the knife under the corner of one of the fillets. **Carefully cut it away from the bones, folding the released fillet back as you do so.** Keep the blade of the knife almost flat and as close to the bones as possible. Remove the adjacent fillet in the same way.

Turn the fish over and repeat on the other side.

Skinning Fillets of Fish

1. Place the fillet skin-side down on a chopping board, with the narrowest (tail) end nearest to you. Angling the blade of the knife down towards the skin, start to cut between the flesh and the skin until a little flap is released.

2. Flip the flap of fish over. Firmly take hold of the skin and, working away from you, continue to cut along its length, sawing with the knife from side to side and keeping the blade of the knife close against the skin.

Filleting Monkfish

1. You may need to skin the monkfish tail before you start. **Hold the thick end of the tail in one hand and the skin in the other. Briskly tear off the skin, which should come away quite easily.**

2. Cut through the fish along either side of the thick backbone, keeping the blade of the knife as close to the bone as possible.

3. You now need to remove the membrane that encases the fillets of fish otherwise it will shrink during cooking, causing the fish to twist unattractively. Pull away as much as possible with your fingers. Remove as much of the remainder as you can with a sharp knife by releasing a flap of the membrane with the knife and then **cutting it away by sawing from side to side** (as if you are skinning an ordinary fish fillet, see opposite), being careful not to cut away too much of the flesh.

Preparing Squid

1. Grasp the head in one hand and the body in the other. Gently pull the head and it should come away easily, taking the milky white intestines with it. You may like to retain the ink sac which will be in the intestines – it will be pearly-white in colour with a slight blue tinge. You can also save the 2 pieces of muscle running down either side of the intestines. The rest of the intestines can be discarded.

2. Cut off the tentacles from the head, then discard the head. Squeeze out the beak-like mouth from the centre of the tentacles, cut it off and discard. The tentacles can either be separated or left intact if very small.

3. Reach into the body and pull out the plastic-like quill and the soft white roe, if there is any.

4. Pull off the two fins from either side of the body pouch. Then pull away the purple, semi-transparent skin from both the body and the fins. Wash the pouch out with water. If the pouch is too long and narrow for you to reach right down inside when cleaning (and you are not planning to stuff it), a trick for cleaning it out thoroughly is to cut off the very tip and then wash it out with running water, squeezing out any residue as you do so.

Cleaning Mussels

1. Wash the mussels in plenty of cold water and scrub the shells with a stiff brush. **Use a knife to scrape off any barnacles that are sticking to them.**

2. Discard any open mussels that do not close when lightly tapped on the work surface. **Pull out the tough, fibrous beards** protruding from the tightly closed shells.

Opening Oysters

1. Scrub any grit and sand off the oyster shells. Wrap one hand in a tea towel and hold the oyster in it, with the more bowl-shaped half of the shell underneath and the flatter shell on top. Take an oyster knife or small, thick-bladed knife in your other hand. **Push the point of the knife into the hinge of the oyster, located at the narrowest point.** Work the knife forwards and backwards between the two halves of the shell to break the hinge. As the hinge breaks, twist the point of the knife to lever the top shell upwards.

2. Now slide the knife under the top shell to sever the ligament that joins the oyster to the shell. The ligament is slightly right of centre in the shell. **Lift off the top shell,** trying not to let any fragments fall on to the oyster and keeping the bottom shell upright so as not to lose any of the juice. Pick out any little pieces of shell that might have broken off into the oyster.

Preparing Prawns

Preparing Scallops

1. Wash the scallops in plenty of cold water. Hold the scallop flat shell uppermost and **slide the blade of a filleting knife between the shells.** Keeping the blade flat against the top shell, feel for the ligament that joins the shell to the muscle meat of the scallop and cut through it.

1. Firmly twist the head away from the body and discard. or use for stock. Turn the prawn over and **break open the soft shell along the belly, then carefully peel it away from the flesh.** For some recipes you may wish to leave the tail section in place.

2. Lift off the top shell and **pull out the black stomach sac and the frilly 'skirt', which surrounds the white scallop meat and bright orange coral.** Cut the scallop meat away from the bottom shell.

3. Pull off and discard the small white ligament that is attached to the side of the scallop meat.

2. With some large raw prawns you may need to remove the intestinal tract, which looks like a thin black vein running down the back of the prawn flesh. Run the tip of a small knife down the back of the prawn and then **lift up and pull out the vein.**

Removing the Meat from a Cooked Lobster

1. Twist off the larger claw arms and the legs. Cut away any bands binding the claws together. Break the claw arms apart at the joints and then **crack the shell with the back of a knife blade** or a hammer.

2. Remove the meat from each section of the claws in as large pieces as possible.

3. Now cut the lobster in half lengthways. **Lift out the intestinal tract which runs down the centre of the meat,** then remove the meat from the tail section.

4. Remove the soft, greenish tomalley (liver) and any red roe from the head and tail (these are edible). Use the rest of the head, all the shell pieces and the legs to make *Shellfish Stock* (see p. 214).

5. If you wish to remove the tail meat in one piece for slicing into discs, don't cut the lobster in half lengthways; instead, detach the head from the tail and then cut the head in half and remove the tomalley and roe. Turn the tail section over and **cut along either side of the flat under-shell with scissors.** Lift back

the flap and take out the meat. Slice as required and remove the intestinal tract from each slice with the point of a sharp knife.

Removing the Meat from a Cooked Crab

1. Break off the tail flap from the underside of the crab. **Twist off the 2 larger claw arms and the legs.**

2. Break the legs at the joints and, unless the crabs are large, discard all but the first largest joint. Crack the shells with the back of a knife blade or a hammer, then **use a crab pick to remove the meat.**

3. Break the claw arms apart at the joints and then crack the shells as before, trying not to shatter them completely. **Remove the meat from each section in as large pieces as possible.**

4. Remove the meat from the claws, discarding the very thin, flat bone from the centre of the meat.

5. Detach the body of the crab from the back shell by inserting a sturdy knife between them and giving it a **firm twist,** then lifting out the body.

6. To remove the meat from the body, first **pull off and discard the inedible 'dead men's fingers'.** These are the feathery-looking gills attached to either side of the body and there will be about 12 of them, varying in size.

7. Now cut the body section into quarters with a large knife. **Using a crab pick, extract the white meat from the little channels in the body,** being careful not to let any small pieces of the wafer-thin shell get mixed in.

8. To remove the brown meat from the back shell, first remove the stomach sac by **pressing firmly on a little piece of shell located just behind the eyes. The bone and the stomach will come away together.**

9. Pour away any excess water from the back shell and then **scoop out the thin layer of brown meat.** If it is still firm, you will be able to lift it out in one piece; otherwise, scrape it out with a teaspoon. Cut it into small pieces if you wish.

Unusual Ingredients

Most of the ingredients used in this book, particularly the seafood, are easy to get hold of, but one of my real enthusiasms as a cook is borrowing ideas from cuisines all over the world, and inevitably there are some things that haven't quite made it to the main high-street shops or supermarkets yet. However, I continue to be delighted by the speed with which supermarkets get new products on to their shelves these days. It is a competitive game from which we customers can only benefit. Just in case you might think that everything to do with food is better in France, I do think that our supermarkets have a much bigger range of food than those in France. Try buying a jar of fennel seeds or star anise there, and, as for wine, I wouldn't be surprised if the average Frenchman was unaware that wine is produced in Australia, California and South Africa. We still lag behind a bit with fresh food and I keep hoping that one day I will sit down at a simple enamel table in an out-of-town shopping centre and eat freshly opened oysters, mussels, just boiled whelks and prawns, all served up with mayonnaise, shallot vinegar and a cold bottle of white Côtes du Rhone – which was just what I did last time I was in France.

All of the ingredients mentioned here are now quite easy to get hold of but for those of you who are unfamiliar with them the following advice and information might be useful.

Candle Nuts and Macadamia Nuts Candle nuts are originally from Indonesia, and macadamias from Australia. Both are round with exceptionally hard shells and are similar in flavour, being rich and creamy. Candle nuts are much used in Malaysian and Indonesian cookery for adding richness and as a thickener for curries. Either is pretty essential to the Malaysian *Laksa* (p.40) but I find that cashew nuts, though different in flavour, have a similar rich, sweet creaminess.

Chillies In order to try to establish some sort of common heat factor I mention just two types of chillies – finger and birdseye. The difference between red and green chillies is merely a question of ripeness. In Britain, our understanding of different types of chilli is not yet advanced enough to be more specific. By finger chilli I mean cayenne chillies, those most commonly available which are thin, about as long as your finger and medium hot. There are also some slightly more snub-nosed chillies readily available which are less hot but can be used instead of finger chillies in the recipes. Birdseye chillies are those tiny red or green ones often found in oriental food shops which are always blindingly hot. The heat-producing substance in chillies is called capsaicin and is measured in Scoville units which have been simplified into a chart from 1 (very mild) to 10 (awfully hot). Finger chillies are about 3 and birdseye 9.

The hottest chillies I know are called Habanero which are a clear 10.

Pasilla chillies, from Mexico, are particularly good with seafood. You can buy these from an enterprising American called Dodie Miller, who runs a mail order service with an enormous variety of imported dried chillies: The Cool Chile Company, PO Box 5702, London W10 6WE. Tel: 0171 229 9360.

Crab Meat There are many recipes using crab meat in this book and, though I tend to say that freshly dressed crab meat is best, I think that either chilled pasteurized crab meat or frozen is a perfectly good substitute, since the task of dressing crabs is time-consuming. Personally, though, when time allows, I like jobs like picking crab. I get myself a couple of bowls and a bucket for the debris, pour myself a glass of wine, put on some Mozart, then sit outside next to the herb garden and relax.

Creamed Coconut and Coconut Milk

Creamed coconut is sold in a small, hard block. Small pieces chipped straight off the block are ideal stirred into sauces and curries to thicken them towards the end of cooking. It can also be dissolved in an equal quantity of hot water to make coconut milk, also best added at the end of cooking as it has a tendency to separate quite quickly.

Coconut milk can be bought in cans and is used in most soupy Thai curries and a lot of southern Indian, Sri Lankan and South East Asian dishes. By not shaking the can before opening it, you can lift off the cream that forms on the top of the milk and use it separately as required. But, in most cases, just shake well before opening. If you want to make your own fresh coconut milk, simply remove the flesh from the coconut shell and peel off the brown skin. Finely grate the flesh, put it into a liquidizer with 450 ml (15 fl oz) of very hot water to every 225 g (8 oz) of coconut and blend for a few seconds. Strain through a muslin-lined sieve and then squeeze out all the liquid. The liquid can be left to settle for a while and the cream skimmed off the top to use separately.

Curry Leaves

These lend a distinctive flavour to curries and other Indian dishes and fresh ones can often be found in Asian groceries and some of the larger supermarkets. They can be frozen in plastic bags for later use. There is no real substitute so simply omit them if you can't find any.

Fennel Seeds

I share a passion with Italians for fresh fennel seeds. I love those dishes of pork and rabbit with garlic, white wine and fennel seeds which you get in parts of Umbria. Fennel seeds go exceptionally well with fish, too. They're a bit hard to get hold of but a shop with a serious spice rack will normally have them. Otherwise, try collecting your own from hedgerows in late September.

Fish Sauce

Fish sauce, or *nam pla*, as it is known in Thailand, is a salty fish liquid derived from the salting of anchovies. It is an essential ingredient in Thai and other South East Asian cuisines. It has a slightly fishy but not unpleasant salty taste and, when combined with lime, lemon grass, chilli and coriander, forms a basic flavouring alliance for many Thai, Vietnamese and Laotian dishes. Available in most supermarkets, it should be fairly clear and not too brown. If you can't get hold of it the best alternative is a light soy sauce or anchovy essence.

Galangal

Galangal, a rhizome root related to ginger, is available in most oriental food shops. You may find it a bit too unusual on the first few tries; all I can say is persevere. Ginger is a perfect substitute.

Kaffir Lime Leaves

The leaves of a gnarled and thick-skinned lime which has almost juiceless fruit. You can buy dried kaffir lime leaves in spice jars quite easily now. Use the pared zest of lime as a substitute. If you can get the fruit of the kaffir lime, the pared zest is well worth adding to dishes such as the *Green Monkfish and Prawn Curry* on p.66.

Lemon Grass

I think this is the single most recognizable flavour in Thai cooking, the thick, moist stem of a tropical grass with a lovely lemony taste and smell. Incidentally, lemon grass does grow reasonably well in greenhouses over here and even outdoors in summer. Just buy a stem or two and put in moist potting compost. There is no real alternative to lemon grass but, at a push, you could use pared lemon zest.

Palm Sugar

A moist, light, soft brown sugar made from the sap of the coconut palm, palm sugar is ideal for use in Thai dishes. Indeed, sugar is used to great effect in Thai savoury cooking, as the dipping sauce for the *Thai Fish Cakes with Green Beans* on p.57 will confirm. The secret lies in combining sugar with lime juice or vinegar, fish sauce and often chilli. This pleasing combination of opposites — sweet and sour, salty and hot — is a system which underlies much Chinese cooking. It is an approach that I think Western cooking could use a lot more, though, funnily enough, this is what has made fish and chips with salt and malt vinegar such a winner. A good substitute would be dark soft brown sugar or muscovado sugar.

Prawns There are lots of recipes using prawns in this book, largely because good-quality, large cooked and raw prawns are now so easy to get hold of.

North Atlantic Prawns Very good value, and the most commonly seen in fishmongers, these are sold both peeled and in the shell. The shells and the whole prawns are ideal for making *Shellfish Stock* (p.214).

Mediterranean Prawns or Crevettes These are long, thin prawns with very curly antennae, usually sold cooked. They are common throughout the Mediterranean but these days, although the small ones are still fished locally, the larger prawns usually come from the waters of Madagascar. They are especially good served with an olive oil mayonnaise.

Tiger and other Raw Prawns I have rather unceremoniously lumped together all the raw prawns, which make up a number of different species. In Australia they have 13 different commercial species, all of which are probably represented in what you buy in fishmongers' and supermarkets both frozen and chilled. Generally I have specified headless unshelled prawns in the recipes but occasionally the look of a whole prawn will make all the difference as with the *Tandoori Prawns* on p.64.

Preserved Lemon This is a North African way of keeping lemons. You just leave then in brine and in three or four weeks they soften and lose their bitterness. They are great in salads and finely chopped in sauces, as in the *Moroccan Fish Tagine* on p.30. See p. 220 in the Basics chapter for my own recipe for preserved lemons.

Rices There are numerous types of rice available today from all around the world. Each one is very individual in both taste and texture.

Basmati Rice This is from the northern regions of India and has a distinctive flavour and delicate texture. It must be rinsed with water before cooking to remove the excess starch so that the grains remain separate and fluffy during cooking. You can soak the rice too if you wish. Some claim that it needs soaking for up to 20 minutes but I find that the grains break up too much during cooking and that 5 minutes is sufficient.

Thai Jasmine Rice As the name suggests, this is a jasmine-scented rice from Thailand. It is similar in appearance to basmati rice but is more sticky and tends to cling together in small clumps during cooking. The perfect authentic accompaniment to all the Thai curries in this book.

Arborio Rice This is just one type of Italian short grain rice, essential for making risotto because it breaks down during cooking to produce the creamy texture required in the final dish. Other varieties include Carnaroli, Maratelli, Roma or Vialone. There is no substitute for risotto rice but happily it is now widely available.

Valencia Rice This is the classic Spanish rice used to make the authentic paella. Unfortunately, it is not easily available in Britain, unless of course you are lucky enough to live near a Spanish deli or specialist food shop. However, through trial and error, I have found arborio rice is a very respectable alternative.

Rice Vinegar A clear vinegar called for in many Chinese dishes, especially the well-known sweet and sour sauces. It's not easily available but a good substitute is to mix three parts white wine vinegar with one part water and a little caster sugar.

Rice Wine This is used extensively in China and is made from glutinous rice, yeast and water. It is usually only available from Chinese supermarkets but a dry/fino sherry makes a good substitute.

Salted Black Beans and Black Bean Sauce
Salted black beans are available in oriental food shops and are much used in Chinese cooking – so much so that I would identify them as one of the definitive flavours. I haven't yet seen them in supermarkets but I wouldn't be surprised if they are on our shelves by the time this book is published. They need to be rinsed to remove the excess salt and chopped before using. If you can't get them, use black bean sauce instead, but preferably the variety in which the beans are not totally puréed.

Sesame Oil I use both cold pressed and roasted sesame oil. The cold pressed oil is light, delicate and fragrant and ideal for dishes such as the *Warm Crab Pancakes with Lemon Grass and Coriander* on p.173, whereas roasted sesame oil, which is much stronger, is ideal for robust dishes full of spice.

Shrimp Paste, Blachan, Balachow, Dried Shrimps The process of salting and drying tiny shrimps is common all over the tropical and equatorial countries of the world. The result is sold as either a dry block or a paste, or simply loose as dried shrimps. The block and paste have a pretty unpalatable smell and taste but a little stir-fried with garlic and ginger gives a background flavour to many memorable dishes, like *Tom Yam Gung* from Thailand (p.32) or *Laksa* from Malaysia and Indonesia (p.40). With shrimp paste I'm always reminded of that phrase from the Bible: 'the stone that the builders rejected has become the head of the corner'. I feel much the same way about whelks and the humble winkle. With a willingness not to waste what is, after all, good food, and a little adroitness, those seemingly unimportant raw materials can be transformed into the main attraction.

Soy Sauce Made from fermented and salted soya beans, soy sauce can be either dark or light and varies in flavour from salty to sweet. In most of my recipes I use dark soy sauce, and in my opinion the Japanese variety is the one to go for as it has a superior, slightly sweeter flavour. Having said that, Chinese soy sauce does the job very well too.

Spring Roll and Wonton Wrappers Both of these are only available from Chinese supermarkets and some very well stocked delicatessens. There is no real substitute for the characteristic texture of wonton wrappers, but for the recipe for *Deep-fried Prawn Wontons with Chilli Jam* (see p.86) and for the *Spring Rolls with Squid, Crab, Bean Sprouts and Shiitake Mushrooms* (see p.188) you could use filo pastry instead.

Star Anise This is a very useful spice for fish cookery. It is quite easy to get in good food shops and is always on sale in oriental food stores. I often sprinkle some in a fish stock for a subtle aniseed hint.

Sichuan Pepper A characteristic flavour of Chinese cookery which manages to be both peppery hot and yet slightly tart and has the effect of numbing the mouth a little. Also called anise pepper, it is not in fact a true pepper but comes from a type of ash tree.

Tamarind The pods of the tamarind tree, tamarind is usually sold in a rectangular block complete with seeds, which are as hard as small black stones. You normally mix the pulp with warm water and pick out the seeds. The paste can then be used in many types of curries, where its acid and scented flavour acts like the juice of citrus fruits, lime or lemon, both of which can be used as an alternative. Tamarind is now also available ready-prepared in jars.

Wasabi Paste This fiercely hot Japanese green horseradish paste is fairly easy to get hold of now in larger supermarkets and oriental food stores. It is the essential accompaniment to the Japanese raw fish dish *sashimi*.

White Pepper In most of my recipes I use freshly ground black pepper but in one or two instances I have called for white pepper. This is because it has a less assertive flavour than its black counterpart, and is better suited to some dishes made with delicately flavoured fish. I also use it in butter sauces and in mayonnaise simply because it is less visible in the finished product.

SOUPS, STEWS AND CLEAR BROTHS

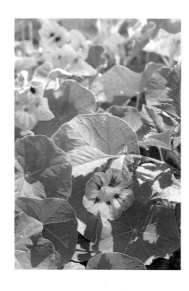

I've just come back from a week in Provence of *bouillabaisses* and *bourrides*. I've certainly never eaten so many robust fish stews in such a short time. After a particularly fierce *bourride* I woke up in the middle of the night thinking I was going to die of indigestion from the garlic. *Bourride* is not a dish for eating at night and I think the Marseillais would regard it as very odd if you did, but then I was a foolish tourist.

At Restaurant Patalain near the Vieux Port of Marseilles I ate a *bouillabaisse* of such distinction that a nagging doubt I have about most fish stews was temporarily dispelled. Since then it has returned: fish stews usually involve boiling all the goodness out of the fish so that you are left with a well-flavoured bouillon but a lot of dry and tasteless fish. It seems to me that, unless the fish is combined with overwhelming flavours, the only way to make fish stews successfully is to cook the fish and soup separately – or, if you do want to cook the fish in the bouillon, to add it at the very last minute. Most of the fish stews in this chapter have been made with this principle in mind, particularly the *bouillabaisse-* and *bourride-* inspired dishes, *Mediterranean Fish Soup* (see p.28) and *A Small Stew of Bass, Squid, Mussels and Prawns with a Warm Aïoli Sauce* (see p.34). The *Moroccan Fish Tagine* on p.30 was entirely changed from the original recipe because that just didn't work for me.

One of my favourite recipes in this chapter is *Seafood in a Crab and Ginger Broth* (see p. 36). It does require a great deal of work but the result is well worth it. When we were filming it, it occurred to me that cooking dishes like this is a bit like ballet dancing. The dancers look as light as feathers, their movements effortless, the pirouetting as if it were just an extension of walking, but then, if you saw them behind the stage afterwards, sweating, their joints aching, you would realize the labour of love that has gone into their performance. And, in a way, it's the same cooking this dish. The broth seems to be an effortless, clear, clean, light creation but in fact a long process of boiling, clarifying, straining and neat cutting has gone into making it. I like that.

Seafood in a Crab and Ginger Broth (see p.36).

MEDITERRANEAN FISH SOUP

1 small gurnard or grey
    mullet, weighing about
    450 g (1 lb)

1 red mullet, weighing
    about 350 g (12 oz)

1 small monkfish tail,
    weighing about 450 g
    (1 lb)

100 g (4 oz) prepared
    squid (see p.16)

20 small mussels, cleaned
    (see p.17)

150 ml (5 fl oz) white wine

1 fennel bulb, trimmed

1 red onion, peeled

1 leek

2 celery sticks

1 red pepper

5 plum tomatoes, skinned

6 small new potatoes,
    weighing about 175 g
    (6 oz) in total

120 ml (4 fl oz) olive oil

6 garlic cloves, thinly sliced

2 strips of orange zest, cut
    into very thin shreds

A good pinch of dried
    chilli flakes

2 teaspoons sun-dried
    tomato paste

2 young, fresh bay leaves,
    finely shredded

Leaves from 1 sprig of
    fresh thyme, finely
    chopped

2 tablespoons chopped
    fresh fennel herb or dill

3 tablespoons Pernod or
    Ricard

This soup contains the type of fish you would normally associate with the Mediterranean and the flavours are those of a bouillabaisse: saffron, orange, tomato, fennel, olive oil and a little Pernod. The vegetables are cut very neatly into small pieces, as is the fish, so that you are left with a sort of mini bouillabaisse to serve as a first course. The supreme advantage of this dish is that the fish is cut into such small pieces that it can be cooked very quickly at the last minute and tastes fresh and clean. The problem with most versions of bouillabaisse is that the fish often tastes as though all the flavour has been boiled out of it and while you get a very well-flavoured soup the fish itself is rather dull.

I like to serve some fresh baguettes with this that you dip into a little good olive oil and sea salt.

Fillet the gurnard or grey mullet, red mullet and monkfish (see p.13 and p.15). Make a fish stock with the bones (see p.212), using 2.75 litres (5 pints) of water.

Cut the squid lengthways along one side of the pouch and open it out. Cut the squid and the fish fillets lengthways into strips 2 cm (¾ in) wide, then cut across each strip into slices 1 cm (½ in) wide. All the pieces of fish should be the same size and shape.

Put the mussels in a pan with a splash of the white wine, cover and cook over a high heat for 3–4 minutes, until they have opened. Discard any that remain closed. Strain the mussel cooking liquor into the fish stock, then shell the mussels, discarding the shells.

Cut the fennel bulb and red onion into 6–8 wedges so that each wedge measures about 2 cm (¾ in) at its thickest part. Cut the leek lengthways into quarters and the celery sticks lengthways in half. Cut the red pepper lengthways into strips 2 cm (¾ in) wide and the tomatoes and potatoes lengthways into 4 wedges. Then cut each of the vegetables across into thin, arc-like slices, making sure that they are all roughly the same size and shape – this is very important to the final look of the soup.

Heat the olive oil in a large pan – if you have a suitable oven-to-table one, this would be ideal. Otherwise just use a large saucepan and transfer the soup to a tureen to serve. Add the fennel, red onion, leek, celery, red pepper, garlic, orange zest and dried chilli. Cook over a low heat for about 4 minutes, until the vegetables are just softened. Add the sun-dried tomato paste, fish stock, remaining white wine, tomatoes, potatoes, salt and pepper. Bring to the boil and simmer for 5 minutes.

Add the fish, plus the bay leaves, thyme, half the fennel herb or dill and the Pernod or Ricard. Simmer for 3 minutes only (otherwise you will overcook the fish), adding the mussels for the final 30 seconds.

Sprinkle the soup with the remaining fennel or dill and take to the table, together with little bowls of extra virgin olive oil and coarse sea salt and the bread. Serve in large soup plates and instruct your guests to dip the bread in the oil and then the salt to eat with the soup.

Salt
20 turns of the black pepper mill
Extra virgin olive oil, coarse sea salt and sliced ciabatta or French bread, to serve

BASQUE SQUID STEW

This recipe comes from a Basque girl, Rosie, who works a trawler with her husband Billy, fishing out of Padstow. She does all the same work — hauling nets, gutting, stowing fish and hosing down the decks — and still finds time to cook the sort of food that any fisherman would be completely happy with, even if they didn't like fish. I would call this the boeuf bourguignonne *of fish stews — it is so deep and rich and the squid becomes very tender after long, slow cooking. This dish is great eaten on its own with crusty French bread or it can be used as a base for a more substantial fish stew. Add extra seafood such as seasoned sliced scallops, halved small skinned fillets of flat fish, langoustines, large prawns or pieces of cooked lobster, bring back to the boil and simmer for another 2 minutes.*

Clean the squid (see p.16). Cut the pouches across into rings and separate the tentacles if large.

Heat the oil in a large, heavy-based pan. Add the squid and cook over a high heat, stirring from time to time, until lightly browned.

Add the onion and garlic to the pan and cook for about 5 minutes, until softened. Stir in the tomatoes, red wine, water and thyme and bring up to the boil. Cover and simmer very gently for 2 hours. Season with the salt and pepper and eat as it is or use as a base for a fish stew (see above).

Serves 4

750 g (1 ½ lb) squid
3 tablespoons olive oil
1 onion, chopped
3 garlic cloves, finely chopped
400 g (14 oz) can of chopped tomatoes
150 ml (5 fl oz) red wine
300 ml (10 fl oz) water
1 teaspoon chopped fresh thyme
1 teaspoon salt
20 turns of the black pepper mill

MOROCCAN FISH TAGINE

2 tablespoons olive oil, plus
   extra for brushing
2 celery sticks, chopped
1 carrot, chopped
1 small onion, chopped
¼ preserved lemon, finely
   chopped
4 plum tomatoes, sliced
600 ml (1 pint) *Fish Stock*
   (see p.212)
8 small new potatoes, cut
   lengthways into quarters
2 red mullet, ocean perch
   or grey mullet, weighing
   about 450 g (1 lb) each,
   filleted (see p.13)
8 black olives, halved
1 teaspoon chopped fresh
   coriander
1 teaspoon chopped fresh
   mint
Salt and freshly ground
   black pepper

FOR THE CHARMOULA
2 tablespoons roughly
   chopped fresh coriander
3 garlic cloves, chopped
1½ teaspoons ground
   cumin
½ red finger chilli, seeded
   and roughly chopped
½ teaspoon saffron strands
4 tablespoons extra virgin
   olive oil
Juice of 1 lemon
1½ teaspoons paprika
1 teaspoon salt

Andy West, one of the chefs at the Seafood Restaurant, described this dish to me after he had been to Essouria, a fishing port between Agadir and Casablanca. He showed me an enchanting picture of Essouria — old white houses, fishing boats, nets, blue skies, blue sea — and told me a story about meeting Arab carpet dealers and sitting on rugs in their house eating this fantastic fish stew — just about the best he'd ever had. So enthusiastic was his description that I decided to cook the dish on television without ever having tried it before, just to see what happened. It didn't go according to plan but, in a way, I thought it was quite interesting that it didn't. First of all the recipe called for large chunks of fish and vegetables, so the tagine ended up looking very ungainly. The taste was fine but, like so many fish stews, all the goodness seemed to go into the sauce, leaving some rather tasteless bits of fish. When my son Edward saw the tagine he said it looked like python stew, and in fact the mullet skin does look a bit like snake! My youngest son Charles just couldn't bear to eat any of it and Jill, my wife, got a large bone stuck in her teeth. I ended up saying to the camera, 'Well, it hasn't quite worked — back to the drawing board!' So I turned it into what I would call restaurant food, by taking the basic elements of the dish, refining them and presenting everything in a neat and tidy package. The result is quite wonderful and, I think, reveals a great deal about how recipes evolve.

For the charmoula, put all the ingredients into a food processor and blend until smooth.

Heat the oil in a large pan, add the celery, carrot and onion and fry gently for 5 minutes, until softened but not browned. Add half the chopped preserved lemon, 2 tablespoons of the charmoula, the tomatoes and the stock. Bring to the boil and simmer for 30 minutes, then add the potatoes. Simmer for 6–8 minutes until tender.

Pre-heat the grill to high. Brush the fillets of fish with olive oil, season with salt and pepper and then cut each diagonally in half. Grill, skin-side up, for about 6 minutes.

Stir the olives, the rest of the charmoula and the remaining preserved lemon into the sauce and check the seasoning. Put the fish in 4 warmed soup bowls, spoon over the sauce and sprinkle with the chopped coriander and mint.

450 g (1 lb) raw, unshelled, headless prawns

1 tablespoon sunflower oil

1 small garlic clove, finely chopped

A pea-sized piece of *blachan* (shrimp paste)

2 lemon grass stalks

1.2 litres (2 pints) *Light Asian Chicken Stock* (see p.213)

2 tablespoons Thai fish sauce (*nam pla*)

3 tablespoons freshly squeezed lime juice

1 red finger chilli, thinly sliced into rings

½ teaspoon palm sugar or muscovado sugar

1 green finger chilli, thinly sliced into rings

2 kaffir lime leaves or 1 strip of pared lime zest, very thinly sliced

Fresh coriander leaves, to garnish

TOM YAM GUNG
(HOT AND SOUR PRAWN SOUP)

This Thai soup is, I think, one of the world's great dishes. It's just a simple, clear chicken stock with prawns, lemon grass, lime and chilli but the vital ingredient is the dried shrimp paste, or blachan, which comes in blocks and smells perfectly revolting. However, a little bit fried in the oil – and I mean just a trace – adds the right oriental touch to this great soup.

Shell the prawns, leaving the tail section in place, then de-vein them (see p.18).

Heat the oil in a large saucepan. Add the prawn shells, plus the garlic and shrimp paste and fry over a medium-high heat for 2 minutes. Cut each stalk of lemon grass in half and crush slightly with a rolling pin. This helps release the flavour. Add the lemon grass and chicken stock to the pan, bring to the boil and simmer for 10 minutes.

Strain the stock through a fine sieve, then return it to the cleaned pan and add the fish sauce, lime juice, red chilli, sugar and prawns. Bring back to the boil and simmer for 3 minutes. Add the green chilli and the lime leaves or zest and simmer for just 30 seconds. Serve garnished with whole coriander leaves.

CULLEN SKINK

Serves 4

2 medium onions
2 cloves
1.2 litres (2 pints) full-fat
  milk
1 fresh bay leaf
225 g (8 oz) Finnan
  smoked haddock fillet,
  or other good-quality
  undyed smoked
  haddock
50 g (2 oz) butter
350 g (12 oz) potatoes, cut
  into 1 cm (½ in) dice
85 ml (3 fl oz) double
  cream
2 tablespoons roughly
  chopped fresh parsley
Salt and freshly ground
  black pepper

When I was writing the recipe for this traditional Scottish smoked haddock soup I was tempted to rename it Smoked Finnan Haddock Soup with Potato, Onions and Parsley, on the grounds that Cullen Skink sounds like something you wouldn't want to give to your pet Jack Russell. But it's a fine Scottish soup of great taste and simplicity. We're all a bit wet in Britain when it comes to naming dishes: if it sounds a bit offputting we call it something else. On the restaurant menu we can never use words such as 'boiled', as in boiled leg of lamb with caper sauce or boiled fish heads, but why not? If that's how you cook the thing, that's how it should be named.

This soup is very easy to prepare. Do make sure that you get the best undyed haddock possible, preferably Finnan haddock, and don't overcook it; the soup really is so much nicer if the flakes of haddock are moist and fresh. Overcooked smoked fish always has a slightly harsh aftertaste. Serve with a chilled Alsace or Gewürztraminer wine.

Peel one of the onions, cut it in half and stud each half with one of the cloves. Put into a pan with the milk and bay leaf, bring just to the boil and simmer for 5 minutes. Add the fish and simmer for 4–5 minutes or until just firm and opaque – a good guide is to allow 10 minutes per 2.5 cm (1 in) thickness of the fillet. Lift the fish out on to a plate and strain the liquid through a fine sieve into a jug. When the fish is cool enough to handle, remove the skin and bones and discard. Flake the fish into large pieces and set aside.

Peel and finely chop the remaining onion. Melt the butter in a large pan, add the onion and cook over a gentle heat for 5 minutes, until softened but not browned. Add the reserved milk and the diced potatoes. Bring to the boil, then simmer gently for 10 minutes, until the potatoes are cooked but still just firm.

Blend half the soup in a liquidizer until smooth. Return to the pan with the double cream and flaked haddock, season with a little salt and pepper and warm through for 1–2 minutes. Serve in a warmed soup tureen, scattered with the chopped parsley.

Serves 4

4 large cooked
   Mediterranean prawns
   (*crevettes*)
900 ml (1½ pints) *Roasted
   Fish Stock*
   (see p.212)
12 mussels, cleaned
   (see p.17)
1 orange
1 teaspoon lemon juice
2 plum tomatoes, roughly
   chopped
6 tablespoons *Olive Oil
   Mayonnaise* (see p.217)
3 garlic cloves, crushed
   with a little salt
2 tablespoons double
   cream
175 g (6 oz) sea bass fillet,
   skin on, cut into 8 thin
   slices
100 g (4 oz) prepared
   squid (see p.16),
   cut into rings
1 teaspoon finely chopped
   fresh flatleaf parsley
Salt and freshly ground
   black pepper

A SMALL STEW OF BASS, SQUID, MUSSELS AND PRAWNS WITH A WARM AÏOLI SAUCE

I have taken the flavourings of bourride, *the Provençal fish stew, to make this elegant starter. The seafood is cooked separately, grilled to produce some colour. The sauce, flavoured with garlic mayonnaise, surrounds a pile of seafood on the plate and is sprinkled with a little chopped parsley.*

Remove the shells from the prawns and reserve. Cut the prawns lengthways in half. Make the fish stock, adding the prawn shells to the other fish bones before roasting.

Put the mussels in a pan with a splash of the stock, then cover and cook over a high heat for 3–4 minutes until they have opened. Discard any that remain closed. Strain the mussel liquor into the stock. Cover the mussels and keep warm.

Remove a strip of zest from the orange with a potato peeler and then squeeze out the juice from the orange. Put the fish stock, orange zest, 2 tablespoons of the orange juice, the lemon juice and the tomatoes into a large saucepan. Bring to the boil and simmer for 15 minutes, until reduced to 600 ml (1 pint). Strain into a jug and discard the residue.

Pre-heat the grill to high. Put the mayonnaise, garlic and cream into a bowl, add a good splash of the warm stock and stir together until smooth. Gradually stir in the remaining stock. Return the mixture to the pan and heat gently to the temperature of an egg custard (hot enough to be just uncomfortable to your little finger), stirring all the time until slightly thickened. Remove from the heat, stir in ½ teaspoon of salt and keep warm while you cook the rest of the fish.

Put the sea bass and squid on to the greased rack of a grill pan and sprinkle with a little salt and pepper. Grill for 2 minutes, adding the prawns towards the end to warm through. Arrange the squid, prawns, sea bass and mussels in 4 warmed soup bowls and surround with the warm garlic cream sauce. Sprinkle with the chopped parsley and serve.

2.5 cm (1 in) piece of fresh
    root ginger
2 limes
1.75 litres (3 pints) *Light
    Asian Chicken Stock
    (see p.213)*
1 lemon grass stalk
1 red birdseye chilli, cut in
    half lengthways
1 tablespoon Thai fish
    sauce (*nam pla*)
1 tablespoon light soy
    sauce
8 raw headless unshelled
    prawns
1 small cooked spider crab
    or brown crab
15 g (½ oz) rice vermicelli
2 spring onions
25 g (1 oz) fresh spinach or
    Chinese cabbage such
    as pak choi
100 g (4 oz) monkfish fillet,
    cut across into very thin
    slices
25g (1 oz) bean sprouts
Fresh coriander leaves, to
    garnish

TO CLARIFY THE STOCK
100 g (4 oz) piece of coley
    or other inexpensive
    white fish fillet, skinned
    and finely chopped
1 small leek, thinly sliced
2 egg whites

SEAFOOD IN A CRAB AND GINGER BROTH

Prawns, monkfish and crab are lightly cooked in a clear, oriental-flavoured broth with some Chinese leaves, rice noodles and bean sprouts. I like to serve it with little side plates of chopped mint and coriander and also some sliced red chilli in rice vinegar, which you stir into the soup as you wish. A great deal of work goes into making this soup and the amazing thing is it looks so simple and clean that your guests will think it is just as simple to make. How wrong could they be!

Peel the ginger, reserving the peel, and cut into very thin slices. Remove a strip of zest from 1 lime with a potato peeler, then squeeze out the juice from both limes. Pour the chicken stock into a large pan and add three-quarters of the sliced ginger, the ginger peel, the strip of lime zest and juice, the outer leaves of the lemon grass, the birdseye chilli and fish sauce. Gradually bring to the boil.

Meanwhile, shell and de-vein the prawns (see p.18), then cover and set aside in the fridge. Pull off the claws and legs of the crab and crack the shells with a rolling pin. Pull the body of the crab away from the shell and add to the boiling stock with the crab legs (but not the claws) and the prawn shells. Bring back to the boil, cover and simmer very gently for 25 minutes.

Pour the stock through a large sieve into another pan, discarding all the solids except the crab. Leave the stock to cool slightly. Meanwhile, remove the white meat from the claws, legs and main body of the crab in as large pieces as possible.

Next you need to clarify the stock. This is worth doing because it is such a pleasure in the final dish to see the white fish, noodles and green vegetables through a sparkling-clear but deeply flavoured liquid. Add the coley, leek and egg whites to the pan and whisk steadily over a medium heat until the mixture boils. Stop whisking immediately, lower the heat and leave to simmer very gently for 5 minutes. Line a fine sieve or conical strainer with a double sheet of muslin and rest it over a clean pan. Carefully pour the stock into the sieve and leave until all the liquid has dripped through. The stock is now ready to use.

Bring a pan of lightly salted water to the boil. Turn off the heat, add the noodles, loosen with a fork and leave for 3 minutes. Cut the spring onions into 5 cm (2 in) pieces and then cut lengthways into very thin shreds. Cut the spinach or Chinese cabbage into 2.5 cm (1 in) pieces. Finely chop the remaining ginger and half the remaining lemon grass.

Bring the stock up to a very gentle simmer, then add the prawns, monkfish, ginger and lemon grass and cook gently for 1 minute. Drain the noodles and add to the pan with the crab meat, spring onions, spinach or Chinese cabbage and bean sprouts. Simmer for 30 seconds, then remove from the heat.

Mix the mint and coriander together in one small bowl and the chillies and vinegar in anotherl. Divide the noodles between 4 large soup plates and then ladle the soup over them. Garnish with whole coriander leaves. Serve with the soup, instructing your guests to season their soup to their own taste.

TO SERVE

1 tablespoon chopped fresh mint

1 tablespoon chopped fresh coriander

2 birdseye chillies, thinly sliced

2 tablespoons rice vinegar or white wine vinegar

¼ teaspoon coriander
   seeds
¼ teaspoon cumin seeds
1 kg (2¼ lb) mussels,
   cleaned (see p.17)
50 ml (2 fl oz) dry white
   wine
50 g (2 oz) unsalted butter
2 shallots, finely chopped
¼ teaspoon turmeric
   powder
¼ teaspoon cayenne
   pepper
2 teaspoons softened
   butter
2 teaspoons plain flour
600 ml (1 pint) *Fish Stock*
   (see p.212)
120 ml (4 fl oz) double
   cream
Salt and freshly ground
   black pepper

MUSSELS WITH TURMERIC, CUMIN AND CORIANDER

In France you often get mussel and other seafood dishes flavoured with what the French call le curry *and this is always a bland, boring powder bought, I expect, in vast quantities so it is completely old and tasteless by the time it is used. The French seem to have the same attitude towards Indian spicing that we had about 30 years ago, when a curry was flavoured with a stale powder and lots of raisins and sliced onions. Today, thanks to the plethora of Indian, Pakistani and Bangladeshi restaurants, most people in Britain have a far more sophisticated idea of spicing than those in any other country in Europe. So this dish, although quite Northern European in content, uses freshly roasted spices instead of some innocuous powder.*

Put the coriander and cumin seeds into a small dry frying pan and roast over a high heat until they begin to smell aromatic. Tip into a pestle and mortar or a coffee grinder and grind to a fine powder.

Put the cleaned mussels in a pan, add the white wine, cover and cook over a high heat for about 3–4 minutes, shaking the pan until the mussels have opened. Strain the liquor through a colander into a bowl, shaking the colander well to drain off the juice lodged in the shells. Shell about two-thirds of the mussels; set all the mussels aside.

Heat half the unsalted butter in a large pan. Add the shallots and fry for 2 minutes, until softened but not browned. Add the ground roasted spices together with the turmeric and cayenne and fry for 1 minute. Mix the softened butter and flour together to make a paste. Add the fish stock and the mussel cooking liquor to the pan with the cream, remaining unsalted butter and butter/flour paste. Simmer for 10 minutes. Add the mussels to the soup, warm through, and then serve with plenty of crusty French bread.

**8 raw, unshelled, headless
  prawns**
5 tablespoons vegetable oil
**900 ml (1½ pints) *Light
  Asian Chicken Stock*
  (see p.213)**
**225 g (8 oz) medium egg
  noodles**
100 g (4 oz) rice vermicelli
100 g (4 oz) bean sprouts
**400 ml (14 fl oz) can of
  coconut milk**
**100 g (4 oz) prepared
  squid (see p.16)**
**2 teaspoons palm sugar or
  muscovado sugar**
1–1½ teaspoons salt
1 lime cut into wedges

FOR THE SPICE PASTE
**3 medium or large dried
  red chillies**
**25 g (1 oz) dried shrimps
  (optional)**
**2 lemon grass stalks, outer
  leaves removed and the
  remainder chopped**
**25 g (1 oz) candle nuts,
  macadamia nuts or
  cashew nuts**
2 garlic cloves, chopped
**2.5 cm (1 in) piece of fresh
  galangal or root ginger,
  roughly chopped**
**1 teaspoon turmeric
  powder**
1 small onion, chopped
**1 teaspoon ground
  coriander**
3 tablespoons water

LAKSA
(MALAYSIAN SEAFOOD AND NOODLE SOUP)

*A spice paste fragrant with lemon grass, chilli, garlic and dried shrimps is
fried in oil. Chicken stock and coconut milk are simmered with the paste,
then seafood is cooked quickly in the soup. Pre-cooked noodles are added
and the whole dish is sprinkled with shredded cucumber, coriander, mint,
spring onions and a bit of extra chilli.*

*With a recipe like this, I always get a little bit anxious that nobody
will ever cook it because of the enormous quantity of ingredients
involved. I first had laksa in Australia and then discovered that you
could buy jars of fantastic laksa paste made by a very well known Sri
Lankan now living in Australia, Charmaine Solomon. It is a pity that, as
yet, small quantities of carefully made masalas and other spice pastes are
not readily available in Britain. I doubt if any domestic cook in Malaysia
would feel the need to make a laksa paste; they just go out and buy it
from their favourite laksa paste shop. Once you have the paste the rest is
easy. The one in this recipe works extremely well and keeps for a couple of
months in the fridge, so it is worth making a large quantity of it.
Anyway, once you've made the dish you probably won't mind making the
paste over and over again. It is so very good.*

For the spice paste, put the dried red chillies and dried shrimps into a bowl,
cover with warm water and leave to soak for 15 minutes. Drain and put into a
food processor with all the remaining spice paste ingredients. Blend until
smooth, then set aside.

Peel and de-vein the prawns (see page 18). Heat 1 tablespoon of the oil in a
pan, add the prawn shells and fry for a few minutes until lightly browned. Add
the chicken stock, bring to the boil and simmer for 10 minutes. Meanwhile, cut
along one side of the squid pouch and open it out flat. Score the inner side first
one way and then the other to make a grid pattern (this not only looks
attractive but tenderizes the squid). Cut into 2.5 cm (1 in) squares and set aside.

Strain the stock and discard the prawn shells. Heat the remaining oil in the
cleaned pan, add the spice paste and fry gently for 5–6 minutes, until it smells
very fragrant and the spices are separating from the oil. Add the stock, bring to
the boil, then cover and simmer for 20 minutes.

Bring a pan of salted water to the boil, add the egg noodles, cover, then take off the heat and leave for 4 minutes. When they are tender but still have a bit of bite, drain and set aside. Bring another pan of water to the boil, drop in the vermicelli, then take the pan off the heat and leave for 2 minutes. Add the bean sprouts and leave for another minute, then drain and mix with the egg noodles.

Add the coconut milk to the stock and simmer for 3 minutes. Add the prawns, squid, sugar and salt and simmer for 4 minutes.

Divide the noodles between 4 large warmed soup bowls. Spoon over the hot soup and garnish each bowl with the cucumber, coriander, mint, spring onions and red chilli. Serve with the lime wedges.

FOR THE GARNISH

5 cm (2 in) piece of
 cucumber, cut into fine
 matchsticks
I tablespoon chopped
 fresh coriander
I tablespoon chopped
 fresh mint
4 spring onions, thinly
 sliced
I red finger chilli, thinly
 sliced across into rings

LIGHT LUNCH DISHES

When I am testing a new dish I always cook it for lunch first. I love lunch, particularly with a cold Loire wine. In the middle of the day you are at your most energetic and optimistic. Is it such a bad idea to enter into imaginative business deals over a long lunch, I wonder? I think that our senses are much more acute at lunch time. One's whole system is ready to enjoy a good meal, tastes and smells are most appreciated and, as for wine, it never tastes as good at night. The fact that most people think of the evening as the right time to enjoy good cooking is more to do with the way we live; lunch may be better but not if you have to work in the afternoon. I believe that if you really want to understand all the thought or lack of thought that goes into a restaurant dish, you should eat it for lunch. So the dishes in this chapter are designed to be really enthused about when your tastebuds are at their most critical, and I suggest that you serve them on their own as a light lunch so they can be fully appreciated. But I also think that they make really great first courses in a more elaborate dinner menu.

When I thought up these recipes I had in mind a table I saw once in Deruta in Umbria, Italy. Deruta is a town near Perugia, where it seems that almost every other building is a ceramics shop or factory. The table would have seated about eight and the top consisted of eight segments of beautifully hand-painted tiles showing blue and yellow fruit and vines on a white background. The vendor wanted tons of money for it and almost more to send it to Britain, but I imagine these dishes on that table in a light, vine-fringed conservatory in the English summer.

Thai Fish Cakes with Green Beans (see p.57).

12 sardines

50 g (2 oz) plain flour,
    seasoned with salt and
    pepper

150 ml (5 fl oz) olive oil

85 ml (3 fl oz) red wine
    vinegar

1 medium onion, thinly
    sliced

5 cm (2 in) strip of orange
    zest

1 sprig of fresh thyme

1 sprig of fresh rosemary

1 fresh bay leaf

4 garlic cloves, crushed

2 dried red chillies

1 teaspoon salt

1 small bunch of fresh
    flatleaf parsley, roughly
    chopped

ESCABÈCHE OF SARDINES

Although the word escabèche *is of Spanish origin, this is a classic Provençal dish, reflecting the fact that fish is cooked in this way all around the Mediterranean. First the fish is fried in olive oil, then a hot marinade of red wine vinegar, chilli, garlic, herbs and, in Provence, orange peel, is poured over it. I have added some roughly chopped flatleaf parsley to produce a simple and delightful dish. I made this in Marseilles under the critical eye of Madame Forte, whose* cabano, *a charming old-fashioned beach chalet, I had borrowed while an episode of my television series,* Fruits of the Sea, *was being filmed. Monsieur Forte assured me that his wife had made* escabèche *all her life and knew everything there was to know about it. She pronounced mine too vinegary and without enough olive oil. I have since made these essential adjustments and hope that when I send her the book she'll try it again and approve.*

Gut, scale and remove the heads from the sardines (see p. 11), then dust them in the seasoned flour. Fry them in half the olive oil for 1 minute on each side, then transfer to a shallow dish. Add everything except the parsley and the remaining oil to the pan, bring to the boil and simmer for about 15 minutes. Add the parsley and the rest of the olive oil, pour the hot marinade over the sardines and leave until cold.

OYSTERS WITH BEURRE BLANC AND SPINACH

I would normally only consider eating oysters raw, but I must say that in this dish, where the oysters are just 'set' in a steamer and accompanied by that classic butter sauce, beurre blanc *I'm more than happy to eat the lightly cooked ones.*

Pour a couple of inches of boiling water into a large saucepan and place some sort of trivet in the bottom. Thoroughly wash the oysters, place them on a plate and rest it on the top of the trivet. Cover the pan and steam for about 4 minutes. Remove the oysters from the pan and open, taking care to save all the juices that come out of them. Put the spinach leaves in the steamer and steam for 2 minutes. Remove and set aside.

Preheat the grill to high. Meanwhile, to make the *beurre blanc*, put the shallot or onion, vinegar, wine and water into a small pan. Add the juice from the oysters and simmer until only 2 tablespoons of liquid are left. Take the pan off the heat and gradually whisk in the pieces of butter, a few at a time, to build up a light emulsion.

Remove the oyster meats from their shells and place a folded leaf of spinach into the base of each one. Place the shells onto a baking tray and push very briefly under the grill to warm the spinach. Remove and place the oysters on top. Pour a little beurre blanc over each one and slide back under the grill for about 15-20 seconds to warm through. Serve immediately.

Serves 4

16 oysters in the shell, well scrubbed

16 fresh spinach leaves, washed and stalks removed

25 g (1 oz) finely chopped shallot or onion

1 tablespoon white wine vinegar

1 tablespoon dry white wine

50 ml (2 fl oz) water

150 g (5 oz) unsalted butter, cut into small pieces

12 large prepared scallops
(see p. 18)

100 g (4 oz) duck livers

300 ml (10 fl oz) *Fish Stock*
(see p. 212)

120 ml (4 fl oz) double
cream

120 ml (4 fl oz) Muscat de
Beaumes de Venise or a
similar sweet white
wine

175 g (6 oz) dried
spaghettini or other
thin pasta such as
capellini

25 g (1 oz) unsalted butter

Salt and freshly ground
black pepper

Sprigs of fresh flatleaf
parsley, to garnish
(optional)

SCALLOPS WITH DUCK LIVERS AND SPAGHETTINI

This dish is designed to be cooked at the last minute, so you need to be well prepared beforehand. It is most successful if you can use fresh duck livers. These are hard to get hold of, however, and you will probably have to make do with frozen ones. You need to be careful with frozen livers because if they've been frozen for too long they tend to go soft and don't plump up nicely during cooking. Freshly frozen ones should be bright red — the older they are, the greyer they become.

A perfect wine to go with this would be a chilled Gewürztraminer or a Tokay Pinot Gris from Alsace.

Bring 1.75 litres (3 pints) of water and 1 tablespoon of salt to the boil in a large pan. Meanwhile, slice the scallops in half and cut the duck livers into similar-sized pieces, being sure to remove any traces of the greeny-yellow gall bladder. Put the fish stock, 85 ml (3 fl oz), of the cream and the wine into a wide-based pan and boil rapidly until reduced to 150 ml (5 fl oz).

Add the pasta to the pan of boiling water and cook for 4 minutes or until al dente. Drain, then cover and keep warm.

Melt a small knob of the butter in a frying pan over a high heat. Add the scallop slices and fry for 1 minute, turning them over after about 30 seconds. Transfer to a plate and keep warm. Add the rest of the butter to the pan with the duck livers and fry for just 1 minute, turning them over as they colour. Set aside with the scallops. Add the reduced stock and wine mixture to the pan and bring to the boil, scraping up all the bits from the bottom of the pan. Strain through a sieve into a small pan. Stir in the rest of the cream, check the seasoning and heat through.

To serve, pile the pasta on to 4 warmed plates and arrange the scallops and duck livers on top. Pour the sauce around the pasta and serve garnished with sprigs of flatleaf parsley if you wish.

100 g (4 oz) fresh spinach

25 g (1 oz) butter

225 g (8 oz) white crab
    meat

50 g (2 oz) brown crab
    meat

A pinch of freshly grated
    nutmeg

A pinch of cayenne pepper

8 sheets of fresh lasagne

20 g (¾ oz) Parmesan
    cheese, finely grated

Salt and freshly ground
    black pepper

FOR THE TOMATO SAUCE

1 medium onion, finely
    chopped

1 garlic clove, finely
    chopped

2 tablespoons olive oil

400 g (14 oz) can of
    chopped tomatoes

50 ml (2 fl oz) red wine
    vinegar

2 teaspoons caster sugar

10 fresh basil leaves, thinly
    shredded

CRAB AND SPINACH CANNELLONI WITH BASIL AND TOMATO SAUCE

Rolls of pasta stuffed with flaked white crab meat and spinach, topped with a rich tomato sauce with plenty of basil, then sprinkled with grated Parmesan cheese and browned under the grill — what could be nicer? I can't claim that this is an authentic Italian recipe, it's one of mine, but all I've done is substitute crab for meat in a classic cannelloni and added some basil to the sauce. I think it is almost better than the traditional version. You can use fresh, pasteurized or frozen crab meat.

For the sauce, fry the onion and garlic in the olive oil for 5 minutes, until softened. Add the chopped tomatoes and simmer for 15–20 minutes. Meanwhile, put the vinegar and sugar in a separate pan and boil down until reduced to about 1 teaspoon. Stir into the tomato sauce and season with salt and pepper. Add the basil and set aside.

Pre-heat the oven to 190°C/375°F/Gas 5.

Remove any large stalks from the spinach and wash the leaves well in cold water. Shake off the excess water, put the leaves into a pan and cook over a high heat for 2 minutes, until wilted. Drain well, chop finely and return to the pan with the butter. Cook for 1 minute, until all the excess moisture has evaporated, then stir in the crab meat and season with the nutmeg, cayenne and some salt and pepper.

Bring 1.75 litres (3 pints) of water and 1 tablespoon of salt to the boil in a large pan. Add the lasagne, take the pan off the heat, cover and leave for 5 minutes. Drain the pasta and lay out on a sheet of food-grade clingfilm. Spoon some of the crab mixture along one short end of each sheet and roll up. Lay the rolls side by side, seam-side down, in a lightly greased shallow ovenproof dish. Spoon over the sauce, sprinkle over the Parmesan cheese and bake for 20 minutes or until golden.

SALAD OF HARBOUR PRAWNS WITH ROASTED TOMATOES AND FENNEL

I got this recipe from Leigh Stone-Herbert, a chef friend of mine in Australia. The roasting of large tomatoes with aromatic vegetables which are left to go cold and then made into a salad is exciting and unusual and tastes fantastic. This dish was originally made with Sydney harbour prawns. Nothing quite beats the intensely sweet taste of these prawns but it is really well worth making with tiger prawns.

Preheat the oven to 230°C/450°F/Gas 8.

Peel the prawns (see p.18). For the roasted vegetables, heat the oil in a large pan. Add the prawn heads and shells and fry over a high heat for 1-2 minutes until they are quite crisp. Tip into a sieve resting over a bowl and press out all of the oil. Discard the shells. Cut the fennel into 4 lengthways. Cut the leeks in half. Place the fennel and the leeks into a roasting tin with the beef tomatoes. Mix the crushed garlic and fennel seeds into the prawn-flavoured oil and pour over the vegetables, making sure that they are all well-coated. Season well with salt and pepper and roast for 25 minutes, until the tomatoes blacken. Remove, peel and leave to go cold.

To cook the prawns, mix the oil with the crushed garlic in a bowl. Add the prawns and some seasoning and toss together well. Heat a large heavy base pan until very hot. Add the prawns and toss over a high heat for 2 minutes. Leave to cool.

To serve, cut a deep cross into the top of each tomato, almost down to the base. Open out each one and place into the centre of 4 large plates so that they look like the petals of a flower. Arrange the pieces of roasted fennel in between the 'petals'.

For the salad dressing, squeeze the liquid out of the roasted leeks, strain all the juices into a small bowl and whisk in the oil, lime juice and some seasoning to taste. Put the curly endive into a bowl and toss with a little of the dressing. Pile this into the centre of the tomatoes and arrange the prawns on top.

Drizzle the rest of the dressing around the edge of the plate and then garnish with a few sprigs of the sorrel and lambs lettuce.

Serves 4

750 g (1 ½ lb) raw, unshelled prawns
2 tablespoons olive oil
1 clove garlic, crushed
Salt and freshly ground black pepper

FOR THE ROASTED VEGETABLES
75 ml (3 fl oz) olive oil
2 small heads of Florence fennel
2 leeks, trimmed
4 beef tomatoes
8 cloves peeled garlic, halved
½ teaspoon fennel seeds, lightly crushed

FOR THE SALAD DRESSING
1 tablespoon olive oil
1 teaspoon lime juice
Salt and freshly ground white pepper
50 g (2 oz) curly endive lettuce
50 g (2 oz) baby sorrel leaves or lambs lettuce

1 skate wing, weighing
    about 900 g (2 lb)
4 tablespoons chopped
    fresh parsley
2 shallots, finely chopped
Salt and freshly ground
    black pepper
3 tablespoons cold water
1 x 11g (0.4 oz) sachet of
    gelatine powder
Salad leaves, to garnish

**FOR THE COURT
BOULLION**
1 bottle of dry white wine
1.2 litres (2 pints) water
2 fresh bay leaves
12 black peppercorns
1 onion, chopped
2 carrots, chopped
2 celery sticks, chopped
1 teaspoon salt
2 slices of lemon
2 star anise
1 fennel bulb, chopped

FOR THE SAUCE GRIBICHE
3 large eggs
1 tbsp white wine vinegar
1 teaspoon Dijon mustard
120 ml (4 fl oz) olive oil
3 small gherkins, very
    finely chopped
1 tablespoon capers, very
    finely chopped
1 tablespoon chopped
    fresh tarragon
1 tablespoon chopped
    fresh parsley

SKATE PERSILLÉ WITH SAUCE GRIBICHE

Skate is particularly suited to serving cold because it has lots of flavour and an attractive soft texture. This dish is based on a real favourite of mine, jambon persillé, and uses similar flavouring. The skate stock has a naturally gelatinous quality and needs only a little extra gelatine to set everything. The stock calls for a whole bottle of wine. It needn't be expensive but you do need this much to achieve the necessary concentration of flavour.

The sauce gribiche is a mayonnaise made with gherkins, capers and a little chopped egg and makes a very pleasant accompaniment to the dish. I would suggest serving a cool white wine from the Languedoc with it — one of the new grape varieties like Rousanne, Marsanne or Viognier.

Put all the ingredients for the court bouillon into a pan and bring to the boil. Simmer for 15 minutes. Put the skate into the pan and simmer for 12 minutes, then lift out and leave to cool. Strain the court bouillon, return it to a clean pan and boil vigorously until reduced to 600 ml (1 pint). Leave to cool.

Lift the skate flesh off the bones and pull it apart a little. Put it into a bowl and mix with the parsley, shallots and a little salt and pepper.

Put 3 tablespoons of cold water into a small pan, sprinkle over the gelatine powder and leave for 5 minutes. Heat gently until clear, then stir into the cool stock.

Line a 900 g (2 lb) loaf tin or terrine with cling film. Spread one-third of the skate mixture over the bottom and pour over enough cooled stock just to cover it. Chill until almost set. Add another third of the skate and stock and chill again. Repeat once more. Cover and chill for 4 hours or overnight, until really firm.

You can make the sauce in advance. Boil the eggs for 5 minutes, then drain and leave in cold water to cool. Peel the eggs, cut them in half and scoop the still-runny yolks into a bowl. Reserve one egg white (discard the rest). Whisk the yolks until pale and creamy. Whisk in the vinegar and mustard and then gradually whisk in the oil to give a mayonnaise-like consistency. Very finely chop the reserved egg white and stir into the sauce with the gherkins, capers, tarragon, parsley and salt and pepper.

To serve, turn the terrine out on to a board and remove the cling film. Cut into slices with a serrated knife or electric carving knife. Put a slice on each plate, spoon a little of the sauce to one side and serve with a few salad leaves.

**225 g (8 oz) hot-smoked
salmon**

**6 tablespoons crème
frâiche**

**2 tablespoons capers,
drained and chopped**

**1 tablespoon chopped
fresh chives**

**4 large or 8 small slices of
sourdough or other
crusty white bread**

**50 g (2 oz) mixed salad
leaves, such as rocket,
curly endive, radicchio,
watercress and oakleaf
lettuce**

**Salt and freshly ground
black pepper**

HOT-SMOKED SALMON SANDWICH WITH CRÈME FRAÎCHE AND CAPERS

This recipe and the three variations that follow it are served in our coffee shop in Padstow and are all based on the same principle. You take some good bread such as sourdough, Granary or ciabatta and toast it lightly, preferably on a cast-iron ribbed pan to give that slightly chargrilled flavour. Then you build up salad leaves on top of it with the main components of the dish and a flavoured mayonnaise or dressing and serve the sandwich with a knife and fork. This formula has proved immensely successful for us and I think it's because it's the sort of light dish that everybody wants to eat these days. The salmon version is fantastic, particularly if you can get hold of hot-smoked salmon. This is salmon cured in the same way as smoked mackerel — in other words, it is actually smoked and cooked at the same time but then served cold. It is becoming more readily available but if you cannot get hold of it use cold-smoked salmon instead.

Remove the skin and bones from the salmon and break the fish into large flakes. Mix the crème frâiche with the capers, chives and a little salt and pepper. Put a cast-iron ribbed pan over a high heat and, when hot, grill the slices of bread for 1 minute on each side. Cut each one diagonally into 3 and fan out slightly on 4 plates. Arrange the salmon, crème frâiche and salad leaves at random on top of the bread and serve immediately.

Hot-Smoked Mackerel with Mustard Dressing

Substitute smoked mackerel for the smoked salmon, Granary bread for the sour dough and baby dandelion leaves and curly endive for the mixed salad leaves. Mix 2 teaspoons Dijon mustard with 2 teaspoons white wine vinegar and 4 tablespoons extra virgin olive oil. Stir in 1 finely chopped shallot, ½ crushed garlic clove and some salt and pepper. Toss the leaves with this dressing and arrange over the grilled bread with the flaked mackerel, 4 quartered hard-boiled eggs and 100 g (4 oz) quartered cherry tomatoes.

Smoked Eel with Horseradish Mayonnaise

Substitute smoked eel fillet, broken into small pieces, for the smoked salmon and replace the sourdough bread with a wholemeal-style bread – I like to use walnut bread from our bakery (see p. 219). Mix 6 tablespoons mayonnaise (see p. 217) with 2 tablespoons of horseradish sauce and some salt and freshly ground black pepper. Arrange the smoked eel and horseradish mayonnaise over the grilled bread with some slices of cucumber and mixed salad leaves.

Prawns and Avocado in Mary Rose Sauce

This is a variation on the theme of prawn cocktail. Replace the salmon with good-quality North Atlantic cooked peeled prawns mixed with 1 teaspoon lemon juice and some salt and pepper. Substitute ciabatta for the sourdough bread and use Little Gem lettuce and watercress sprigs for the salad. Mix together 3 tablespoons each of mayonnaise (see p. 217) and Greek yoghurt, 1 tablespoon tomato ketchup, a few drops of Tabasco sauce, the finely grated zest of ½ lemon, 2 teaspoons lemon juice and some salt and cayenne pepper. Arrange the prawns, sauce, salad leaves and 1 peeled, stoned and sliced avocado on top of the grilled bread.

OYSTERS CHARENTAIS

This classic dish from the south-west coast of France combines oysters with hot spicy sausages and is wonderful with a cold glass of Sauvignon.

Put all the sausage ingredients (except the caul fat) into a food processor and blend until the mixture is coarse. Remove, portion the mixture into 12 balls about the size of a golf ball and mould into rough sausage shapes. Wrap them in 10 cm (4 in) squares of caul fat.

Twenty minutes before serving, open the oysters but keep them flat, taking care not to spill too much of the salty liquor. Divide the oysters between four plates.

Pre-heat the grill to high and grill the sausages. Place three sausages beside each serving of oysters.

Serves 4
20 Pacific oysters

FOR THE SAUSAGES
350 g (12 oz) belly pork
½ teaspoon salt
½ teaspoon paprika
½ teaspoon black pepper
½ teaspoon thyme
½ teaspoon cayenne
    pepper
75 g (3 oz) *chorizo*
    sausages, skin removed
100 g (4 oz) caul fat or
    pork back fat for
    wrapping the sausages

**225 g (8 oz) white crab
 meat**
**50 g (2 oz) brown crab
 meat**
2 egg yolks
**85 ml (3 fl oz) double
 cream**
A pinch of cayenne pepper
**50 g (2 oz) Gruyère
 cheese, finely grated**
**Salt and freshly ground
 black pepper**

FOR THE PASTRY
225 g (8 oz) plain flour
½ teaspoon salt
65 g (2 ½ oz) butter
65 g (2 ½ oz) lard
1½ tablespoons cold water
1 egg white

CRAB AND GRUYÈRE TARTLETS

Made with the freshest white crab meat, a little brown meat, some Gruyère cheese and the shortest of shortcrust pastry, this dish needs no accompaniment except perhaps a single sprig of parsley – and a chilled glass of premier cru *Chablis. One large cooked brown crab should supply the right amount of crab meat for the tarts.*

For the pastry, sift the flour and salt into a food processor, add the butter and lard cut into small pieces and process until the mixture looks like fine breadcrumbs. Tip into a large mixing bowl and stir in the water with a round-bladed knife until everything starts to stick together. Bring together into a ball, turn out on to a work surface lightly dusted with flour and knead once or twice until smooth. Roll out the pastry thinly and use to line 4 shallow 11 cm (4½ in) loose-based tartlet tins. Chill for 20 minutes.

Pre-heat the oven to 220°C/425°F/Gas 7.

Line the pastry cases with crumpled greaseproof paper, cover the base with a generous layer of baking beans and bake blind for 15 minutes. Remove the paper and beans, brush the inside of each pastry case with a little unbeaten egg white and return to the oven for 2 minutes. Remove from the oven and lower the temperature to 200°C/400°F/Gas 6.

Mix the crab meat with the egg yolks, cream, cayenne and some salt and pepper. Spoon the mixture into the tartlet cases and sprinkle with the grated Gruyère cheese. Bake at the top of the oven for 15–20 minutes, until lightly golden. Serve warm.

2 tablespoons salt

1 teaspoon Chinese five-
spice powder

1 teaspoon ground Sichuan
peppercorns

1 teaspoon ground black
pepper

Sunflower oil for deep-
frying

900 g (2 lb) raw, unshelled,
headless prawns

STIR-FRIED SALT AND PEPPER PRAWNS

The idea for this recipe came from a dish I had on Lamma Island, Hong Kong, where I was struck by the starkness of the accompaniments — just salt and pepper. Actually, there is a bit more to it than that. I finally tracked down a recipe in Yan-Kit So's Classic Chinese Cookbook, *so here it is.*

Heat a dry wok over a medium heat. Add the salt and stir constantly for about 4 minutes, until it has turned a slightly greyish colour. Transfer to a small bowl and mix with the five-spice powder, Sichuan pepper and black pepper.

Pour some oil into a large pan until it is about one-third full and heat to 180°C/350°F or until a small piece of white bread dropped into the oil browns and rises to the surface in 1½ minutes. Add half the prawns and fry for 30 seconds, until they have curled up and turned pink. Remove and repeat with the remaining prawns.

Reheat the dry wok, add 2 tablespoons of the spiced salt and the cooked prawns, then flip the prawns over in the salt for 30 seconds so that it can permeate them. Tip on to warm serving plates and serve the remaining salt separately.

Serves 4

2 large garlic cloves, peeled

100 g (4 oz) unsalted
butter, softened

1 teaspoon lemon juice

1 teaspoon brandy

24 large, cooked, unshelled
prawns

15 g (½ oz) chopped fresh
parsley

Salt and freshly ground
black pepper

PRAWNS FRIED WITH GARLIC BUTTER

There is really very little to this recipe except a first-rate set of ingredients but it's just one of those dishes that is totally irresistible and can be knocked up in, let us say, 5 minutes flat.

For the garlic butter, roughly chop the garlic cloves, then add a good pinch of salt and crush to a paste with the back of a knife. Mix with the butter, lemon juice and brandy.

Melt 25 g (1 oz) of the garlic butter in a large frying pan. Add the prawns and gently fry for 2 minutes or until they are heated through. Season with salt and pepper. Stir the chopped parsley into the remaining garlic butter, add to the pan and, when it has melted and is hot and foaming, spoon the prawns into 4 warmed gratin dishes. Serve immediately, with lots of freshly baked French bread to mop up the garlic butter.

Thai Fish Cakes with Green Beans (Tod Man Pla)

I think this is a pretty authentic recipe for those delightful little flat fish cakes that are served as a starter in Thai restaurants, always quite spicy but not terribly hot. However, the sauce that accompanies them is usually hot and this one is no exception. I have put two birdseye chillies in it. In all my recipes using chilli, I tend to include the amount you might expect to get in a dish made by Thais or Indians, not an English chef worried about customers overdosing on chillies. If you are at all unsure about the heat in this dish, remove the seeds from the chillies (see notes on chillies on p. 22).

For the sauce, gently heat the vinegar, sugar and water in a small pan until the sugar has dissolved. Bring to the boil and boil for 1 minute, then remove from the heat and leave to cool. Stir in the fish sauce, cucumber, carrot, onion and chillies. Pour into 4 small dipping saucers or ramekins and set aside.

For the fish cakes, put the fish in a food processor with the fish sauce, curry paste, kaffir lime leaf or lime zest, chopped coriander, egg, sugar and salt. Process until smooth, then stir in the sliced green beans.

Divide the mixture into 16 pieces. Roll each one into a ball and then flatten into a 6 cm (2 ½ in) disc. Heat the oil in a large frying pan and fry the fish cakes in batches for 1 minute on each side, until golden brown. Lift out and drain on kitchen paper, then serve with the sweet and sour cucumber sauce.

Serves 4

450 g (1 lb) ling or coley fillets, skinned and cut into chunks

1 tablespoon Thai fish sauce (*nam pla*)

1 tablespoon *Red Curry Paste* (see p. 219)

1 kaffir lime leaf or 1 strip of lime zest, very finely shredded

1 tablespoon chopped fresh coriander (leaves and stalks)

1 egg

1 teaspoon palm sugar or muscovado sugar

½ teaspoon salt

40 g (1 ½ oz) French beans, thinly sliced into rounds

150 ml (5 fl oz) groundnut or sunflower oil

FOR THE SWEET AND SOUR CUCUMBER SAUCE

50 ml (2 fl oz) white wine vinegar

100 g (4 oz) caster sugar

1 ½ tablespoons water

2 teaspoons Thai fish sauce (*nam pla*)

50 g (2 oz) cucumber, very finely diced

25 g (1 oz) carrot, very finely diced

25 g (1 oz) onion, very finely chopped

2 red birdseye chillies, thinly sliced

Serves 4

12 sardines

40 g (1 ½ oz) Parmesan
cheese, finely grated

1 ½ tablespoons chopped
fresh parsley

50 g (2 oz) fresh white
breadcrumbs

50 g (2 oz) plain flour

2 eggs, beaten

Salt and freshly ground
black pepper

Sunflower oil for deep-
frying

Sprigs of fresh flatleaf
parsley, to garnish
(optional)

Lemon wedges, to serve

FRIED BUTTERFLIED SARDINE FILLETS WITH PARMESAN CRUMBS

The heads are removed from whole sardines and most of the backbone is taken out, leaving an inch or so at the tail end which gives the deep-fried fish a very pretty shape. The process of removing the bones is easier if the sardines are fresh but this is not a recipe where frozen fish need be ruled out. The delight is the remarkably pleasant, crisp Parmesan and parsley crust sandwiching a moist but thin sheet of sardine fillet — served with nothing more than lemon wedges.

First butterfly the sardines (see below). Season the fish on both sides with a little salt and pepper.

Pre-heat the oven to 150°C/300°F/Gas 2. Line a baking tray with plenty of kitchen paper.

Butterflying Sardines

1. Trim the fins off the sardines with kitchen scissors. Cut off the heads and then cut along the belly from the gut cavity right down to the tail and pull out the guts with your fingers.

2. Open out each fish and place belly-side down on a chopping board. Gently but firmly, press along the backbone with your thumb or the palm of your hand, so that you gradually flatten out the fish.

3. Turn the fish over and carefully pull out the backbone, snipping it off at the tail end with scissors. Remove any small bones that are left behind with a pair of tweezers or pliers.

Mix together the Parmesan cheese, parsley, breadcrumbs and some seasoning. Dip the butterflied sardines into the flour, then into the beaten egg and finally into the breadcrumb mixture, pressing it on well to give an even coating.

Pour the oil into a large pan and heat to 180°C/350°F or until a small piece of bread dropped into the oil browns and rises to the surface in about 1½ minutes. Deep-fry the sardines one or two at a time for 1 minute, flipping them over half-way through so that they brown on both sides. Lift out with a slotted spoon on to the paper-lined tray and keep hot in the oven while you cook the rest. Garnish with sprigs of parsley, if liked, and serve with lemon wedges.

Salmon Rillettes

100 g (4 oz) butter

300 ml (10 fl oz) water

1 teaspoon salt

2 slices of lemon

2 bay leaves

10 black peppercorns

350 g (12 oz) salmon

¼ teaspoon ground mace

A good pinch of ground
allspice

Freshly ground white
pepper

Walnut Bread (see p. 219)
or wholemeal bread,
to serve

**FOR THE GREEN
CHUTNEY**

2 teaspoons English
mustard powder

1 tablespoon finely
chopped capers

1 small gherkin, cut into
fine matchsticks (about
1 tablespoon)

1 tablespoon chopped
fresh *fines herbes*, i.e.
parsley, chervil, chives
and tarragon

2 tablespoons extra virgin
olive oil

1 teaspoon white wine
vinegar

½ teaspoon salt

I first came across this dish in a restaurant near the rather unfortunatley named town of Condom in South West France. I suppose in Britain you might call it potted salmon, but rillettes seems more appropriate because the idea is to try and shred the salmon rather like duck or goose rillettes. Like its poultry counterpart it is designed to use valuable trimmings, such as the heads and tails, which would normally be thrown away but actually contain plenty of good-tasting fillet. It is flavoured with the sort of spices you would find in something like potted shrimps and served with a simple, fresh, green chutney made with capers, gherkins and herbs.

Leave the butter somewhere warm until it is really soft but not melted. Meanwhile, put the water, salt, lemon, bay leaves and peppercorns in a small pan, bring to the boil and simmer for 10 minutes. Add the salmon and simmer for 8–10 minutes. Leave to cool in the cooking water. Remove the skin and bones from the fish, place the flesh in a bowl and shred by pulling apart with 2 forks.

Add the butter to the salmon with the mace, allspice and 3 twists of freshly ground white pepper. Mix together gently with a fork, then cover and chill for 2 hours or until just firm. If it gets too hard, leave to soften at room temperature for about 30 minutes before serving.

For the green chutney just mix together all the ingredients in a small bowl and season with freshly ground white pepper, then cover and chill. Serve the rillettes and chutney with lightly toasted walnut or wholemeal bread.

PLAICE WITH LEEKS, MINT AND BEAUJOLAIS

This is one of the most successful dishes for plaice — we've had it on the menu in my restaurant for twelve years.

I think its success lies in the almost indefinable satisfaction of the three components — the watery fragrance of the plaice, the tartness of the Beaujolais sauce and the freshness of mint with the leeks, with the slight taste of smoke from the bacon.

Cut the leeks in half lengthways and once more into quarters if they are quite large. Cut across these strips into 1 cm (½ in) pieces.

Bring a small pan of salted water to the boil, add the leeks and simmer for a few minutes until tender but still *al dente*. Drain them well. Melt 15 g (½ oz) butter in a small pan, add the bacon and leeks and cook gently until all the excess water has evaporated. Stir in the mint and season with some salt and pepper. Set aside and keep warm.

Pre-heat the grill to high.

Put the Beaujolais, port, fish stock and sugar into a large pan and boil rapidly until reduced by three-quarters.

Melt another 15 g (½ oz) butter and brush over both sides of each plaice fillet. Season with salt and pepper and lay them on the lightly oiled rack of the grill pan. Grill for 2 minutes.

Dice the remaining butter. Bring the reduced wine and stock back up to the boil and then whisk in the butter, a few small pieces at a time. Adjust the seasoning if necessary.

To serve, spoon the leeks on to 4 warmed plates. Put the plaice fillets on the plates, and pour the sauce around. Garnish with sprigs of fresh mint.

Serves 4

100 g (4 oz) leeks
100 g (4 oz) butter
1 smoked back bacon rasher, cut into thin strips
1 teaspoon chopped fresh mint
175 ml (6 fl oz) Beaujolais
500 ml (2 fl oz) port
300 ml (10 fl oz) *Fish Stock* (see p. 212)
¼ teaspoon caster sugar
4 plaice fillets, weighing about 75 g (3 oz) each, skinned
Salt and freshly ground white pepper
Sprigs of fresh mint, to garnish

HOT AND SPICY FISH

One of the mystifying questions about Great Britain is why, for a country surrounded by some of the richest fishing waters in the world, are we so relatively uninterested in fish cookery? I find it terribly difficult to answer that one. If you ask Cornish people why they don't like fish, many of them reply that they were brought up on it and so it isn't a great delicacy to them. Then you argue that the people of Brittany, with a similar coastline and similar fish, have made much more of what's on offer, as have virtually all the people on the coastline from Brittany to Finland, and you come up with no real reason why.

But suppose that in Britain we were used to eating the sort of seafood dishes they cook in Goa, would our attitude be the same? I think not, because most of us love spicy food. One only has to observe the enormous popularity of Indian and Thai restaurants in this country to realize how different the case would be if we were much more relaxed about using plenty of heat and spice in our cooking, and that's why I think this is such an important chapter. I believe that fish cookery in this country will more and more feature ingredients such as chilli, turmeric, cardamom, ginger, kaffir lime leaves, coriander, *nam pla* and everything else that still seems so exotic to us.

So what dishes would I particularly like to bring to your attention in this chapter? I think above all the *Thai Red Seafood* (see p.70). If you want a fish stew that you'll never forget, this is it. I cooked it for the annual staff barbecue on Harlyn Beach near Padstow and I honestly think it was the best fish dish for large numbers I have ever cooked. We invited about 150 people and 200 came. We asked a band to play on the beach. We bought three barrels of beer and about 100 bottles of wine, plus a stack of soft drinks for the kids. We had prawn tandoori and chicken tandoori, spare rib teriyaki and the *Rice-shaped Pasta* on p.104. We always make a salad of fusilli and pesto, plus a tomato, onion and coriander salad with cumin and chilli like the one served with *Tandoori Prawns* on p.64, some couscous salad with mint, a potato salad with lots of spring onions chopped into it, and loads of freshly baked baguettes. The weather helped; it was one of those still, balmy summer evenings that make me think there is nowhere else in the world I would rather be than Cornwall.

Tandoori Prawns (see p.64).

**32 large, raw, unshelled
    prawns**
175 g (6 oz) Greek yoghurt

**FOR THE LEMON CHILLI
MARINADE**
1 teaspoon cayenne pepper
1 teaspoon salt
Juice of 1 lemon

**FOR THE TANDOORI
MASALA PASTE**
15 g (½ oz) fennel seeds
**1 tablespoon coriander
    seeds**
1 tablespoon cumin seeds
**25 g (1 oz) fresh root
    ginger, roughly chopped**
6 garlic cloves, chopped
**4 red finger chillies, seeded
    and roughly chopped**
2 teaspoons paprika
**1 teaspoon turmeric
    powder**
Juice of 1 lemon
1–2 tablespoons cold water

**FOR THE KACHUMBER
SALAD**
3 tomatoes
1 medium onion
**2 tablespoons roughly
    chopped fresh coriander**
¼ teaspoon ground cumin
**A large pinch of cayenne
    pepper**
**1 tablespoon white wine
    vinegar**
½ teaspoon salt

TANDOORI PRAWNS

*The tandoori spice mix that I use for my prawns is quite unconventional.
Although it includes all the standard tandoori marinade ingredients, such
as yoghurt, lemon juice, chilli and curry spices, I also put in a great deal of
pounded fennel seed, which I find gives the marinated prawns an
incomparable texture and aromatic flavour. Do splash out on the best-
possible whole uncooked prawns for this dish; it is well worth it.*

Mix together all the ingredients for the lemon chilli marinade. Make 3 small slits
in either side of each prawn between the shell segments to allow the marinade
to penetrate. Put the prawns and marinade in a bowl, turning the prawns to
coat them, and set aside for 20 minutes.

   For the tandoori masala paste, grind the fennel, coriander and cumin seeds
in a coffee grinder or a pestle and mortar. Put the spices in a food processor
with all the rest of the ingredients and the cold water and blend until smooth.
Stir the paste into the yoghurt. Add the prawns, stir together well and leave for
20 minutes.

   Thread the prawns on to metal skewers or bamboo skewers that have been
soaked in water, piercing them just behind the head and through the tail. Cook
them over a barbecue or under a very hot grill for 4 minutes, turning them
over half-way through.

   While the prawns are cooking, prepare the salad. Halve and thinly slice the
tomatoes and onion, then mix with all the remaining salad ingredients. Serve
with the prawns, together with some warm naan bread.

MILD POTATO CURRY TOPPED WITH SMOKED HADDOCK AND A POACHED EGG

This dish must be made! The idea of putting spiced potatoes underneath smoked haddock with a poached egg turns a homely, well-known English dish into something much more elevated. It is not hard to do and it has a sort of joyous sophistication to it which, to me, is what good cooking is all about.

Poaching eggs carries the same sort of fear of failure as making omelettes. The restaurant way is to use plenty of water and a fairly deep pan. Once the water is boiling, the pan is pulled slightly to one side to create a rolling boil and the eggs are then broken into the middle and roll up into a pleasing oval shape. But to avoid any possibility of failure in this recipe I have suggested using a shallow pan and a small amount of water, which should be heated to the merest tremble of a boil. I always add vinegar to the poaching water, not because it helps the eggs to set but because I like the faint flavour which lingers in the eggs.

For the potato curry, cook the potatoes in a pan of boiling water for 6–7 minutes, until tender, then drain. Meanwhile, heat the oil in a pan, add the mustard seeds and, when they begin to pop, add the turmeric and onions. Fry for 5 minutes or until the onions are soft and lightly browned. Add the potatoes and some salt and pepper and fry for 1–2 minutes. Add the tomatoes and cook for 1 minute. Stir in the chopped coriander, then set aside and keep warm.

Bring a pan of water to the boil, add the pieces of smoked haddock and simmer gently for 3–4 minutes, until cooked. Lift out with a slotted spoon, cover and keep warm.

Pour about 4 cm (1½ in) water into a frying pan and bring to a very gentle simmer; the water should be just trembling and there should be a few bubbles rising up from the bottom of the pan. Add the vinegar, break in the eggs and poach for 3 minutes, basting the top of the eggs with a little of the hot water as they cook. Lift out with a slotted spoon and drain briefly on kitchen paper.

To serve, put the potato curry on 4 warmed plates, lay a piece of smoked haddock on top and a poached egg on top of that. Serve garnished with sprigs of coriander.

Serves 4

350 g (12 oz) undyed smoked haddock, cut into 4 pieces
2 teaspoons white wine vinegar
4 eggs
Sprigs of fresh coriander, to garnish

FOR THE POTATO CURRY
350 g (12 oz) waxy main-crop potatoes, such as Wilja, peeled and cut into 1 cm (½ in) dice
2 tablespoons sunflower oil
½ teaspoon yellow mustard seeds
¼ teaspoon turmeric powder
100 g (4 oz) onions, finely chopped
2 tomatoes, skinned and chopped
1 teaspoon roughly chopped fresh coriander
Salt and freshly ground black pepper

GREEN MONKFISH AND PRAWN CURRY

3 tablespoons sunflower
  oil
1 quantity of *Green Curry
  Paste* (see p.215)
400 ml (14 fl oz) can of
  coconut milk
175 ml (6 fl oz) water
2 tablespoons Thai fish
  sauce (*nam pla*)
2 teaspoons palm sugar or
  muscovado sugar
4 kaffir lime leaves or
  1 pared strip of lime
  zest, cut into very fine
  shreds
Juice of 1 lime
100 g (4 oz) very small
  new potatoes, cut in
  half if large
50 g (2 oz) baby
  aubergines or
  mangetout, quartered
12 raw, unshelled, headless
  prawns
350 g (12 oz) monkfish
  fillet, cut across into
  slices 1 cm (½ in) thick
50 g (2 oz) canned
  bamboo shoots
2 tablespoons finely
  shredded fresh basil
1 green finger chilli, thinly
  sliced across into rings

If you put the maximum amount of green chillies in this recipe that I've suggested, you will create a curry of such heat and intensity that you could be sitting in Bangkok. If you like your curries a little milder, use only two chillies. Either way, I hope you'll agree that this is probably the best recipe for green fish curry you have ever tasted. It is fragrant and blindingly hot but also sweet and delicious with the background flavour of coconut.

Heat the oil in a large pan, add the green curry paste and fry for 5–6 minutes, until the ingredients begin to separate from the oil and it starts to smell aromatic. Add the coconut milk, water, fish sauce, sugar, lime leaves or zest, lime juice, potatoes and the aubergines, if using. Simmer for about 10 minutes, until the potatoes and aubergines are tender. Meanwhile, shell the prawns and de-vein them (see p.18). Cut each one in half lengthways.

Add the prawns to the pan with the monkfish, bamboo shoots and the mangetout, if using. Simmer for another 2 minutes. Stir in the shredded basil and serve sprinkled with the sliced green chilli.

6 tablespoons vegetable oil

2 medium onions, finely
    chopped

6 garlic cloves, finely
    chopped

2 tablespoons red wine
    vinegar

1 tablespoon palm sugar
    or muscovado sugar

450 g (1 lb) cooked peeled
    prawns

4 fresh curry leaves or
    2 young fresh bay leaves,
    very finely shredded

GOAN MASALA PASTE

1 teaspoon cumin seeds

2 teaspoons coriander
    seeds

2 teaspoons black
    peppercorns

2 teaspoons cloves

1 teaspoon turmeric
    powder

100 g (4 oz) red finger
    chillies, roughly
    chopped

1 teaspoon salt

6 garlic cloves, peeled

1 teaspoon palm sugar or
    muscovado sugar

2 tablespoons prepared
    fresh tamarind
    (see p.25)

5 cm (2 in) piece of fresh
    root ginger, roughly
    chopped

2 tablespoons red wine
    vinegar

GOAN PRAWN BALCHAO

This Goan dish comes in two forms: either as a curry made with small prawns or as a preserve, where more vinegar is added and the curry is cooked out longer. The preserve is served with such great Goan dishes as pork Vindaloo. In this recipe the prawns are served freshly cooked as a curry. It makes a very pleasant dish that needs only plain boiled rice and, perhaps, a tomato and coriander salad to accompany it.

For the Goan masala paste, grind the cumin seeds, coriander seeds, peppercorns and cloves in a coffee grinder or pestle and mortar. Transfer to a food processor with all the remaining paste ingredients and process until smooth. Spoon into a sterilized glass jar, seal and store in the fridge.

Heat the oil in a medium-sized pan, add the onions and garlic and fry for 8 minutes, until golden. Add the masala paste and fry for 2 minutes, until the spices start to separate from the oil. Mix the red wine vinegar and sugar together, add to the pan and simmer for 1 minute. Add the prawns and the shredded curry or bay leaves and turn the mixture over gently for about 2–3 minutes, until the prawns are hot. Serve with plain boiled rice.

GOAN FISH CURRY

I have chosen steaks of cheap and readily available fish for this popular curry from Goa — either conger eel or huss. Very easy to make, it is what I would call a wet curry because there is plenty of sauce, rich in coconut milk and flavoured with garlic, ginger and coriander.

For the curry paste, blend all the ingredients in a food processor until smooth.

Season the fish steaks well with salt and pepper. Heat the oil in a deep frying pan, add the onion and fry for about 10 minutes, until richly golden. Add the curry paste and fry for 2 minutes. Stir in the tomatoes and fry for 1 minute, then add the coconut milk and bring to the boil. Add the fish and chillies to the pan, cover and simmer for 10–12 minutes, turning the fish over half-way through.

Lift the fish steaks out of the pan, put them in a serving dish and keep warm. Season the sauce with salt and pepper, add the coriander and boil for a minute or two to reduce a little. Return the fish to the sauce and serve with boiled rice.

Serves 4

4 conger eel or huss steaks, weighing about 175 g (6 oz) each
85 ml (3 fl oz) sunflower oil
1 medium onion, sliced
2 tomatoes, skinned and chopped
250 ml (8 fl oz) canned coconut milk
4 green or red chillies, split open
2 tablespoons chopped fresh coriander
Salt and freshly ground black pepper

FOR THE CURRY PASTE
6 red finger chillies, seeded and roughly chopped (leave the seeds in if you want extra heat)
2 tablespoons ground coriander
2 teaspoons ground cumin
1 teaspoon turmeric powder
3 garlic cloves, roughly chopped
5 cm (2 in) piece of fresh root ginger, roughly chopped
2 tablespoons prepared fresh tamarind (see p.25)

THAI RED SEAFOOD

1 cooked lobster, weighing
    about 450 g (1 lb)
1 cooked crab, weighing
    about 750 g (1½ lb)
225 g (8 oz) prepared
    squid (see p.16)
1 red mullet, weighing
    about 350 g (12 oz),
    filleted (see p.13)
3 tablespoons sunflower oil
1 quantity of *Red Curry
    Paste* (see p.219)
1.2 litres (2 pints) *Chicken
    Stock* (see p.213)
100 g (4 oz) creamed
    coconut
3 tablespoons Thai fish
    sauce (*nam pla*)
2 limes
3 fresh or dried kaffir lime
    leaves (optional)
12 large, raw, unshelled
    prawns
24 large mussels, cleaned
    (see p.17)
1 small bunch of fresh
    basil, finely shredded

FOR THE GARNISHES

4 red birdseye chillies,
    thinly sliced
85 ml (3 fl oz) rice vinegar
    or white wine vinegar
300 ml (10 fl oz) sunflower
    oil
4 shallots, thinly sliced
6 garlic cloves, thinly sliced
50 g (2 oz) cashew nuts,
    split in half

There was a bit of a toss-up whether I was going to put this recipe in this chapter or the one on soups and stews. But because it is particularly hot and deliciously full of Thai spices and coconut milk, I decided it belonged here. It is an expensive dish to make but well worth it as it has so much of interest in it: pieces of lobster, crab, prawns, a delicious sauce, and accompaniments of deep-fried garlic, shallots and nuts, chilli-flavoured vinegar and fresh basil.

Pull the claws off the lobster, break them into 3 and lightly crack the shells with a rolling pin (see p.19). Detach the head and legs from the tail section and discard (or save for *Shellfish Stock*, see p.214). Cut the tail into 3 sections through the shell. Detach the legs and claws from the crab, break them into 3 and lightly crack the shells. Remove the body from the back shell (see pp.20–21). Scoop the brown meat out of the back shell and set aside, discarding the shell. Remove the dead man's fingers from the body (see p.20) and then cut the body section into quarters. Slice the squid across into rings and each red mullet fillet into 3 pieces.

For the garnishes, mix the chillies with the vinegar in a small bowl. Heat the oil in a frying pan, add the shallots, garlic and cashew nuts and fry for about 3 minutes, until crisp and golden. Lift out with a slotted spoon, drain on kitchen paper and then spoon into another small bowl. Set aside.

Heat the oil in a large pan, add the red curry paste and fry for 2 minutes, until the paste starts to separate from the oil. Add the stock, creamed coconut and fish sauce and heat gently until the coconut dissolves.

Meanwhile, pare 2 strips of zest from 1 lime and cut them across into very fine shreds. Squeeze out the juice from both limes. Add the zest and juice to the pan with the dried kaffir lime leaves, if using, and simmer everything together for 2 minutes.

Add the lobster and crab pieces to the pan and simmer for 2 minutes. Add the prawns and simmer for 1 minute. Add the squid and red mullet and simmer for 2 minutes. Add the mussels, cover and simmer for 2 minutes until they have opened. Discard any that remain closed.

Stir in the basil and the fresh kaffir lime leaves, if using, then transfer everything to a large shallow serving platter and serve with the little bowls of prepared garnishes and *Baked Rice* (see p.218) made with Thai jasmine rice.

MALAYSIAN FRIED LEMON SOLE

Serves 4

3 lemon sole, weighing
about 450 g (1 lb) each,
filleted and skinned
(see pp.14–15)
175 g (6 oz) cornflour
Sunflower oil for deep-
frying
Salt and freshly ground
black pepper

FOR THE CHILLI SAUCE
6 red finger chillies,
roughly chopped
4 garlic cloves, roughly
chopped
1 teaspoon turmeric
powder
5 cm (2 in) piece of fresh
root ginger, roughly
chopped
4 tablespoons sunflower oil
1 teaspoon salt
2 tablespoons vinegar
4–6 tablespoons cold water

Here, lemon sole is dipped in a sauce made with red chilli, garlic, ginger and turmeric, then dusted with cornflour and deep-fried. It is a simple and delightfully spicy way of serving up any fillets of flat fish, such as plaice, dab or flounder, and can be accompanied by a simple green salad and maybe some plain rice (see p.218). However, I've added a couple of satellite recipes to the main one which I suggest you try after you have done the deep-fried fish a few times. I think that the total idea comprising three separate recipes is too much to attempt straight away. In addition to the deep-fried fish there is a Roasted Tomato and Chilli Sambal, which is a hot Indonesian salsa made with dried chillies, and Nasi Goreng, which is egg-fried rice with prawns.

Put all the ingredients for the chilli sauce into a liquidizer and blend until smooth. Pour into a pan and simmer gently for 10 minutes or so until the mixture begins to separate.

Pour the sunflower oil into a large pan until it is about a third full. Heat to 190°C/375°F or until a small piece of white bread dropped into the oil browns and rises to the surface in 1 minute. Put the chilli sauce in one shallow dish and the cornflour in another. Season the fish fillets and dip them first into the chilli sauce and then into the cornflour, making sure that it coats the fish evenly. Cook the fillets in the hot oil, 2 or 3 at a time, for about 2 minutes or until crisp and golden. Lift out with a slotted spoon and drain on kitchen paper.

Roasted Tomato and Chilli Sambal

Ideally, this should include dried pasilla chillies, which are available from good delicatessens, larger supermarkets, and by mail order (see p.22). Pasilla is a fruity chilli with overtones of smoke and liquorice (I sound a bit like a wine writer!) and is fantastic with seafood. See p.22 for a more general discussion on types of chilli.

If using the dried chillies, cover them with boiling water and leave to soak for 15 minutes or until soft. Pre-heat the grill to high. Put the tomatoes, whole red chillies and shallots on a grilling tray and grill for 5–10 minutes, turning now and then, until well blackened. Cool slightly, then chop roughly by hand. Drain the soaked chillies and chop them finely, then mix with the roasted vegetables and the lime juice and fish sauce.

Serves 4

2 dried pasilla chillies (optional)
350 g (12 oz) tomatoes, cut in half
6 red finger chillies
3 shallots, peeled
2 tablespoons lime juice
2 tablespoons Thai fish sauce (*nam pla*)

Nasi Goreng

Beat the eggs with the sesame oil and salt. Heat the oil in a wok or a large frying pan, add the garlic, ginger and the white part of the spring onions and stir-fry for about 3 minutes, until golden. Add the beaten eggs and stir-fry for 1 minute. Add the cooked rice and stir until it is thoroughly heated through, then add the prawns and heat through. Finally, sprinkle over the green spring onion tops and the coriander, then serve.

Serves 4

2 eggs
2 teaspoons sesame oil
½ teaspoon salt
2 tablespoons sunflower oil
2 garlic cloves, very finely chopped
2.5 cm (1 in) piece of fresh root ginger, very finely chopped
6 spring onions, thinly sliced
½ quantity of *Baked Rice* (see p.218)
100 g (4 oz) cooked peeled prawns
1 tablespoon chopped fresh coriander

DEEP-FRIED FISH

One day I'm going to open a fish and chip shop. I think that the satisfaction of serving good fish and chips would be as great as serving up a plate of Helford oysters in my restaurant with a bottle of *premier cru* Chablis, followed by a thick fillet of bass with some *beurre blanc*. It's got to be done with a bit of style, though. Of course I would serve cod, haddock and plaice but also gurnard, skate in batter, and marinated and deep-fried monkfish. There would be whole prawns, mackerel and fennel fish cakes, salmon and tarragon fish cakes and a variety of batters – not just the yeast and beer batter I enjoy so much (see p.80) but also tempura batter for deep-frying scallops and fish wrapped in wonton or spring roll wrappers and, while we're at it, we'd sell some cold fried fish in matzo meal, to be eaten with horseradish and beetroot.

Most of us feel just a shade guilty about enjoying deep-fried food because it's not held to be too healthy. Lightly cooked fish and salads, Mediterranean fish cooked in olive oil, and Indian or Chinese fish dishes containing almost no oil are the sort of thing people feel safest eating because they taste good and don't do you any harm either, but oh the charm of deep-fried fish. Who cares if it is high in fat? Just don't eat it very often.

Fish and shellfish are the perfect foods for deep-frying. Their white delicacy and tenderness make the perfect contrast to crisp batter or breadcrumbs. But there is one essential point about deep-frying which makes all the difference: be extravagant with the oil. Change it regularly. The charm of deep-fried food is seeing it dipped into a bubbling inferno of clear, sparkling oil and then emerge cloaked in bright, crisp batter. The alternative is a bit like cooking new potatoes fresh from the garden in water that you have used ten times already. I'm not being totally purist about this and suggesting that you discard oil after one frying, but go and look at your oil now and throw it out!

Salmon Fish Cakes with Sorrel and Watercress Salad in a Caper and Lemon Dressing (see p.77).

FRITTO MISTO OF SCALLOPS, PRAWNS AND SQUID WITH LEMON

Serves 4

8 prepared scallops
(see p.18)

100 g (4 oz) prepared
squid (see p.16)

12 large, raw, headless
prawns, shelled and
de-veined (see p.18)

1 litre (1¾ pints) olive oil

75 g (3 oz) plain flour,
seasoned with salt and
black pepper

2 lemons

Salt

This is my version of the classic Italian dish, fritto misto di mare, *where small pieces of seafood are tossed in seasoned flour and then deep-fried in olive oil. Much as I've enjoyed this dish on many occasions, I've always balked at putting it in a recipe book because of the high price of olive oil — there's no point in writing recipes if you have a suspicion that nobody is ever going to cook them. However, I spent some time trying to work out the minimum amount of oil you'd need to deep-fry 4 portions of this superb dish successfully and I now present my own version of fritto misto, specially adapted to use just one bottle of olive oil.*

Pre-heat the oven to 150°C/300°F/Gas 2. Line a large baking tray with plenty of kitchen paper.

Detach the coral from each scallop and slice it in half lengthways (this prevents them exploding during cooking). Then slice the scallop meat horizontally in half as well. Cut the squid across into thick rings. Season all the seafood with a little salt.

Pour the oil into a large saucepan and heat to 190°C/375°F or until a small piece of white bread dropped into the oil browns and rises to the surface in 1 minute. Toss the fish in the seasoned flour and deep-fry in batches for 30 seconds–1 minute, until the floury coating is just beginning to be tinged with brown. Lift out with a slotted spoon, arrange on the baking tray and keep hot in the oven while you cook the rest. Slice each lemon across into chunky halves and serve with the seafood.

SALMON FISH CAKES WITH SORREL AND WATERCRESS SALAD IN A CAPER AND LEMON DRESSING

These fish cakes have plenty of fresh tarragon in them, which goes very well with salmon I always think, and they're served with a simple salad and quite a sharp dressing to cut the richness of the deep-frying. If you can't get sorrel leaves, don't worry, just use some other small salad leaves, but sorrel does add a slightly tart accent which is most pleasing with the fish cakes.

Cook the potatoes in boiling salted water until tender. Drain well, tip back into the pan and mash until smooth. Leave to cool slightly.

Break the salmon into small flakes, removing any bones and skin. Put into a bowl with the mashed potatoes, melted butter, herbs, salt and some black pepper. Mix together well. Shape the mixture into 8 rounds about 2.5 cm (1 in) thick, cover with cling film and chill for 20 minutes.

Meanwhile, whisk all the ingredients for the dressing together and season to taste.

Pour the oil into a pan until it is no more than half full and heat to 180°C/350°F, or until a small piece of bread dropped into it browns and rises to the surface in 1½ minutes. Dip the fish cakes into the seasoned flour, then the beaten eggs and finally the breadcrumbs, pressing them on well to give an even coating. Deep-fry them in batches for about 4 minutes, until crisp and golden. Lift out and drain briefly on kitchen paper. Keep warm in a low oven while you cook the rest.

Toss the sorrel and watercress with 1 tablespoon of the dressing. Put the fish cakes on 4 warmed plates, pile the dressed salad leaves to one side and spoon a little more dressing over the remainder of the plate.

Serves 4

900 g (2 lb) potatoes, peeled and cut into chunks

750 g (1 ½ lb) cooked salmon

25 g (1 oz) butter, melted

1 tablespoon chopped fresh dill

15 g (½ oz) chopped fresh parsley

1 teaspoon salt

50 g (2 oz) plain flour, seasoned with salt and pepper

2 eggs, beaten

150 g (5 oz) fresh white breadcrumbs

15 g (½ oz) sorrel leaves, torn into small pieces

15g (½ oz) watercress, divided into sprigs

Freshly ground black pepper

Sunflower oil for deep-frying

FOR THE CAPER AND LEMON DRESSING

Juice of 1 small lemon

85 ml (3 fl oz) olive oil

2 tablespoons capers, well drained, rinsed and finely chopped

1 small garlic clove, crushed

1 tablespoon chopped fresh chives

1 tablespoon chopped fresh dill or fennel herb

**4 sea bass or black bream,
weighing about 350 g
(12 oz) each, cleaned
(see p.11)**
**50 g (2 oz) plain flour,
seasoned with salt and
pepper**
**Sunflower oil for
deep-frying**

FOR THE CHILLI SAUCE
**2 tablespoons finely
chopped garlic**
**2 large red chillies, finely
chopped**
2 tablespoons sunflower oil
**2 tablespoons palm sugar
or muscovado sugar**
**3 tablespoons Thai fish
sauce (nam pla)**
**1 tablespoon tamarind
mixed with 1
tablespoon water, or
2 tablespoons lemon
juice**

FOR THE GARNISHES
4 shallots, sliced
2 garlic cloves, thinly sliced
**50 g (2 oz) cashew nuts,
halved**
**2 kaffir lime leaves, finely
shredded (optional)**
**25 g (1 oz) fresh basil
leaves**

DEEP-FRIED SEA BASS WITH CHILLI SAUCE

I ate a whole fish served this way a few years ago at Hua Hin, in Thailand. The interesting thing about it is that I can't quite remember what the dish was like so I keep on coming up with approximations, and each one seems almost nicer than the last. That reveals quite a lot about how one thinks up new recipes: little scraps of information bob around in one's mind and gradually build up into a firm idea. This dish is rather good. The fish is just dusted in seasoned flour, deep-fried, then served with deep-fried sliced garlic, shallots, lime leaves, cashew nuts and basil, and a hot and sweet chilli sauce.

For the sauce, pound together the garlic and chillies in a pestle and mortar until they form a coarse paste. Heat the oil in a small saucepan, add the garlic and chilli paste and fry for 1 minute. Stir in the sugar, fish sauce and tamarind water or lemon juice, bring to a simmer and keep warm.

Next prepare the garnishes. Fill a pan large enough to accommodate the fish about one-third full with sunflower oil. Heat to 190°C/375°F or until a small piece of white bread dropped into it browns and rises to the surface in 1 minute. Add the sliced shallots, garlic and cashew nuts and fry for 2 minutes. Lift out with a slotted spoon and drain on kitchen paper. Add the shredded lime leaves, if using, and the basil leaves and fry for about 30 seconds. Drain and set aside.

Rinse the fish and pat dry. Coat in the seasoned flour and deep-fry, one at a time, for 5–6 minutes, until crisp and golden. Lift out, drain briefly on kitchen paper and keep warm while you cook the remaining fish.

Put the fish on 4 warmed plates and spoon over the sauce. Scatter with the garnishes and serve.

900 g (2 lb) Maris Piper
  potatoes, peeled and
  cut lengthways into
  chips 1 cm (½ in) thick
4 thick pieces of cod fillet
  from the loin end, not
  the tail, weighing about
  175 g (6 oz) each
Sunflower oil for
  deep-frying
Sprigs of flatleaf parsley, to
  garnish (optional)
Salt and freshly ground
  black pepper

**FOR THE YEAST AND
BEER BATTER**
15 g (½ oz) fresh yeast
300 ml (10 fl oz) beer
225 g (8 oz) plain flour
1 teaspoon salt

FOR THE TARTARE SAUCE
½ quantity of *Mustard
  Mayonnaise* (see p.216)
1 teaspoon finely chopped
  green olives
1 teaspoon finely chopped
  gherkins
1 teaspoon finely chopped
  capers
2 teaspoons chopped fresh
  chives
2 teaspoons chopped fresh
  parsley

DEEP-FRIED COD IN A YEAST AND BEER BATTER WITH TARTARE SAUCE AND CHIPS

The best ever! I used to think that the only decent chips were the thin and crispy French-style frites *because, on the whole, my experiences of chips in British fish and chip shops have been rather limp and soggy, greasy and unappetizing. But the other day, while walking down London's Kings Road, I nipped into a place called Ed's Easy Diner because it looked so friendly in an American chrome-and-formica sort of way. I had a burger and a side order of American fries, which were big, thick chips but, as the current saying goes, these chips were 'to die for'. They were crisp and fat but also slightly grainy and sandy on the outside, like the best roast potatoes. I hope I've managed to recreate them here. I have specified only one type of potato, Maris Piper, which we find makes consistently the best chips. In summer most recently dug potatoes make great chips but for the rest of the year potatoes tend to absorb the oil and look greasy. I don't find that the floury varieties normally recommended for chips, such as King Edward, Désirée and Pentland Dell, work very well, and sometimes even Maris Pipers fry up greasy and soggy too. A good chip potato fries dry and crisp. When we get a good one we buy a tonne or so but every time we buy in a new batch we have to test them.*

I think you will very much enjoy the batter, which is lightened by yeast and beer. It has a taste and smell almost of fresh bread and remains perfectly crisp. Guinness gives it a pleasing dark appearance but any beer will do.

For the batter, cream the yeast to a smooth paste with a little of the beer. Gradually stir in the rest of the beer. Sift the flour and salt into a bowl, make a well in the centre and pour in the beer mixture. Gradually whisk the liquid into the flour to make a smooth batter. Cover and leave at room temperature for 1 hour.

Pre-heat the oven to 150°C/300°F/Gas 3. Line a baking tray with plenty of kitchen paper and set aside. Mix together all the ingredients for the tartare sauce and set aside.

If you don't have a thermostatically controlled chip fryer you will need to use a fairly good sized friture, a pan that will take about 4.5 litres (8 pints) with a frying basket to fit. Use about 2.25 litres (4 pints) of oil; it is never sensible to fill a deep-frying pan more than that.

Cooking chips in 2 stages makes them crisp on the outside and fluffy inside. First you blanch them. Heat the oil to 140°C/275°F and fry the chips in 2 batches for about 5 minutes, emptying them into a roasting tin afterwards. The object is to cook the potatoes through without colour.

To fry the fish, heat the oil to 160°C/325°F, season the pieces of fish with salt and pepper and then dip them into the batter. Fry 2 pieces at a time for 7–8 minutes, until crisp and a deep golden brown. Lift out and drain on the paper-lined tray, then keep hot in the oven while you cook the other 2 pieces.

Raise the temperature to 190°C/375°F and fry the chips, again in 2 batches, until crisp and a deep golden brown. Serve immediately, with the tartare sauce. At the restaurant we finish the frying by dropping sprigs of parsley into the fryer for a few seconds, which we serve as a garnish.

Serves 4

FOR THE PESTO BUTTER

15 g (½ oz) fresh basil

2 large garlic cloves,
   roughly chopped

15 g (½ oz) Parmesan
   cheese, grated

15 g (½ oz) pine kernels

3 tablespoons olive oil

½ teaspoon salt

25 g (1 oz) butter, softened

DEEP-FRIED COD STUFFED WITH PESTO BUTTER

The contrast between a crisp, golden breadcrumb coating, delicate flakes of moist white fish and a just-melted centre of fragrant basil, garlic and pine kernel pesto is a delight. It is important to get the right cut of fish for this dish. A good thick fillet of cod cut from just behind the head of a large fish is ideal.

First make the pesto butter. Put all the ingredients except the butter into a food processor and blend until smooth. Scrape the mixture into a bowl and beat in the softened butter. Spoon the pesto butter on to a sheet of cling film in a line about 10 cm (4 in) long, then roll it up in the cling film into a sausage shape, twisting the ends of the cling film to secure it. Put in the freezer until hard. When the butter is firm, use to stuff the fish (see below).

Stuffing the Cod with Pesto Butter

1. Trim away the thinner belly flap from the fillet and cut the rest into four 175 g (6 oz) pieces, each about 12.5 cm (5 in) long.

2. To make a pocket in the pieces of cod, **make a deep cut, 7.5 cm (3 in) long, in the side of each piece of fish with a small, sharp knife,** taking care not to cut right through to the other side.

3. Remove the butter from the freezer, unwrap and cut into slices 1 cm (½ in) thick. **Gently poke 2 pieces of butter into the pocket of each piece of fish** and then close up the pocket so that no butter is visible.

Pour the oil into a large pan so that it is about one-third full. Heat to 180°C/350°F or until a small piece of white bread dropped into the oil browns and rises to the surface in 1½ minutes. Dip the pieces of fish in the seasoned flour, making sure that they are all well coated. Then dip them into the beaten egg and lastly the breadcrumbs, pressing them on well to give a thick, even coating. Deep-fry the fish, 2 pieces at a time, for 5 minutes or until crisp and golden. Lift out and drain on kitchen paper, then serve straight away.

Sun-dried Tomato, Roasted Red Pepper and Chilli Butter

Finely chop ½ roasted red pepper, 2 sun-dried tomatoes and ½ red finger chilli, then mix together with a little salt. Beat in 25 g (1 oz) softened butter, then continue as for the main recipe.

1 x 1.25kg (2 ½ lb) thick fillet of cod, skinned
40 g (1 ½ oz) plain flour, seasoned with salt and pepper
1 large egg, beaten
75 g (3 oz) fresh white breadcrumbs
Sunflower oil for deep frying

12 raw, unshelled, headless
    prawns
175 g (6 oz) plaice fillets,
    skinned
100 g (4 oz) prepared
    squid (see p.16), sliced
    into rings
4 shiitake mushrooms, cut
    in half
8 chrysanthemum leaves
    (optional)
1 small courgette, cut
    lengthways into slices
    3 mm (⅛ in) thick
12 sugarsnap peas
6 spring onions, cut into
    7.5 cm (3 in) lengths
8 asparagus tips
40 g (1½ oz) cornflour
Groundnut or sunflower oil
    for deep-frying
Salt

FOR THE DASHI
1.5 litres (2½ pints) water
15 g (½ oz) dried kelp
    (kombu)
15 g (½ oz) shaved dried
    bonito fillet
    (katsuobushi)

TEMPURA

Small pieces of fish and vegetables are dipped in the lightest batter imaginable and cooked in sparkling-fresh hot oil. The secret of making good tempura is to prepare the batter at the very last minute, keep the oil at the right temperature, and serve and eat the pieces as quickly as possible. For this reason I have specified cooking in a small pan with a small amount of oil and only frying a few pieces at a time. These are bought to the table and eaten by your guests while you, unfortunately, have to go back and deep-fry the next batch. But it is this sort of communal cooking and eating that is what relaxed and informal meals with friends are all about. You really should eat this dish with chopsticks and the idea is that you pick up a deep-fried morsel and dip it into the sauce.

Dashi, used to make the dipping sauce, is a Japanese stock but if you cannot get the ingredients you can substitute chicken stock. You may wonder at the inclusion of chrysanthemum leaves in the tempura but the Japanese use a number of different leaves of the chrysanthemum family in their cooking. They have a slightly bitter, scented flavour.

Shell the prawns, leaving the last tail segment in place, and de-vein them (see p.18). Sprinkle the prawns, plaice and squid with a little salt.

For the dipping sauce, first make the dashi. Bring the water to the boil, add the dried kelp and stir around for 3–4 minutes to release the flavour. Remove the kelp with a slotted spoon and add the shaved bonito. Bring to the boil, then remove from the heat and leave for a few minutes until the flakes settle to the bottom. Strain through a muslin-lined sieve and set aside 250 ml (8 fl oz) to use in the dipping sauce (the remainder can be frozen for later use).

Pour the mirin or dry sherry, soy sauce and dashi into a small pan, add a pinch of salt and bring to the boil. Keep warm over a low heat while you fry the fish and vegetables. Mix together the grated mooli and ginger and set aside.

Pour some oil into a medium-sized saucepan until one-third full and heat to 190°C/375°F. Meanwhile, make the tempura batter. Put the egg and iced water into a bowl and stir together until well mixed. Sift over the flour and cornflour and mix very briefly until just combined – there should be a few little lumps of flour still remaining. The batter should be as thin as single cream; if it is any thicker, add a little more iced water.

To test the temperature of the oil, drizzle a little batter into the pan; it should sink slightly, then rise to the surface and brown in 45 seconds. If the oil is too hot the batter will stay on the surface, while if it is too cool it will sink to the bottom and rise to the top only very slowly.

The fish, mushrooms and chrysanthemum leaves can be dipped directly into the cornflour and then the batter; the other vegetables need to be dipped into cold water before the cornflour and batter to help the coating stick. Coat 6 pieces of fish and vegetables at a time, drop into the hot oil and fry for 1–1½ minutes, until crisp and golden. Lift out with a slotted spoon and drain briefly on kitchen paper. As soon as a small selection of tempura is cooked, arrange on a large plate. Pour the warm dipping sauce into 4 shallow dishes or ramekins and pile the grated mooli and ginger into the centre of each dish. Take the tempura and dipping sauce to the table and top up the plate with the remaining batches of tempura as you cook them.

FOR THE DIPPING SAUCE

3 tablespoons mirin or dry sherry

3 tablespoons Japanese soy sauce

15 cm (6 in) piece of mooli (white radish), coarsely grated

2 tablespoons finely grated fresh root ginger

FOR THE TEMPURA BATTER

1 egg

120 ml (4 fl oz) iced water

3 tablespoons plain flour

1 tablespoon cornflour

**20 raw, unshelled, headless
prawns**
**20 Chinese wonton
wrappers**
Oil for deep-frying
Salt

FOR THE CHILLI JAM
**50 ml (2 fl oz) sunflower or
vegetable oil**
**15 g (½ oz) peeled garlic
cloves, very finely
chopped**
**15 g (½ oz) peeled fresh
root ginger, very finely
chopped**
**225 g (8 oz) onions, very
finely chopped**
**5 large red finger chillies,
seeded and very finely
chopped**
**100 ml (3½ fl oz) red wine
vinegar**
**25 ml (1 fl oz) Japanese soy
sauce**
**½ teaspoon ground star
anise**
**15 g (½ oz) palm sugar or
muscovado sugar**
Salt

DEEP-FRIED PRAWN WONTONS WITH CHILLI JAM

*Here, the prawns are enclosed in wonton wrappers but the tails are left on
and, to highlight the appearance, are not wrapped, otherwise they look a
bit like Egyptian mummies. They are served with a dark chilli and onion
relish flavoured with garlic, ginger and soy sauce. Large raw prawns in the
shell are now available at most supermarkets and wonton wrappers can be
bought in oriental food shops. Try to use Chinese rather than Japanese
wrappers as they puff up nicely during frying.*

Peel the prawns, leaving the last tail segment in place (see p.18), and reserve
the shells. Heat the sunflower or vegetable oil for the chilli jam in a medium-
sized pan, add the prawn shells and fry over a high heat for 1–2 minutes, until
they are quite crisp. Tip everything into a sieve resting over a small pan and
press really well to remove all the oil. The oil will now be pleasantly flavoured
with prawn.

To make the jam, re-heat the oil, add the garlic and ginger and fry quickly
until both are beginning to colour. Add the onions and chillies and fry fiercely
for 3–4 minutes. Stir in the vinegar, soy sauce, star anise, sugar and some salt to
taste. Bring to the boil and simmer gently for 20–30 minutes, until the onions
are very soft and the jam is well reduced and thick. Leave to cool, then spoon
into 4 small dipping bowls or ramekins.

Wrap each prawn in one of the wonton wrappers, leaving the tail end
uncovered, and seal with a little water. Pour the oil into a pan until it is about
one-third full. Heat to 190°C/375°F or until a small piece of white bread
dropped in the oil browns and rises to the surface in 1 minute. Fry the prawns
in batches for about 1–1½ minutes, until crisp and golden. Lift out and drain
briefly on kitchen paper. Serve hot with the chilli jam.

Mackerel Fish Cakes with Fennel

**450 g (1 lb) floury potatoes
such as Maris Piper,
peeled and cut into
chunks**

**900 g (2 lb) whole
mackerel**

**2 tablespoons chopped
fresh fennel herb or dill**

25 g (1 oz) butter, melted

1 teaspoon salt

**10 turns of the black
pepper mill**

**1 tablespoon Pernod or
Ricard (optional)**

**50 g (2 oz) plain flour,
seasoned with salt and
pepper**

2 eggs, beaten

**150 g (5 oz) fresh white
breadcrumbs**

**Sunflower oil for
deep-frying**

**Salt and freshly ground
black pepper**

I'm very fond of mackerel in fish cakes. The taste takes me right back to my childhood in Cornwall, when we used to go out feathering for mackerel around Padstow or the Scilly Isles. Couple it with some fresh fennel and a simple fish cake becomes something much more special. Except that the only sauce to go with this is tomato ketchup!

Cook the potatoes in boiling salted water until tender, drain well and then mash.

Pre-heat the grill to high. Make 2–3 shallow cuts in either side of each mackerel – this helps the heat penetrate the fish – and season well with salt and pepper. Grill for about 5 minutes on each side, then cool slightly. When the mackerel are cool enough to handle, flake the flesh, discarding the skin and bones.

Mix the mashed potato and flaked mackerel with the chopped fennel herb or dill, melted butter, salt, pepper and the Pernod or Ricard, if using. Divide the mixture into 8 and shape into rounds 2.5 cm (1 in) thick. Chill for about 20 minutes, until firm.

Pour the oil into a large pan so that it is no more than half full and heat to 180°C/350°F, or until a small piece of bread dropped into it browns and rises to the surface in 1½ minutes.

Dip the fish cakes first in the seasoned flour, then in the beaten eggs and finally in the breadcrumbs, pressing them on well to give an even coating. Deep-fry for about 4 minutes, until crisp and golden, then lift out and drain briefly on kitchen paper before serving.

DEEP-FRIED FISH PIES

I'm really pleased with this dish. What I did was take the filling for a good fish pie — a creamy velouté sauce, flaked white fish, parsley and hard-boiled egg — pour it into round moulds lined with cling film and chill it. When I took them out the mixture had formed fish-cake shapes. I floured, egged and breadcrumbed them, then deep-fried them.

Bring the stock to the boil in a deep frying pan or a saucepan. Add the smoked haddock and the fresh fish, bring back to a simmer and cook for 5–7 minutes, until firm and opaque. Lift the fish out of the stock and, when cool enough to handle, flake the flesh, discarding any bones and skin.

Melt 50 g (2 oz) of the butter in a clean pan, add 50 g (2 oz) of the flour and cook, stirring, for 1 minute. Remove from the heat and gradually stir in the stock. Return to the heat, bring to the boil, then add the cream and leave to simmer over a very low heat for 15 minutes, stirring now and then, until you have a very thick sauce.

Melt the remaining butter in a small pan, add the mushrooms and fry briskly over a high heat for 1 minute. Stir into the sauce with the grated cheese, hard-boiled eggs, parsley and flaked fish, then season to taste.

Put four 10 cm (4 in) plain pastry cutters or egg poaching rings on a baking sheet and line each one with a sheet of cling film, leaving the edges overhanging. Divide the fish mixture between the rings, level the tops and then cover with the overhanging cling film. Chill for at least 6 hours or until very firm.

To cook, lift off the rings from each 'pie' and remove the cling film. Pour the oil for deep-frying into a large pan until it is about one-third full. Heat to 160°C/325°F. Meanwhile, carefully dip each pie into the remaining flour, then the beaten egg and finally the breadcrumbs, pressing them on well to give an even coating. Deep-fry for about 9 minutes, until crisp and golden. Serve immediately, with *Tartare Sauce* and a crisp green salad.

Serves 4

600 ml (1 pint) *Fish Stock* (see p.212)
175 g (6 oz) undyed smoked haddock
175 g (6 oz) haddock fillet or Greenland halibut
65 g (2 ½ oz) butter
75 g (3 oz) plain flour
50 ml (2 fl oz) double cream
25 g (1 oz) button mushrooms, finely chopped
15 g (½ oz) Cheddar cheese, very finely grated
2 hard-boiled eggs, peeled and chopped
2 tablespoons roughly chopped fresh parsley
1 egg, beaten
75 g (3 oz) fresh white breadcrumbs
Salt and freshly ground black pepper
Sunflower oil for deep-frying
Tartare Sauce (see p.80), to serve

SUMMER FISH AND SALADS

I was sitting on the lawn the other evening, drinking a glass of chilled Chenin Blanc, and eating some lobster with salad and mayonnaise that had been made with a divinely smoky Italian olive oil. I ruminated – as one does at tranquil times such as this, when all that is needed to set off the most perfect evening is the occasional firefly in the gathering dusk, flitting by with little bursts of yellow light – on barbecues and how the smell of barbecues on a summer's evening is quite often pretty repulsive.

A typical barbecue in many a garden involves flavouring pieces of meat and fish with the exhaust fumes from igniting oil coupled with the burning effect of sheets of flame. The smell is of burnt oil and firelighters. The barbecue is lit but there are never enough coals on it in the first place, nor does anyone wait long enough for them to burn down and produce intense heat. Then the grid is loaded with far too much heavily oiled food. The oil drops into the coals, bursts into flame, and everything acquires that all-too-familiar blackened flavour. Charred lumps of meat and fish are then served up with little else but a green salad and everyone thinks they're having a great time. Plenty of beer and Chardonnay and the world is a fine and sunny place. This chapter is designed to take a slightly fresher look at outdoor eating. Not all the recipes are cooked on a barbecue but they are all the sort of food that you can imagine eating outdoors and that tastes all the better for it. So I've got a fantastic monkfish dish, which is started off on a charcoal grill and then finished on the stove on a bed of ratatouille. I've got raw salmon and smoked salmon made into a neat shape with slices of avocado, a little chopped onion and olive oil and served with a basil and tomato dressing. I've got a beautiful salad that I first ate on Christmas day overlooking a beach in Australia, made with rice-shaped pasta, sun-dried tomatoes, chargrilled vegetables and lots of seafood. I've got fried squid served with a simple Greek salad, all cut very small. I've got chargrilled shark steaks with a simple tomato and cumin chutney but best of all, I've got paella, that superb, much messed-about dish from Valencia. I've made it as simple as I can, with the minimum of ingredients – just really good rice, the finest saffron and the best-quality seafood.

Rice-shaped Pasta with Seafood, Rocket and Roasted Vegetables (see p.104).

Seared Tuna with Rice Noodle and Coriander Salad

Serves 4

4 x 200 g (7 oz) tuna steaks

6 tablespoons dark soy sauce

4 tablespoons balsamic vinegar

FOR THE SALAD

1 tablespoon sesame seeds

2 oz bunch coriander

6 springs onions, trimmed

Coarsely grated zest and juice of 1 lime

2 tablespoons Thai fish sauce

75 ml (3 fl oz) water

2 teaspoons roasted sesame oil

2 tablespoons sunflower oil

75 g (3 oz) rice vermicelli noodles

3 green finger chillies, seeded and finely chopped

2 tablespoons Japanese pickled ginger, cut into shreds

Small bunch garlic chives (optional), chopped

1 bunch watercress, larger stalks removed and broken into sprigs

I cooked this on my last trip to Australia after we'd been out on a yellofin tuna boat off Ulludulla – can you think of a more Australian sounding name than Ulludulla! This recipe sums up how I feel about Australian cooking at its best. The tuna is served very rare and the accompanying salad is designed to be served warm, not hot. I have suggested that you use three green chillies for this recipe because it needs to be quite punchy, but it will depend on how hot they are and how much you like chilli, so feel free to adjust this to your own taste.

For the salad, preheat the grill to high. Spread the sesame seeds onto a baking tray and toast, shaking the pan now and then, until golden. Pick the leaves off the coriander and discard the stalks – if they are quite large, very roughly chop them. You will need about 6 tablespoons in all. Very thinly slice the spring onions on the diagonal. Mix together the lime juice, fish sauce, water, sesame and sunflower oils.

Bring a pan of water to the boil, drop in the noodles and take it off the heat. Leave for 3 minutes, drain well and tip back into the pan. Cover and keep warm. Heat a heavy-based frying pan until very hot. Brush with a little oil, add the tuna steaks and cook for 2 minutes on each side. Add the soy sauce and balsamic vinegar to the pan and boil vigorously, turning the steaks once, until they become coated in a rich brown glaze. Remove from the heat and keep warm while you finish the salad.

Add the sesame seeds, coriander, spring onions, lime zest, green chilli, pickled ginger, the garlic chives if using and the watercress to the noodles. Add the dressing ingredients and toss everything together.

Pile some of the salad into the centre of 4 warmed plates, slice each tuna steak into 3 on the angle and rest them on top of the salad. Serve the rest of the salad separately.

SALAD OF CHARGRILLED GARFISH WITH FENNEL SEEDS

The idea for this recipe came from Australia, where garfish are available from most fishmongers. The same species swims in British waters but is not so easy to buy — I suspect that people are put off by the bright turquoise bones. However, it's a delicious fish, firm in texture and eminently suitable for chargrilling. Should you ever see it on sale, snap it up; otherwise use grey mullet, gurnard, Dover sole or even mackerel.

It is important to arrange the components of the salad on the plates without flattening the delicate leaves too much, gradually building up the dressed salad leaves, tomato strips and grilled fish in layers. It should be served with a big bowl of chips (see p. 80) in the centre of the table, so you can eat the salad while dipping in and out of the chips with your fingers.

Cut the fish fillets diagonally into 7.5 cm (3 in) pieces. Mix together the olive oil, lemon juice, thyme, fennel seeds, chilli, salt and pepper. Brush a little of this mixture over both sides of the fish and leave for 5 minutes to allow the flavours to permeate it.

Put the rocket and curly endive in a large bowl. Break the parsley and chervil into small sprigs and add to the bowl.

Put a lightly oiled cast-iron ribbed pan over a high heat until really hot. Add the pieces of fish, skin-side down, and cook for 1–1½ minutes, turning them over half-way through. Transfer to a plate and keep warm. Add the olive oil/fennel seed mixture and sherry vinegar to the hot pan and swill around. Remove from the heat.

Arrange the leaves, sun-dried tomato strips and fish in layers on 4 serving plates, poking in the pieces of the fish so that they don't flatten the salad leaves. Pour the warm dressing all around the salads and a little over the top. Serve immediately.

Serves 4

4 garfish, weighing about 275–350 g (10–12 oz) each, filleted (see p. 13)
2 tablespoons olive oil
Juice of ¼ lemon
1 teaspoon chopped fresh thyme
1 teaspoon fennel seeds
A good pinch of dried flaked chilli
½ teaspoon salt
A few twists of freshly ground black pepper
4–6 sun-dried tomatoes in oil, drained and thinly sliced

FOR THE SALAD

4 tablespoons extra virgin olive oil
1 sprig of fresh oregano, finely chopped
1 tablespoon sherry vinegar
25 g (1 oz) rocket
25 g (1 oz) curly endive
15 g (½ oz) flatleaf parsley
15 g (½ oz) chervil

STIR-FRIED CRAB WITH BLACK BEANS, GINGER AND SPRING ONIONS

Serves 4

1 cooked brown crab,
    weighing about 1.5 kg
    (3 lb)
100 g (4 oz) rice noodles
3 tablespoons sunflower oil
5 cm (2 in) piece of fresh
    root ginger, cut into fine
    matchsticks 2.5 cm
    (1 in) long
8 spring onions, sliced
1 tablespoon salted black
    beans or black bean
    sauce
4 garlic cloves, finely
    chopped
2 tablespoons Chinese rice
    wine or 1 tablespoon
    dry sherry
1 tablespoon dark soy
    sauce
85 ml (3 fl oz) water
½ teaspoon salt

Serve this with the Chinese Cabbage with Oyster Sauce *below. Some people hate the idea of fiddling around with crab in the shell but if, like me, you find it a pleasure, do try this recipe, where pieces of crab in the shell are served with a pile of steaming fresh noodles with ginger and spring onions. I have used a brown crab but if by any chance you can get hold of a live crab the flavour will be incomparably better. Kill it first by inserting a screwdriver or skewer between the eyes, then follow the method below but increase the cooking time for a raw crab to 5 minutes.*

Put the crab upside down on a chopping board and twist off the claws and legs. Break the claws in half at the joint and lightly crack the shells with a rolling pin. Twist and remove the bony tail flap and discard. Prise the body away from the back shell, remove the dead man's fingers (see pp.20–21) and cut the body into quarters. Remove the brown meat from the shell and reserve; discard the shell.

Cook the rice noodles in boiling water for 3 minutes or until just tender, then drain and keep warm. Heat the oil in a wok or a large, deep frying pan. Add the ginger, the white part of the spring onions, the black beans and garlic and stir-fry over a high heat for 1 minute. Add all the crab pieces and the brown meat, the rice wine or sherry, soy sauce, water and salt and stir-fry for 1½–2 minutes, until the crab is heated through. Add the green spring onion tops and the warm noodles, toss quickly and serve with the *Chinese Cabbage with Oyster Sauce* (below).

CHINESE CABBAGE WITH OYSTER SAUCE

Serves 4

2 teaspoons salt
4 tablespoons groundnut
    oil
900 g (2 lb) Chinese
    cabbage such as choi
    sum or pak choi, cut
    into 15 cm (6 in) pieces
3 tablespoons oyster sauce

This can also be made with gow choi, the very long, thick Chinese chives.

Bring 1.75 litres (3 pints) of water to the boil in a large pan. Add the salt, 2 tablespoons of the oil and the cabbage, bring back to the boil and boil for 1 minute, until the cabbage is tender but still retains a bit of bite. Drain well, return to the pan with the remaining oil and 2 tablespoons of the oyster sauce and toss lightly. Spoon on to a serving dish and drizzle with the remaining oyster sauce.

Warm Salad of Pink Fir Apple Potatoes with Matjes Herring, Chives and Soured Cream Vinaigrette

Pink fir apple potatoes, a beautiful waxy salad variety, are in the shops from late summer until the end of the year. If you can't find them, any waxy salad potato will do just fine. Cured with sugar, salt and saltpetre, matjes herrings are the most delicious cured herrings on earth, popular in Holland, Belgium and Germany. The word matjes *means virgin, and the herrings are young, with the roe not fully developed. These days they are only very lightly salted and normally sold pre-soaked, filleted and ready to eat. If you cannot get matjes herrings (they are not difficult to find), any cured but not smoked herring fillets will do instead.*

Cook the potatoes in boiling water until tender, then drain and leave to cool slightly. Meanwhile, mix together the soured cream, shallot, mustard, vinegar, chives and garlic. Cut the potatoes into thick slices and put them into a bowl with the herrings and the soured cream dressing. Season with a little salt and pepper and stir together gently. Spoon the mixture on to 4 plates and garnish with a few chive stems.

Serves 4

450 g (1 lb) Pink Fir Apple potatoes or other waxy new potatoes
85 ml (3 fl oz) soured cream
1 large shallot, very finely chopped
1 teaspoon English mustard
1 tablespoon white wine vinegar
½ tablespoon chopped fresh chives, plus a few whole chives to garnish
1 small garlic clove, crushed
225 g (8 oz) matjes herring fillets, cut into slices 2.5 cm (1 in) wide
Salt and freshly ground black pepper

STUFFED SQUID

Serves 4

8 squid

50 g (2 oz) pine kernels

1 medium onion, finely
chopped

2 garlic cloves, finely
chopped

4 tablespoons olive oil

75 g (3 oz) long-grain rice

25 g (1 oz) raisins

2 tablespoons chopped
fresh flatleaf parsley

400 g (14 oz) can of
chopped tomatoes

2 sun-dried tomatoes in
oil, drained and finely
chopped

120 ml (4 fl oz) dry white
wine

Salt and freshly ground
black pepper

This is the classic Greek recipe for stuffing the bodies of squid or cuttlefish. You will need to use medium-sized squid with a body section measuring about 13–15 cm (5–6 in) in length.

Pre-heat the oven to 180°C/350°F/Gas 4.

Clean the squid (see p.16), taking care not to split the pouches. Rub the outside of the pouches liberally with 1 teaspoon of salt, leave for 5 minutes and then rinse well with cold water. Chop the tentacles into small pieces.

Spread the pine kernels over a baking tray and toast in the oven for about 7 minutes or until lightly browned. Remove from the oven and set aside.

Fry the onion and garlic in 2 tablespoons of the olive oil for 5 minutes, until softened and lightly browned. Add the chopped squid tentacles and fry for 3 minutes. Stir in the rice, pine kernels, raisins and parsley and season with salt and pepper. Leave to cool slightly and then spoon into the squid pouches, making sure they are only two-thirds full to allow room for the rice to swell up. Secure each one with a cocktail stick, if you wish.

Heat the remaining oil in a large flameproof casserole dish. Add the squid and fry for a few minutes on all sides until lightly browned. Add the tomatoes, sun-dried tomatoes, wine, salt and pepper, then cover and bake in the oven for 1 hour. Serve hot or cold.

GRILLADE OF TUNA WITH OLIVE OIL MASH

I cooked this when we were filming the thrid programme in the second television series, in Sormiou, an idyllic beach just outside Marseilles in the Calanques. We arrived in Marseilles, typically, with no cooking equipment and nowhere to cook but we managed to borrow a cabano, *a terracotta-tiled holiday cabin, just up from the beach, with a tiny kitchen to film in and a nice big terrace that had a glorious view over the limestone hills behind, dotted with wild thyme, mallow and great clumps of daisies. The fish in that case were sea bass and daurade royale, also known as gilt head bream, but tuna works well too, as do swordfish and shark.*

The dressing for the grillade is a difficult concept to grasp. I start with a simple, well-reduced, sharp tomato sauce and add lots of chopped aromatic herbs — what I loosely call Provençal herbs — in an olive oil and red wine vinegar dressing. The idea is that the finished dressing should look split, i.e. the tomato should appear to have separated from the dressing. It just looks much more fresh and appetizing than a smooth tomato sauce. Texture is very important visually as well as for the taste in my cooking.

Make the tomato sauce and then pass it through a conical strainer into a clean pan. If necessary, simmer for a few minutes until the sauce is thick enough to coat the back of a spoon. Adjust the seasoning and keep warm.

Put all the ingredients for the dressing into a bowl, season with black pepper and whisk together. Stir into the tomato sauce and keep warm.

For the olive oil mash, cook the potatoes in boiling salted water until tender, then drain. Add the cream, olive oil, chicken stock, garlic and salt and mash until smooth. Set aside and keep warm.

Place a lightly oiled cast-iron ribbed pan over a high heat. Mix the olive oil with the thyme leaves. Brush the tuna with the thyme oil and season well with sea salt and black pepper. When the pan is very hot, put the tuna on it and cook for about 4–5 minutes on each side, pressing down firmly with the back of a fish slice to help mark the fish with the lines from the griddle.

To serve, put the tuna on 4 warmed plates and spoon the olive oil mash to one side. Using a teaspoon, spoon little pools of the sauce to the other side of the fish.

Serves 4

½ quantity of *Tomato Sauce* (see p.48), made without the basil

3 tablespoons olive oil

Leaves from 2 sprigs of fresh thyme

4 tuna steaks, weighing about 175 g (6 oz) each

Sea salt and freshly ground black pepper

FOR THE DRESSING

120 ml (4 fl oz) extra virgin olive oil

2 tablespoons red wine vinegar

3 tablespoons chopped mixed fresh herbs, such as dill, young bay leaf, thyme, rosemary, oregano, savory

1 teaspoon salt

FOR THE OLIVE OIL MASH

900 g (2 lb) floury potatoes, such as King Edward, Maris Piper or Wilja, peeled and cut into chunks

25 ml (1 fl oz) double cream

85 ml (3 fl oz) olive oil

50 ml (2 fl oz) *Chicken Stock* (see p.213)

2 garlic cloves, crushed

½ teaspoon salt

1 kg (2¼ lb) monkfish tail

1 head of garlic, cloves
    peeled and thinly sliced

1 teaspoon ground fennel
    seeds

2 red and 2 green peppers

150 ml (5 fl oz) olive oil,
    plus extra for brushing

2 aubergines, sliced into
    rounds 5 mm (¼ in)
    thick

2 large onions, sliced

450 g (1 lb) courgettes,
    sliced

3 beefsteak tomatoes,
    skinned and cut into
    quarters

Leaves from 1 sprig of
    fresh thyme

2 fresh bay leaves, very
    thinly sliced

Salt and freshly ground
    black pepper

MONKFISH ROASTED OVER CHARCOAL WITH RATATOUILLE

This dish is far better cooked on a charcoal or gas-fired barbecue because not only does the monkfish get that wonderful chargrilled flavour but you can also barbecue the peppers and aubergines for the ratatouille, which lends it a marvellously smoky taste. However, if you don't have a barbecue, you can do all the cooking indoors and the dish will still taste good.

The secret of making a great ratatouille is to cook the vegetables thoroughly so that the flavours are concentrated and you end up with something full of flavour rather than everyone's weak and watery nightmare vegetarian dish! Although this ratatouille is made with grilled vegetables you can also serve the monkfish with a more conventional ratatouille. Try following the recipe in the poem called 'Ratatouille' on p.154. I've done it and it works perfectly.

Remove the skin from the monkfish and cut off most of the membrane (see p.15), otherwise the tail will curl up rather unattractively while it cooks. Make 10 small incisions all over it with the point of a small knife. Take 10 slices of the garlic and turn them over in the ground fennel to coat. Slide them down the blade of the knife into the monkfish.

For the ratatouille, brush the peppers with some of the oil and grill on a barbecue, turning them as they blacken and blister. Put the sliced aubergines in a shallow dish with 4 tablespoons of the olive oil, sprinkle with salt and turn them over in the oil until well coated. Cook on the barbecue for a few minutes on both sides until soft. If you don't have a barbecue, you can cook the vegetables on a cast-iron ribbed pan or cook the peppers under a domestic grill and fry the aubergines in the same amount of oil.

Heat half the remaining oil in a heavy-based flameproof casserole dish, add the onions and cook very gently for about 30 minutes, stirring occasionally. Add the remaining garlic and the courgettes, season with salt and pepper and cook for another 5 minutes.

Pour the rest of the oil into a frying pan and fry the tomatoes over a high heat until just beginning to fall apart. Add the tomatoes and all the oil to the casserole.

Remove the blistered skin from the peppers, cut them in half and remove the seeds, taking care not to pour away the delicious juice that will have accumulated inside. Pour this into the casserole. Slice the peppers and add them, too, with the aubergines. Stir in more salt and pepper and the thyme and bay leaves, then cook the ratatouille, uncovered, over a very gentle heat for about 1 hour, by which time the excess moisture in the vegetables will have evaporated and the vegetables should shine with oil.

Meanwhile, brush the monkfish with oil and season well with salt and pepper. Cook over the barbecue for 5 minutes on each side until lightly browned. Alternatively, grill it under a high heat for 5 minutes on each side. Now put it on top of the ratatouille, cover with a lid and simmer for the last 20 minutes of the ratatouille cooking time. Check that the monkfish is cooked by making a small incision in the thickest part right into the centre. The fillet should be white right through. If it still looks a bit translucent in the middle, give it another 5 minutes.

To serve, lift out the monkfish and cut it into slices. Spoon the ratatouille on to 4 warmed plates, place the sliced monkfish on top and serve with a green salad and a bottle of ice-cold Bandol rosé wine.

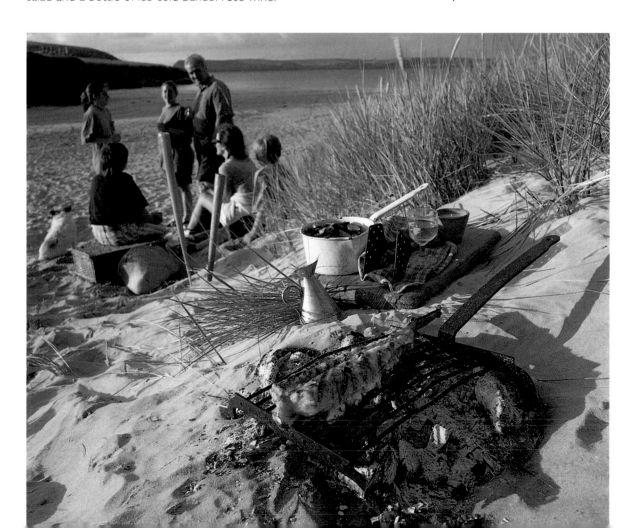

12 prepared scallops or 24
   prepared queen scallops
   (see p.18)
35 g (1¼ oz) unsalted
   butter
3 slices of Granary bread,
   1 cm (½ in) thick, crusts
   removed, cut into 1 cm
   (½ in) dice
100 g (4 oz) bag of mixed
   baby leaf salad
8 slices of Parma ham, cut
   into strips 2 cm (¾ in)
   wide
1 quantity of *Mustard
   Dressing* (see p.216)
1 teaspoon walnut oil
½ tablespoon snipped fresh
   chives
Salt and freshly ground
   black pepper

SEARED SCALLOP SALAD WITH PARMA HAM AND CROÛTONS

A simple salad of young leaves with scallops, strips of Parma ham and Granary bread croûtons, finished with a few snipped chives. The scallops are sautéd in a hot frying pan in which a very small amount of butter has been melted, giving them a really sweet, caramelized exterior. But they are only cooked briefly so that they remain succulent.

If using the larger scallops, slice them horizontally into 2 discs. Leave queen scallops whole. Season with a little salt and pepper and set aside.

To make the croûtons, melt 25 g (1 oz) of the butter in a frying pan, add the cubes of bread and fry for a few minutes, turning them over as they brown. Lift out and drain on kitchen paper.

Arrange the salad leaves on 4 plates. Heat the frying pan until very hot and melt the remaining butter in it, then add the scallops and fry for just 30 seconds on each side. Remove from the pan and tuck them in amongst the salad leaves. Add the strips of Parma ham and the croûtons to the pan and fry briskly over a high heat for just a few seconds to warm through. Sprinkle them over the salad. Now add the mustard dressing and walnut oil to the pan. Bring to the boil, stir in the chives and taste for seasoning. Drizzle over the salads and serve immediately.

SAUTÉD SQUID WITH GREEK SALAD

The squid is cooked very simply with a little thyme, garlic and dried chilli and then is served with one of my favourite salads — Greek salad, made with feta cheese, cucumber, tomato, olives and onion in a good olive oil dressing. Greek salad is usually fairly rustic, with the ingredients in rough chunks, but here they are cut very small so that the salad looks neat on the plate next to the squid.

For the salad, put all the ingredients in a bowl and mix together gently. Whisk together all the ingredients for the dressing and season to taste. Stir it into the salad and set aside.

Cut the body of the squid into rings, the fins into strips and the tentacles into 3. Heat the olive oil and thyme in a frying pan. When hot, add the squid and fry for about 2½ minutes. Add the garlic, chilli flakes, salt and pepper and toss for 1 minute. Serve immediately, with the Greek salad.

Serves 4

350 g (12 oz) prepared
    small squid (see p.16)
2 tablespoons olive oil
2 sprigs of fresh thyme
1 garlic clove, finely
    chopped
A pinch of dried chilli
    flakes
A good pinch of sea salt
10 turns of the black
    pepper mill

FOR THE GREEK SALAD
2 salad tomatoes, skinned,
    seeded and cut into
    1 cm (½ in) pieces
75 g (3 oz) cucumber, cut
    into 1 cm (½ in) pieces
50 g (2 oz) feta cheese, cut
    into 1 cm (½ in) pieces
1 small red onion, finely
    chopped
8 unpitted black olives
½ tablespoon chopped
    fresh fennel herb or dill

FOR THE DRESSING
2 tablespoons extra virgin
    olive oil
½ tablespoon red wine
    vinegar
1 teaspoon retsina
    (optional)

Serves 4

400 g (14 oz) salmon fillet,
    skinned
100 g (4 oz) smoked
    salmon
1 large garlic clove, very
    finely chopped
3 shallots, very finely
    chopped
1 ½ tablespoons lemon
    juice
½ teaspoon salt
12 turns of the black
    pepper mill
A pinch of cayenne pepper
A few drops of
    Worcestershire sauce
2 small avocados
Mixed baby salad leaves,
    to garnish

FOR THE DRESSING
50 ml (2 fl oz) extra virgin
    olive oil
1 tablespoon lemon juice
2 tomatoes, skinned,
    seeded and finely diced
½ teaspoon coarse sea salt
8 basil leaves, very finely
    shredded
A few turns of the black
    pepper mill

TIANS OF LIGHTLY CURED SALMON AND AVOCADO WITH A FRESH TOMATO AND BASIL DRESSING

Smoked and raw salmon are shaped into small discs between which are sandwiched some slices of avocado. The salmon is flavoured with lemon juice, garlic and shallots and accompanied by a sauce of lemon juice, tomato, basil and virgin olive oil. Since the salmon is not cooked, it is essential that it is absolutely fresh. This is not a recipe for making in advance. Everything is just mixed together, moulded and then served so that it all tastes of itself. Serve as a first course or maybe as something exceptional to eat outdoors with that special glass of white wine from the Loire.

Thinly slice the salmon fillet and smoked salmon, then cut them into strips about 5 mm (¼ in) wide. Put them in a bowl with the garlic, shallots, 1 tablespoon of the lemon juice, salt, black pepper, cayenne pepper and Worcestershire sauce and mix together well. Halve the avocados and remove the stone and peel. Cut each half into thin slices, then mix with the remaining lemon juice and a pinch of salt.

Place a 9 cm (3 ½ in) poaching ring or plain pastry cutter in the centre of each of 4 large plates. Divide half the salmon mixture between the rings and lightly level the top; don't press the mixture down – you want it to be loosely packed. Cover each one with avocado slices and then with the remaining salmon mixture, lightly levelling the top once more. Carefully remove the rings.

Lightly stir the dressing ingredients together in a bowl. Arrange 4 small piles of the salad leaves around each tian. Using a teaspoon, spoon little pools of the dressing in between the leaves and then serve.

350 g (12 oz) rice-shaped
   pasta

I small aubergine, cut into
   2.5 cm (I in) cubes

I red onion, cut into thin
   wedges

I red pepper, cut into
   2.5 cm (I in) pieces

I plum tomato, cut into
   thin wedges

2 garlic cloves, finely
   chopped

85 ml (3 fl oz) extra virgin
   olive oil

½ teaspoon coarse sea salt

3–4 tablespoons wine or
   water

450 g (I lb) mussels,
   cleaned (see p.17)

100 g (4 oz) prepared
   squid (see p.16), cut into
   rings

100 g (4 oz) best-quality
   cooked peeled North
   Atlantic prawns

3 sun-dried tomatoes in
   oil, thinly sliced

I red finger chilli, seeded
   and finely chopped

25 g (I oz) Parmesan
   cheese, finely grated

I tablespoon white wine
   vinegar

5 tablespoons chopped
   fresh parsley

50 g (2 oz) rocket

Salt and freshly ground
   black pepper

RICE-SHAPED PASTA WITH SEAFOOD, ROCKET AND ROASTED VEGETABLES

I've seen rice-shaped pasta sold as puntalette, puntine and orzo. Made to look like rice, it provides a bit of a culinary joke, if you like, because a lot of people will think they're eating a rice salad and then be surprised to find they're not. I dreamt up this dish last Christmas in Sydney where I ate a salad using rice pasta with sun-dried tomatoes and olive oil and I thought, what a great base for a seafood salad. We spent Christmas day out at Newport, one of Sydney's beaches, and were asked to bring along a salad. Besides the seafood, rice and sun-dried tomatoes, I put in roasted vegetables, garlic, Parmesan cheese and, lastly, fresh rocket, torn into pieces and folded into the salad at the last minute to give it a nice, peppery bite.

Actually this dish serves as a memory of a very good friend of mine, Ed Ifould, and that Christmas lunch in the hot sun with him and his family. He died a few months ago of a heart attack when he was out in his boat on the sea. Ed was the same age as me and I'd known him ever since I was 19. Every time I went over to Australia we ate lots of good food and drank lots of great Australian wine, and he promised to come over to Cornwall one day but he never made it. His life was a sort of mirror image of mine on the other side of the world. He had similar enthusiasms but he was, unlike me, the most competitive sportsman imaginable, and exceptional at everything he did. I think he would have liked Padstow. He certainly would have liked May Day, 'Obby 'Oss Day in Padstow, when the rebirth of the year and the coming of summer are celebrated with a pagan fertility rite of immense antiquity and a complete lack of whimsical folk-music chumminess. Like many Australians, he liked things that were lacking in pretension, and was practical and full of enthusiasm. He probably would have realized after his visit that although Australia is the finest country in the world, England is not all greyness and drizzle.

Unite and unite and let us all unite
For summer is acome unto day
And whither we are going we shall all unite
In the merry morning of May.
There is a verse that would have suited him well in this May Day song:

O! Where is St George?
O! Where is he O?
He's out on his long boat
All on the salt sea O.

Ed never stopped surfing, sailing or swimming. He was always out on the water somewhere.

Pre-heat the oven to 220°C/425°F/Gas 7.

Bring 1.75 litres (3 pints) of water and 1 tablespoon of salt to the boil in a large pan. Add the pasta and cook for 9 minutes or until *al dente*, then drain and leave to cool.

Meanwhile, put the aubergine, onion, red pepper and tomato in a bowl with the garlic, 2 tablespoons of the olive oil and the sea salt and mix together well. Spread out in a small roasting tin and cook in the oven for about 30 minutes, until well coloured around the edges. Remove from the oven and leave to cool.

Put the wine or water in a saucepan, add the mussels, then cover and cook over a high heat for 3–4 minutes until they have opened. Discard any that remain closed. Shell the mussels and leave to cool.

Heat 1 tablespoon of the remaining oil in a frying pan. Add the squid and fry over a high heat for 2½ minutes, until lightly browned. Season with salt and pepper and leave to cool.

When the pasta, roasted vegetables, mussels and squid are all cold, put them in a large bowl with the remaining olive oil, prawns, mussels, sun-dried tomatoes, chilli, Parmesan cheese, vinegar, 4 tablespoons of the parsley, 1 teaspoon of salt and 10 turns of the black pepper mill. Toss together lightly, then fold in the rocket. Spoon the salad on to a large serving platter and sprinkle with the remaining chopped parsley.

Serves 6

1 cooked lobster, weighing
about 450 g (1 lb)

1.2 litres (2 pints) *Chicken
Stock* (see p.213)

2 fresh bay leaves

1 large leek, sliced

12 mussels, cleaned
(see p.17)

85 ml (3 fl oz) extra virgin
olive oil

450 g (1 lb) monkfish fillet,
cut into slices 1 cm
(½ in) thick

100 g (4 oz) prepared
small squid (see p.16),
sliced

1 medium onion, finely
chopped

8 garlic cloves, 4 finely
chopped and 4 cut into
quarters

1 red pepper, seeded and
thinly sliced

450 g (1 lb) Arborio or
Valencia rice

Scant ½ teaspoon saffron
strands

6 cooked Mediterranean
prawns (*crevettes*)

SEAFOOD PAELLA

I have written this to serve only six people because most recipes for paella feed more people than anybody could possibly have a pan large enough for in their own home. If you are lucky enough to possess an enormous frying pan or, even better, a paellera, *then by all means double up the quantities in this recipe. Paella is one of those dishes that often contain just about everything in the fridge. However, what I like about it are the flavours of olive oil, garlic and saffron together with seafood and some good, large-grained rice. Keep it simple, in other words. The best rice to use is Valencia rice but this is still hard to get in Britain. I use Italian risotto rice, which I think works nearly as well.*

Pull the claws and legs off the lobster and then detach the head from the tail. Cut the tail into pieces at each section and the claws into 3 and set aside. Put the lobster head and legs into a pan with the chicken stock, bay leaves and the green part of the leek. Bring to the boil, then leave to simmer until reduced to 900 ml (1½ pints). Strain the stock through a sieve into a clean pan and set aside.

Put the mussels into a pan with a splash of the stock. Cover and cook over a high heat for 3–4 minutes, until opened. Lift the mussels out of the cooking liquid, discarding any that remain closed, then cover and set aside. Pour all of the liquid back into the stock except the last tablespoonful, which is often gritty.

Heat the oil in a large frying pan or shallow saucepan – you will need one that is about 30 cm (12 in) across. Add the monkfish and fry for 3 minutes, turning it over after 2 minutes. Remove from the pan and set aside. Add the squid and stir-fry for 2–3 minutes, until lightly browned. Set aside with the monkfish. Add the onion, the chopped and the quartered garlic, the white part of the leek and the red pepper to the pan and fry for 4–5 minutes, until softened and lightly browned. Add the rice and stir until all the grains are well coated with the oil. Add the saffron and stock and bring to the boil. Season with salt and pepper, then lower the heat, cover and simmer gently for 15 minutes.

Uncover the rice and lay the pieces of lobster, monkfish, squid, mussels and prawns on top. Cover and cook gently for 5 minutes. Remove from the heat and leave for 5 minutes, then uncover and gently fork the seafood and rice together before serving.

4 x 225 g (8 oz) shark
    steaks or swordfish
    steaks
2 tablespoons olive oil
Finely grated zest of ½
    lime
Salt and freshly ground
    black pepper

FOR THE ROASTED
TOMATO AND CUMIN
CHUTNEY

I tablespoon black or
    yellow mustard seeds
100 ml (3½ fl oz) malt
    vinegar
I kg (2¼ lb) beef tomatoes,
    peeled
75 ml (3 fl oz) olive oil
I tablespoon cumin seeds
50 g (2 oz) fresh root
    ginger, roughly chopped
5 garlic cloves, roughly
    chopped
3 red birdseye chillies,
    roughly chopped
2 teaspoons sambal oelek
    or minced red chilli
1½ teaspoons turmeric
    powder
50 g (2 oz) palm sugar or
    light soft brown sugar
2 tablespoons Thai fish
    sauce (nam pla)

CHARGRILLED SHARK STEAKS WITH ROASTED TOMATO AND CUMIN CHUTNEY

The real pleasure of this dish is the accompanying chutney, which comes from one of my favourite cooks, Gay Bilson, who runs the Bennelong Restaurant in Sydney Opera House. If you ever go to Sydney, you've got to have a meal there. I happened to see a jar of it while looking round Leigh Stone Herbert's outside catering kitchen in Sydney. I insisted on taking off the lid of the chutney and trying a spoonful. It was wonderful, and just made to go with a piece of fish. Naturally I have forgotten exactly how Gay makes it. Leigh rattled off the recipe and I only remember the outline — often a good idea since you get the original recipe and a derivative, too. Incidentally, you can equally well use swordfish instead of shark, which you might find easier to obtain, but shark is what we get in Cornwall. Porbeagle or mako shark have the best flavour but, failing that, blue shark is cheaper and easier to come by.

For the chutney, soak the mustard seeds in the vinegar overnight. If you don't have time to do this you can put them in a small pan and bring to the boil, then take off the heat and leave to soak for 2 hours.

Preheat the oven to 200° C/400° F/Gas 6. Place the tomatoes in a small roasting tin, pour over the oil and roast in the oven for 1½ hours.

Heat a dry, heavy-based frying pan or wok over a high heat. Add the cumin seeds and fry for a few seconds until they begin to darken and smell aromatic. Tip into a pestle and mortar or coffee grinder and grind to a fine powder. Put this powder and the ginger, garlic, chillies, sambal oelek, turmeric, sugar and fish sauce, vinegar and mustard seeds into a liquidizer and blend until smooth. Pour this puree into a pan and simmer very gently for 10 minutes, stirring all the time as it has a tendency to spit quite a lot. Add the roasted tomatoes to the pan and simmer for 10–15 minutes until the chutney has thickened. Season with salt and pepper.

Season the shark steaks with plenty of salt and pepper. Mix the olive oil with the lime zest and then paint it over both sides of the steaks. Heat a lightly oiled cast iron ribbed pan, add the steaks and cook for 3–4 minutes on each side. Transfer the steaks to 4 warmed plates and serve with the chutney.

Poached Salmon with Mayonnaise, New Potatoes and Cucumber Salad

This is the sort of classic dish which is all too often served up at weddings over-cooked. In this recipe I've given you precise cooking times and weights which will always mean that the salmon is slightly pink and moist.

Put the salmon in the fish kettle and pour in enough water to cover. Add the salt, bring to the boil and simmer very gently for 5 minutes. Remove the fish from the heat and set aside to cool for about 20 minutes.

Boil the new potatoes with 1 sprig of mint in salted water until soft. Drain and keep warm.

Peel the cucumber and slice it as thinly as possible, preferably with a mandolin. Chop the leaves of the remaining mint sprigs and mix them together with the sliced cucumber and white wine vinegar. Remove the salmon from the fish kettle and serve with a bowl of new potatoes, the mayonnaise and the cucumber salad.

Serves 4

1 piece salmon, weighing about 1.5 kg (3–3½ lb)
5 tablespoons salt
750 g (1½ lb) new potatoes, preferably freshly dug
3 sprigs of mint
1 cucumber
1 tablespoon white wine vinegar
1 quantity of *Olive Oil Mayonnaise* (see p. 217)

FISH FROM COLDER CLIMATES

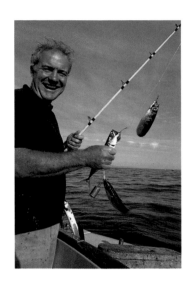

The inspiration for this chapter came from a conversation I had in Sydney in the offices of *Australian Gourmet Traveller*, which is a magazine devoted to the interests of people such as myself, who like to travel around the world and enjoy good food. Why on earth don't we have a similar magazine in this country? I was overwhelmed by the intelligence and enthusiasm of the entire staff and their knowledge of what was going on not only in Australian cooking but everywhere else in the world as well. I had gone to see the editor, Caroline Lockhart, to ask her if she might be interested in visiting the West Country or sending someone over to write about all the good restaurants and hotels we have. When I told her how exciting I found Australian cooking, with its great influences from Thailand, Singapore, Hong Kong, India and the whole of the Pacific, she said, 'Yes, but reading your book [*Taste of the Sea*], we don't half hanker sometimes after some good old European butter sauces.' So I started thinking and realized that we shouldn't spend all our time fretting about calories and trying to stick to salads and grilled fish. Occasionally we should rejoice in those classic sauces, rich in butter, cream and wine, those hefty fish pies whose delicious, heart-warming fillings are topped with a layer of buttery pastry, or mounds of steaming-hot mashed potatoes enriched with a slick of saffron-scented butter or extra virgin olive oil. Well, this chapter is where you'll find all these and more. Long may they survive.

Baked John Dory with Chilli, Cannellini Beans and Thyme (see p.120).

4 pieces of turbot fillet,
 weighing about 175 g
 (6 oz) each
Salt and freshly ground
 black pepper

**FOR THE MONTPELLIER
BUTTER**
25 g (1 oz) fresh spinach
25 g (1 oz) rocket leaves
25 g (1 oz) chopped mixed
 fresh parsley, chives,
 chervil and tarragon
25 g (1 oz) shallots,
 chopped
3 small gherkins, chopped
1 teaspoon capers
2 garlic cloves, chopped
6 anchovy fillets
1 egg yolk
2 hard-boiled egg yolks
100 g (4 oz) butter,
 softened
½ teaspoon salt
85 ml (3 fl oz) olive oil

**FOR THE CREAMED
CABBAGE**
50 g (2 oz) butter
450 g (1 lb) spring
 cabbage, thinly sliced
225 g (8 oz) leeks, thinly
 sliced
1 tablespoon white wine
 vinegar
85 ml (3 fl oz) double
 cream
120 ml (4 fl oz) *Fish Stock*
 (see p.212)

TURBOT FILLET WITH MONTPELLIER BUTTER AND CREAMED CABBAGE

I don't know why I've never used creamed cabbage and leeks before with fish because it's very common in France and every time I eat it I vow to include it in a recipe. The idea is that you cook the cabbage very gently with some leeks and butter, then add cream and a little stock to make a sort of vegetable-come-sauce base for the fish — here, fillets of beautifully white turbot topped with slices of green Montpellier butter. You could also use John Dory, brill, sea bass or a thick fillet of cod.

First make the Montpellier butter. Drop the spinach and rocket leaves into a pan of boiling water for 1 minute, then drain and refresh under cold running water. Press out all the excess water and then put the leaves into a food processor with all the remaining ingredients except the oil. Process to a purée, then with the machine still running, pour in the olive oil in a steady stream. Season to taste, then scrape out on to a large sheet of cling film, shape into a roll 2.5 cm (1 in) thick and chill until firm.

For the creamed cabbage, melt the butter in a large pan, add the cabbage, leeks and vinegar, then cover and cook over a gentle heat for 20 minutes. Add the cream and fish stock and cook, uncovered, over a high heat for about 10 minutes, until the liquid has reduced but the mixture is still quite creamy.

Meanwhile, pre-heat the grill to high. Season the turbot fillets on both sides with salt and pepper, then put them, skin-side up, on the lightly oiled rack of the grill pan and cook for 6 minutes. Carefully peel away the skin from the fillets. Remove the Montpellier butter from the fridge, cut off 8 thin slices and put 2 slices on each piece of fish.

Put the cabbage mixture on 4 warmed plates. Slide the fish back under the grill for a few seconds, until the butter is just beginning to melt. Quickly put the fish on top of the cabbage and serve immediately.

FILLET OF COD WITH SAFFRON MASHED POTATOES

This dish is known in our kitchen as cod and saff mash. I got the idea for the potatoes from Simon Hopkinson, the chef and food writer, whose recipes in the Independent *are not only a pleasure to read but also usually leave me thinking, blast, I wish I'd come up with that one. Cod with saff mash not only has this delightful purée of potatoes with saffron and olive oil but also a mayonnaise-based sauce flavoured with tomato, orange and chilli and, on the side, some tapenade, which is a purée of black olives, anchovy and capers. There is a recipe for* Tapenade *on p.218 but you can buy jars of good-quality tapenade in all the major supermarkets these days, so feel free to go and buy your own.*

For the sauce, chop the carrot, onion and red chilli very finely, then fry them with the orange zest in the olive oil for 5 minutes. Add the orange juice, white wine, tomato and stock and simmer for 20 minutes. Season with salt and white pepper.

Meanwhile, put the potatoes in a pan and barely cover with cold water. Add the saffron and a pinch of salt, then bring to the boil and cook for 20 minutes or until tender. Drain the cooking liquid off the potatoes into a clean pan and boil rapidly until reduced to 4–6 tablespoons. Mash the potatoes until smooth, then beat in the reduced cooking liquid, garlic, olive oil, cream and some salt and pepper to taste. Keep warm.

Strain the sauce into a jug. Put the mayonnaise in a small pan and gradually whisk in the sauce. Cook over a very gentle heat until it thickens and just coats the back of the spoon. Do not let it boil or it will curdle. Keep warm.

Pre-heat the grill to high. Brush both sides of the cod with olive oil and season with coarse sea salt and pepper. Place on the oiled rack of the grill pan, skin-side up, and cook for 8 minutes.

To serve, put the saffron mashed potatoes in the centre of 4 warmed plates and place the cod on top. Pour the sauce around the edge and sprinkle with the diced tomato and chopped parsley. Put 2 small teaspoons of the tapenade on either side of each plate.

Serves 4

4 thick pieces of cod fillet, weighing about 175 g (6 oz) each, skin on

Olive oil for brushing

Coarse sea salt

2 tomatoes, skinned, seeded and diced

1 tablespoon chopped fresh parsley

About 8 teaspoons tapenade

FOR THE SAUCE

50 g (2 oz) carrot

50 g (2 oz) onion

½ red chilli, seeded

5 cm (2 in) piece of pared orange zest

1 tablespoon olive oil

Juice of ½ orange

50 ml (2 fl oz) white wine

1 tomato, chopped

600 ml (1 pint) *Roasted Fish Stock or Fish Stock* (see p.212)

Salt and white pepper

4 tablespoons *Olive Oil Mayonnaise* (see p.217)

FOR THE POTATOES

900 g (2 lb) floury potatoes, peeled and cut into chunks

A good pinch of saffron

½ garlic clove, crushed

50 ml (2 fl oz) olive oil

25 ml (1 fl oz) double cream

Salt and freshly ground black pepper

Serves 6

600 ml (1 pint) milk

300 ml (10 fl oz) *Fish Stock*
(see p.212)

750 g (1½ lb) haddock fillet

275 g (10 oz) leeks

65 g (2½ oz) butter

50 g (2 oz) carrot, finely
diced

50 g (2 oz) celery, finely
diced

50 g (2 oz) onion, finely
chopped

40 g (1 ½ oz) rindless
smoked streaky bacon,
thinly sliced

50 g (2 oz) plain flour

100 g (4 oz) cooked peeled
prawns

100 g (4 oz) Cornish Yarg
cheese, grated

Freshly grated nutmeg

Salt and freshly ground
black pepper

**FOR THE POTATO PASTRY
CRUST**

350 g (12 oz) potatoes,
peeled and cut into
chunks

225 g (8 oz) self-raising
flour

1 teaspoon salt

15 turns of the black
pepper mill

175 g (6 oz) butter, cut
into small pieces

2 tablespoons cold water

1 egg, beaten

HADDOCK AND CORNISH YARG PIE WITH A POTATO PASTRY CRUST

Fish pies are always incredibly popular. This one is a result of my continuing attempts to try and produce some genuinely local dishes. Here I've used all local fish and vegetables and that excellent cheese, Cornish Yarg, which is mild and firm and particularly suited to a pie like this. If you can't get Cornish Yarg, use a mild Cheddar.

For the pastry, cook the potatoes in boiling salted water until tender. Drain well and either mash or pass through a potato ricer. Leave to cool.

Meanwhile, put the milk and fish stock into a large pan and bring to the boil. Add the haddock and simmer for 5–7 minutes, until firm and opaque. Lift the fish out on to a plate and, when cool enough to handle, break the flesh into large flakes, discarding any skin and bones.

Clean the leeks, finely dice 50 g (2 oz) of them and set aside. Thinly slice the remainder. Melt 25 g (1 oz) of the butter in a clean pan, add the sliced leeks and fry gently for 2–3 minutes, until just cooked. Lift out with a slotted spoon and set aside.

Add the diced leek, carrot, celery, onion and bacon to the pan with a little more of the butter if necessary. Fry over a gentle heat for 10 minutes without letting them brown. Add the remaining butter to the vegetables, stir in the flour and cook for 1 minute. Remove the pan from the heat and gradually add the cooking liquid from the haddock, stirring all the time to make a smooth sauce. Bring to the boil, stirring. Tie together all the ingredients for the bouquet garni and add to the pan. Simmer gently for 30 minutes, then remove the bouquet garni from the pan and season the sauce with nutmeg, salt and pepper.

Stir the flaked fish, reserved leeks, prawns and Cornish Yarg into the sauce, spoon into a deep 1.75 litre (3 pint) pie dish and push a pie funnel into the centre of the mixture. Set aside to cool.

Meanwhile, for the pastry, sift the flour, salt and pepper into a bowl. Add the butter and rub it in with your fingertips until the mixture looks like fine breadcrumbs. Add the cold potato and lightly mix into the flour, then add the water and stir with a round-bladed knife until everything starts to stick together. Form it into a ball, turn out on to a lightly floured work surface and knead briefly until smooth. Chill for 20–30 minutes.

Pre-heat the oven to 200°C/400°F/Gas 6.

Roll out the pastry on a floured surface until it is slightly larger than the top of the pie dish. Cut a thin strip off the edge of the pastry, brush with a little water and press it on to the rim of the pie dish. Brush with a little more water. Make a small cut in the centre of the remaining pastry and then lay it over the pie so that the pie funnel pokes through the cut. Press it on to the rim of the dish and crimp the edge decoratively with your fingers. Brush the top with beaten egg and decorate with leaves cut from the pastry trimmings if you wish. Bake in the oven for 35–40 minutes, until the pastry is crisp and golden.

FOR THE BOUQUET GARNI
I bay leaf
I small bunch of fresh parsley with stalks
Leaves from the centre of I head of celery
I small sprig of fresh thyme

75 g (3 oz) unsalted butter

900 g (2 lb) thick cod fillet, skin on, cut into 4 pieces

1 large onion, cut into quarters and finely sliced

4 plum tomatoes, skinned, seeded and chopped

4 sun-dried tomatoes in oil, drained and finely chopped

300 ml (10 fl oz) *Fish Stock* (see p.212)

120 ml (4 fl oz) white wine

2 tablespoons chopped fresh parsley

Salt and freshly ground black pepper

Sprigs of parsley, to garnish

BAKED COD PORTUGUESE

I have never eaten a cod Portuguese that was anything other than fish in a watery sauce, so I thought it would be fun to take such a standard dish and try and restore it to something like the original. The problem with cooking many Portuguese or Mediterranean dishes in Britain is that they never taste the same using vegetables, particularly tomatoes, that have been grown in Northern Europe. You have to zip up these dishes with something to compensate for the lack of sunshine in the vegetables. I have added sun-dried tomatoes to boost the flavour and used fresh plum tomatoes for authenticity. Although the dish is from Southern Europe I don't think of it as particularly summery so I have included it in this chapter. Call me inconsistent, of course I am!

Melt half the butter in a shallow flameproof casserole dish that is big enough to hold all the pieces of cod in a single layer. Fry the cod, skin-side down, for 1 minute, until crisp and golden. Carefully remove from the casserole and set aside.

Add the onion to the casserole and fry gently for 5 minutes, until softened. Add the plum tomatoes, sun-dried tomatoes, stock and white wine. Bring to the boil and simmer for 10 minutes, until slightly reduced and thickened.

Pre-heat the oven to 200°C/400°F/Gas 6.

Place the cod skin-side up on top of the onion and tomato mixture, transfer the casserole to the oven and bake for 5–6 minutes – less if the pieces of cod are thin. Remove from the oven and lift the cod out on to a warm plate. Return the casserole to the stove over a high heat, add the remaining butter and reduce by boiling rapidly for about 4 minutes, stirring now and then, to make a really thick sauce. Stir in the parsley, season with salt and pepper and cook for 30 seconds more. Spoon the sauce on to 4 warm plates, put the cod on top and garnish with parsley sprigs. Serve with boiled potatoes and a green salad.

LOBSTER POT PIE

This is a fish pie from the other side of the Atlantic, where lobsters are cheap and plentiful. I wouldn't expect you to use one of our British lobsters, they're far too expensive. But you can use cheaper North American lobsters.

Remove the meat from the cooked lobster (see p.19). Cut the lobster tail meat and the cod into slices 1 cm (½ in) thick and set aside. Break up the lobster shell into small pieces and use to make the *Shellfish Stock* (see p.214).

Strain the stock into a clean pan. Add the potatoes and the whole baby carrots and simmer for 5 minutes or until just cooked. Add the peas and simmer for 1 minute. Lift the vegetables out with a slotted spoon and set aside. Add the slices of cod to the pan and simmer for 1 minute, then lift out and set aside. You will need 600 ml (1 pint) of stock for the sauce. If you have more than this, boil rapidly until reduced to the required amount.

Melt the butter in a pan, add the onion and cook for 5 minutes, until lightly browned. Stir in the flour and cook for 1 minute. Take the pan off the heat and gradually stir in the stock. Return to the heat and bring to the boil, stirring all the time. Simmer for 5 minutes and then stir in the cream, lobster meat, cod and vegetables. Season with salt and pepper, spoon into a 1.75 litre (3 pint) pie dish and push a pie funnel into the centre of the mixture. Set aside to cool.

Pre-heat the oven to 220°C/425°F/Gas 7.

For the pastry, sift the flour and salt into a food processor, add the butter and lard and process until the mixture looks like fine breadcrumbs. Tip this into a large mixing bowl and stir in the water with a round-bladed knife until everything starts to stick together. Bring together into a ball, turn out on to a lightly floured work surface and knead once or twice until smooth. Roll out the pastry thinly until it is about 2.5 cm (1 in) bigger than the top of the pie dish. Cut a thin strip off the edge of the pastry, brush with water and press it on to the rim of the pie dish. Brush the top of the pastry strip with a little more water. Make a small cut in the centre of the remaining pastry and then lay it over the pie so that the funnel pokes through the cut. Press it on to the rim of the dish and crimp the edge decoratively with your fingers. Beat the egg yolk with the milk, brush it over the top of the pie and then bake for 35–40 minutes, until the pastry is golden, protecting the edge of the pastry with a strip of foil after 20 minutes, if necessary, to stop it going too brown.

Serves 8

1 cooked lobster, weighing about 750 g (1½ lb)
225 g (8 oz) cod fillet
1 quantity of *Shellfish Stock* (see p.214), made with the broken lobster shell instead of prawns
350 g (12 oz) small waxy potatoes, such as Charlotte, peeled and thickly sliced
100 g (4 oz) baby carrots
100 g (4 oz) young peas, fresh if possible
50 g (2 oz) butter
1 medium onion, chopped
40g (1½ oz) plain flour
150 ml (5 fl oz) double cream
Salt and freshly ground black pepper

FOR THE PASTRY
350 g (12 oz) plain flour
¼ teaspoon salt
100 g (4 oz) butter, cut into small pieces
90 g (3½ oz) lard, cut into small pieces
2 tablespoons cold water
1 egg yolk
1 teaspoon milk

1 chicken, weighing about
   1.5 kg (3½ lb)
1 tablespoon olive oil
50 g (2 oz) butter
2 tablespoons tarragon
   vinegar or white wine
   vinegar
300 ml (10 fl oz) *Chicken
   Stock* (see p.213)
300 ml (10 fl oz)
   Chardonnay wine
25 g (1 oz) fresh tarragon
4 garlic cloves, peeled
900 g (2 lb) mussels,
   cleaned (see p.17)
300 ml (10 fl oz) double
   cream
Juice of ½ lemon
Salt and freshly ground
   black pepper

SAUTÉD CHICKEN WITH MUSSELS, TARRAGON AND CHARDONNAY

This is just a simple sautéd chicken dish but live mussels are added right at the end so that there is only time for them just to open in the pan before the dish is served. The cooking liquor from the mussels gives a final salty tang to the tarragon sauce. I took such an aversion to the phrase 'surf and turf' when I first heard it in the early Eighties that it took me over ten years to accept the fact that a combination of meat and seafood can often be excellent.

Joint the chicken into 8 pieces: to do this, pull one leg away from the body and cut through the skin, down towards where the thighbone joins the main carcass. Twist the leg so that the ball and socket joint is exposed and cut through it to detach the leg. Repeat on the other side. Cut each leg in half through the joint and cut off and discard the feet bones from the end of each drumstick. Now cut through the skin down the centre of the breastbone and ease back the breast meat slightly. Cut along either side of the breastbone using kitchen scissors or a sharp knife. Open up the bird and remove the breast and wing joints by cutting horizontally through the rib bones. Cut the breast and wing joint diagonally in half so that each piece has an equal amount of breast meat. Cut off the tips of the wings. The backbone, breastbone, wing tips and feet bones can be discarded or used to make stock (see p.213).

Season the chicken pieces with a little salt and pepper. Heat the oil and butter in a large, deep frying pan, add the chicken pieces and fry, skin-side down, for 10 minutes or until well browned. Turn over and continue cooking for 5 minutes. Transfer the breast meat portions to a plate and continue to fry the leg and thigh portions for another 5 minutes. This means that all the pieces of chicken will be well browned without the breast meat being overcooked.

Remove the remaining chicken from the pan and pour away the excess fat. Add the vinegar to the pan and boil until it has almost all evaporated. Add the chicken stock and wine and boil until reduced to half its original volume.

Return the chicken to the pan and add half the tarragon with its stalks and the whole garlic cloves. Partly cover with a lid and simmer very gently for 30 minutes, until the chicken is tender and cooked through.

Add the mussels to the chicken in the pan, cover and cook over a high heat for about 3 minutes, until the mussels have opened. Discard any that remain closed. Lift the chicken and mussels out of the pan with a slotted spoon and place in a warmed serving dish; cover and keep warm. Strain the cooking liquid to remove the tarragon and garlic, then return it to the pan and bring back to the boil. Boil until reduced by half, then taste; it should be really well flavoured. Chop the remaining tarragon leaves, setting aside a few sprigs for garnish.

Add the cream to the pan and boil for 2–3 minutes, until the sauce thickens slightly. Stir in the lemon juice and chopped tarragon and season with a little salt and pepper if necessary. Simmer for 1 minute to release some of the flavour from the tarragon, then pour the sauce over the chicken and mussels. Serve garnished with the reserved tarragon sprigs and accompanied by a tossed green salad and boiled new potatoes.

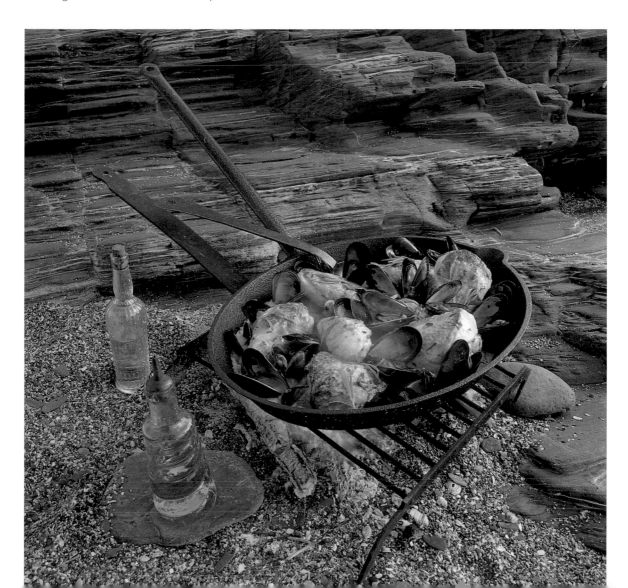

Serves 6

450 g (1 lb) dried cannellini
beans

1 red pepper

150 ml (5 fl oz) olive oil,
plus extra for brushing

3 garlic cloves, very finely
chopped

2 shallots, finely chopped

2 red finger chillies, seeded
and finely chopped

2 tablespoons chopped
fresh thyme

1 John Dory, weighing
about 1.25–1.5 kg
(2½–3 lb), cleaned
(see p.11)

12 black olives, finely
chopped

2 tablespoons white wine
vinegar

Salt and freshly ground
black pepper

BAKED JOHN DORY WITH CHILLI, CANNELLINI BEANS AND THYME

The cannellini beans are mixed with olive oil, garlic, lots of red chilli, roasted red pepper and thyme. Then a whole John Dory is baked on top of them, sprinkled with chopped black olives. Serve with a frisé salad tossed with some Olive Oil Dressing *(see p.216), preferably made with a lemon-flavoured olive oil. You can make this dish equally successfully with red bream, sea bass, tilapia or snapper.*

Cover the beans with plenty of cold water and leave to soak overnight.

The next day drain the beans, return them to the pan with plenty of fresh water to cover and bring to the boil, skimming off any scum as it rises to the surface. Leave to simmer for 40 minutes or until tender. Drain the beans, pour the cooking liquid into another pan and bring back to the boil. Boil rapidly until reduced to 200 ml (7 fl oz).

Meanwhile, pre-heat the oven to 200°C/400°F/Gas 6 and pre-heat the grill to high.

Brush the red pepper with a little oil and grill, turning now and then, until the skin is slightly blackened. Leave until cool enough to handle, then peel off the skin, remove the seeds and cut the flesh into fine dice.

Heat the oil in a flameproof casserole dish large enough to hold the fish. Add the garlic, shallots, chillies, diced red pepper and thyme and fry gently for 5 minutes. Stir in the beans and reduced cooking liquid and season well with plenty of salt and pepper.

Brush the fish inside and out with olive oil and season well with salt and pepper. Put it on top of the beans and sprinkle with the black olives. Cover and bake for 20 minutes. Then uncover and cook for a further 10 minutes, by which time the fish should be done.

To serve, lift the fish off the beans and remove the flesh from the bones. Put it on 4 warmed plates. Stir the vinegar into the beans and serve them alongside the fish.

COD WITH RED WINE SAUCE

This dish originated from one of the best restaurants in the world, Giradet at Crissier, near Lausanne in Switzerland. I got the recipe from a book that has given me a great deal of pleasure, Egon Ronay's The Great Dishes In My Life. *Almost better than an autobiography, it's one of those books that every one who has influenced the way we eat should write. The original recipe calls for a very elaborate fish-scale effect to be made with wafer-thin slices of small potatoes, which are fried and laid on top of the fish. We occasionally do this at the restaurant but it really is three-star cooking and probably, I think, outside the scope of even an advanced cookery book like this!*

A good accompaniment to the cod would be some courgettes fried very gently in butter with chopped tarragon and chives.

Put all the ingredients for the lentils into a pan and simmer until tender. Drain, remove the clove and bay leaf, then cover and keep warm.

Melt 50 g (2 oz) of the butter in a medium-sized pan and brush a little over the cod. Set aside, skin-side up, on the greased rack of the grill pan and sprinkle with sea salt and a little black pepper.

For the sauce, add the carrot, celery, onion and spices to the remaining butter in the pan and fry over a high heat for about 10 minutes, until the vegetables are well browned. Add the red wine, stock, sugar and ¼ teaspoon of salt, bring to the boil and boil until reduced to one quarter of its original volume. Strain the reduced sauce to remove the vegetables, return to the pan and keep warm.

Pre-heat the grill to high. Grill the cod for 8 minutes, until the skin is well browned. Meanwhile, mix the remaining butter with the flour to make a smooth paste. Bring the sauce to the boil and then whisk in the paste, a little at a time. Simmer for 2 minutes until the sauce is smooth and thickened. Adjust the seasoning if necessary.

To serve, put the lentils on 4 warmed plates and place the cod on top, then spoon the sauce around the fish.

Serves 4

75 g (3 oz) unsalted butter

4 pieces of cod, cut from a thick fillet, weighing about 175 g (6 oz) each

50 g (2 oz) carrot, chopped

50 g (2 oz) celery, chopped

50 g (2 oz) onion, chopped

A small pinch of ground allspice

A small pinch of ground cloves

A small pinch of grated nutmeg

A large pinch of curry powder

600 ml (1 pint) red wine

600 ml (1 pint) *Chicken Stock* (see p.213)

1 teaspoon sugar

1 tablespoon plain flour

Coarse sea salt and freshly ground black pepper

FOR THE LENTILS

50 g (2 oz) dried green lentils or Puy lentils

175 ml (6 fl oz) *Fish Stock* (see p.212)

1 clove

1 fresh or dried bay leaf

2 slices of onion

½ teaspoon salt

Serves 4

600 ml (1 pint) *Chicken Stock* (see p.213)

150 ml (5 fl oz) white wine

85 ml (3 fl oz) double cream

4 prepared monkfish fillets (see p.15), weighing about 175 g (6 oz) each

4 thin slices of Parma ham, weighing about 15 g (½ oz) each

50 g (2 oz) unsalted butter

2 teaspoons chopped fresh parsley

Salt and freshly ground black pepper

FOR THE SAUERKRAUT

25 g (1 oz) butter

50 g (2 oz) carrot, very thinly sliced

50 g (2 oz) celery, thinly sliced

50 g (2 oz) onion, thinly sliced

225 g (8 oz) sauerkraut

ROAST MONKFISH WITH PARMA HAM AND SAUERKRAUT

This dish works extraordinarily well because the slight blandness of the monkfish contrasts most pleasingly with the acidity of the sauerkraut. Fillets of monkfish are wrapped in thin slices of Parma ham, tied and roasted in the oven. They are then sliced and served on top of some sauerkraut that has been stewed with carrot, celery and onion, accompanied by a sauce made from the roasting juices, a little fish stock and cream, and finished with parsley.

I'm quite happy to use canned sauerkraut for this. To me, sauerkraut is the heart of warm, glowing winter food and I love its slightly smoky, salty flavour. I got the idea for this dish in Obergurgl during one very cold skiing holiday in January. In central Europe sauerkraut was for centuries the only source of vitamin C in the winter months, when no fresh vegetables were available. We don't have to eat it any more but you ought to know that it's very good for you. The lactic acid in foods like sauerkraut is now thought to be part of the secret of longevity in the Balkan diet. So eat more, it's lovely!

Pre-heat the oven to 200°C/400°F/Gas 6.

For the sauerkraut, melt the butter in a pan, add the carrot, celery and onion and cook gently for 5 minutes, until softened. Add the sauerkraut, cover and cook gently for 20–25 minutes.

Put the chicken stock, white wine and cream into a wide-based pan and boil rapidly until reduced to 175 ml (6 fl oz).

Wrap each monkfish fillet in a slice of the Parma ham and tie securely with string in 2 places. Melt 25 g (1 oz) of the butter in a large, shallow ovenproof pan. Add the monkfish, seam-side up, and fry for 1–1½ minutes, until golden brown underneath. Turn over, transfer the pan to the oven and cook for 10 minutes.

Remove the fish from the oven, transfer to a plate and keep warm. Add the reduced stock, wine and cream mixture to the pan and stir to scrape up all the crusty bits from the bottom. Strain into a small pan, bring back to the boil and then whisk in the remaining 25 g (1 oz) of butter. Season with pepper and a little salt if necessary (but remember that the Parma ham is quite salty. To serve, spoon the sauerkraut into the centre of 4 warmed plates. Cut each piece of monkfish on the slant into 4 and place on top of the sauerkraut. Pour the sauce around and sprinkle with the chopped parsley.

Serves 4

4 pieces of haddock fillet,
   weighing about 175 g
   (6 oz) each, skin on
25 g (1 oz) butter, melted
Coarse sea salt

FOR THE GNOCCHI
550 g (1¼ lb) floury
   potatoes, such as King
   Edward
½ teaspoon salt
2 egg yolks
90 g (3 ½ oz) plain flour,
   sifted

FOR THE BEURRE ROUGE
100 g (4 oz) red onions,
   very finely chopped
150 ml (5 fl oz) red wine
150 ml (5 fl oz) *Fish Stock*
   (see p.212)
65 ml (2 ½ fl oz) red wine
   vinegar
¼ teaspoon caster sugar
175 g (6 oz) chilled
   unsalted butter, cut into
   small pieces
Salt and freshly ground
   black pepper

GRILLED HADDOCK WITH POTATO GNOCCHI AND BEURRE ROUGE

This dish typifies restaurant cooking in that it relies on quite a lot of advance preparation but the actual cooking is very straightforward and easy. The gnocchi can be prepared a long time in advance, as can the base for the beurre rouge. *Then, when you are ready to serve, you just poach the gnocchi, whisk the butter into the sauce and grill the fish — none of which takes more than a few minutes. Everything is then assembled on the plate with no last-minute panics. Every dish has to be more or less like this in a busy restaurant kitchen, otherwise we'd all perish from stress!*

Pre-heat the oven to 200°C/400°F/Gas 6. Bake the potatoes in their skins for 1 hour or until soft.

Meanwhile, for the *beurre rouge*, put all the ingredients except the butter into a saucepan with a pinch of salt, bring to the boil and simmer, uncovered, for 15 minutes. Cover and cook gently for another 20–25 minutes or until the onions are very soft.

Remove the potatoes from the oven and, when cool enough to handle, cut in half and scoop out the cooked potato into a bowl. Mash until very smooth, then beat in the salt, egg yolks and flour to make a soft dough. Turn the mixture out on to a very lightly floured surface and knead briefly until smooth. Divide it into 20 pieces and lightly roll each one into a ball. Press a finger into the centre of each to form an indentation and then put on a floured baking tray. You can cover and refrigerate them at this stage, if convenient.

To finish the dish, pre-heat the grill to high. Brush the top of the haddock liberally with the melted butter and season with pepper. Place skin-side up on the rack of the grill pan and drizzle with more butter, then sprinkle with coarse sea salt. Bring the *beurre rouge* up to a simmer and then whisk in the butter, a few pieces at a time, until thick and creamy. Season and keep warm.

Grill the haddock for 3–6 minutes, depending on the thickness of the fillet. Meanwhile, drop the gnocchi in batches into a pan of simmering water and cook for 2 minutes or until they float to the surface. Lift out with a slotted spoon and put them in a lightly buttered dish as soon as they are cooked.

To serve, put the haddock on 4 warmed plates and pile the gnocchi alongside. Spoon the *beurre rouge* over and around the haddock.

SKATE AU POIVRE WITH BÉARNAISE SAUCE

The skate is strewn with coarsely crushed peppercorns, seasoned and then fried in olive oil and served with a classic butter sauce. Do be careful when buying skate that it doesn't smell at all of ammonia. I don't care what other books say; if you can smell it, don't buy it.

If the béarnaise sauce strikes fear into your heart, use the Quick Hollandaise Sauce *on p.215 and simply add the tarragon, shallot, pepper and vinegar reduction to it.*

Coarsely crush the black peppercorns in a pestle and mortar or simply in a bowl with the end of a rolling pin. Trim about 2.5 cm (1 in) from the edge of the skate, otherwise it will break off during cooking and look unattractive.

For the béarnaise sauce, put the tarragon, shallots, pepper and vinegar in a small pan, bring to the boil and boil until reduced to 1 tablespoon, then set aside. Clarify the butter by melting it in a pan over a low heat, then pouring off the clear butter, leaving the white solids behind. Put the egg yolks and water in a bowl set over a pan of simmering water, making sure the bowl is not touching the water. Whisk until the mixture is voluminous and creamy. Remove the bowl from the heat and whisk in the clarified butter a little at a time. Rest the bowl in a bowl of warm water to keep it warm. Stir the tarragon and shallot reduction into the sauce.

To cook the skate, heat the olive oil in a large frying pan. Brush the peppercorns on both sides of each piece of skate with a pastry brush, then sprinkle with the salt. Fry 2 pieces at a time for about 4–5 minutes on each side, depending on their thickness. Transfer to a warm plate and keep hot while you cook the rest. To serve, put the skate on 4 warmed plates and spoon the béarnaise sauce to one side.

Serves 4

2 tablespoons black peppercorns

4 pieces of skate, weighing about 200 g (7 oz) each, skinned

4 tablespoons olive oil

1 teaspoon salt

FOR THE BÉARNAISE SAUCE

1 tablespoon chopped fresh tarragon

2 shallots, very finely chopped

20 turns of the black pepper mill

50 ml (2 fl oz) white wine vinegar

225 g (8 oz) unsalted butter

2 egg yolks

2 tablespoons water

½ teaspoon salt

20 mussels, cleaned
(see p.17)

3–4 tablespoons dry white
wine or water

450 g (1 lb) puff pastry,
either home-made or
the best-quality bought
puff pastry

6 prepared scallops
(see p.18)

100 g (4 oz) white crab
meat

1 egg, beaten

Salt and freshly ground
black pepper

FOR THE MOUSSELINE

175 g (6 oz) whiting or
pollack fillets, skinned

40 ml (1½ fl oz) *Shellfish
Reduction* (see p.214)

1 egg

1 small shallot, finely
chopped

¾ teaspoon salt

120 ml (4 fl oz) double
cream

FOR THE SAUCE

65 ml (2½ fl oz) *Shellfish
Reduction* (see p.214)

150 ml (5 fl oz) double
cream

75 g (3 oz) chilled unsalted
butter, cut into small
pieces

2 teaspoons lemon juice

TOURTE OF SCALLOPS, CRAB AND MUSSELS

I suppose if any dish typified a slight return in British cooking to more substantial, warming — dare I say, comforting — food, this would be it. We used to sell individual tourtes made with crawfish in the restaurant about ten years ago but then gave up when the wave of Mediterranean food began to sweep over Northern Europe. However, we've slipped the dish back on to the menu recently and it has gone down very well indeed. A tourte is a round, savoury, covered tart from France, made with the very best puff pastry which is glazed with egg to give it a beautiful brown finish and cut in radiating curves like a Pithiviers gâteau. This one is filled with seafood, then a rich shellfish sauce is poured into the tart and served with it. Tourtes are very old in origin. The founder of classic French cookery, Antoine Carême, noted with sadness in the early 1800s that the tourte served by 'our great cooks in the old days at the table of princes' was by then thought to be too common for sophisticated gastronomes because it was round.

Make the *Shellfish Reduction* if you have not already done so (see p.214). Leave to cool.

For the mousseline, cut the fish fillets into small pieces and put them in a food processor with the shellfish reduction, egg, shallot and salt. Process until smooth, then, with the motor still running, add the cream in a steady stream, taking care not to process for more than 10 seconds or the mixture may curdle. Scrape into a bowl, cover and chill for 1 hour.

Put the mussels and white wine or water in a large pan over a fairly high heat, cover and cook for 3–4 minutes, until the mussels have opened. Discard any that remain closed. Shell the mussels and leave to cool.

Pre-heat the oven to 220°C/425°F/Gas 7.

Cut the pastry in half and roll out one piece into a 25 cm (10 in) circle. Roll out the second piece into a 28 cm (11 in) circle. Put the smaller piece of pastry on a lightly greased baking tray and spread half the mousseline over it to within 4 cm (1½ in) of the edge. Cut each scallop in half horizontally and arrange over the mousseline with the crab and the cooked mussels. Season with salt and pepper and then carefully spread the remaining mousseline over the top.

Brush the edge of the pastry with a little water, cover with the larger circle of pastry and press the edges together to seal. Crimp the edges decoratively, then brush the top with the beaten egg. Using the tip of a small, sharp knife, either score criss-cross lines on top or mark radiating curves from the centre. Make a hole in the centre and bake for 25 minutes.

Shortly before the tourte is ready, make the sauce. Put the shellfish reduction and cream into a pan, bring to the boil and simmer for 5 minutes. Whisk in the butter a piece at a time, followed by the lemon juice.

Take the tourte out of the oven, pour about 2 tablespoons of the sauce into it through the hole in the top, then return it to the oven for 5 minutes. Slide the pie on to a warm serving plate and serve the rest of the sauce separately.

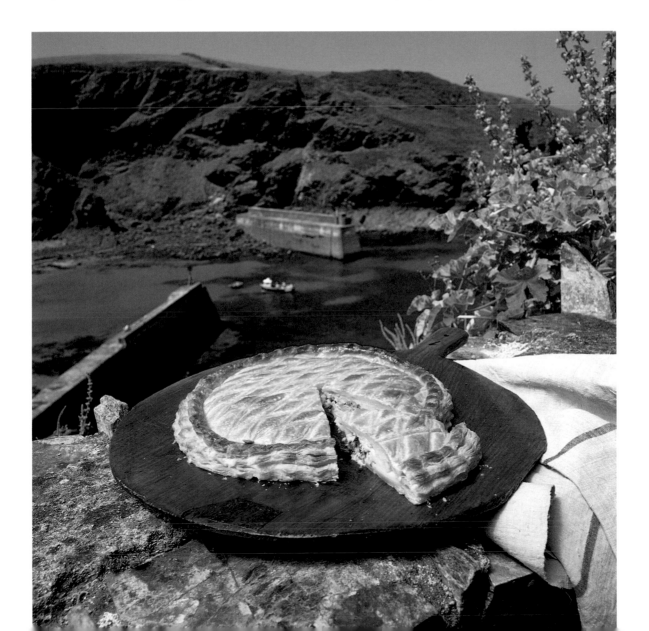

Serves 4

2.25 litres (4 pints) water

I slice lemon

I tablespoon salt

750 g–900 g (1½–2 lb) hake
fillet, skin on

75 g (3 oz) unsalted butter

15 g (½ oz) flour

600 ml (1 pint) full-cream
milk

25 g (1 oz) fresh parsley,
stalks removed and
chopped

CLASSIC HAKE IN PARSLEY SAUCE

This is the joke dish that people always use as an example of boring British cooking but in fact, if you use perfectly fresh hake, haddock or cod and make this simple white sauce properly (i.e. not out of a packet) and use freshly chopped parsley, the joke is on everyone else as it is very good.

Put the water, lemon and salt in a large pan. Bring to the boil, then simmer for 5 minutes. Add the hake and simmer for 2 minutes. Remove the pan from the heat and leave to finish cooking gently in the cooking liquid.

Melt 25 g (1 oz) butter in a heavy-based pan and sprinkle over the flour. Stir continuously with a wooden spoon to mix, then cook until the mixture smells nutty. Gradually pour in the milk, stirring all the time, to make a smooth sauce. Add 300 ml (10 fl oz) of the fish cooking liquid and leave to simmer for 12 minutes.

Drain the hake and cut into 4 portions. Place on 4 warmed plates. Stir the chopped parsley and the rest of the butter into the sauce. Pour the sauce over half the fish. I think dishes like this look more attractive if the fish is only partly covered. Serve with some potatoes boiled in salted water and a sprig of mint.

Serves 4

4 herrings weighing about
225 g (8 oz) each

100 g (4 oz) oatmeal

25 ml (1 fl oz) vegetable oil

4 rashers streaky bacon,
cut into thin strips

Salt and freshly ground
black pepper

I lemon, cut into wedges

HERRINGS IN OATMEAL WITH BACON

We filmed this dish and five or six other dishes on the theme of simplicity in the series and in the end, nothing seems to bring out the creamy, nutty flavour of fresh herrings better than this straightforward British dish.

Fillet the herrings(see p. 13). Season and press with oatmeal until they are well covered. Heat the oil in a frying pan and fry the streaky bacon until crisp. Remove from the pan and keep warm. Fry the herrings in the same pan oil, flesh side first, until golden brown. Sprinkle the fillets with the bacon. Serve with lemon wedges and some boiled potatoes with chopped parsley.

Fillets of Brill with a Ginger and Monbazillac Sauce and Pappardelle Pasta

You can use John Dory or turbot equally successfully in this dish. Like many of my recipes, I look to build up complexity of flavours by combining two or more different, but complementary, tastes on the plate. Here I have combined a butter and ginger sauce with a tomato and olive dressing for the pasta. The trick is to aim to be complex but not over complicated.

Put the fish stock and wine into a pan (the larger the better because it will reduce more quickly) and boil rapidly until reduced to one quarter of its original volume (about 175ml [6 fl oz])

Pre-heat the oven to 200°C/400°F/Gas 6. Meanwhile, lightly grease a shallow ovenproof dish with some of the butter and then sprinkle the base with the chopped shallots. Bring 1.75 litres (3 pints) water and 1 tablespoon of salt to the boil in a large pan.

Season the brill fillets on both sides with salt and pepper and lay on top of the shallots. As soon as the stock is ready, cool slightly and then pour over the fish and cover with a piece buttered greaseproof paper. Bake for 8 minutes.

Put the olive oil, diced tomatoes, basil and lemon juice for the pasta into a small pan and leave over a very low heat to warm through. Drop the pappardelle pasta into the boiling water and cook for 3-4 minutes (or according to the manufacturer's instructions).

Drain the pasta well, return to the pan with the olive oil and tomato mixture and a little salt and toss together gently. Keep warm.

Remove the fish from teh oven and lift the fillets out of the sauce onto a plate. Cover and keep warm. Strain the sauce into a small pan and add the chopped ginger. Bring to the boil and then whisk in the remaining butter a small piece at a time. Season with a little salt and pepper. Keep warm.

To serve, put the brill onto 4 warmed plates and spoon the ginger butter sauce over and around the fish. Place four little piles of pasta to the side and serve with a slightly off-dry white wine such as Vouvray or an Australian Sémillon Chardonnay.

Serves 4

600 ml (i pint) fish stock (see p.212)

75 ml (3 fl oz) Monbazillac (or another sweet wine such as Sauternes or Muscat Beaumes de Venise)

75g (3 oz) unsalted butter

1 shallot, peeled and very finely chopped

4 x 175g (6 oz) fillets of brill, skinned

15g (½ oz) fresh root ginger, peeled and very finely chopped

Salt and freshly ground black pepper

FOR THE PASTA

100g (4 oz) pappardelle pasta

2 tablespoons extra virgin olive oil

2 tomatoes, skinned, seeded and diced

6 fresh basil leaves, very finely sliced

juice of ¼ lemon

ELEGANT FISH DISHES

The dishes in this chapter are not necessarily ones that require hours of commitment in the kitchen, though some of them do. They are more a collection of recipes that you might even feel embarrassed to serve at anything but a formal occasion. You would feel a bit self-conscious about bringing out a plateful of *Braised Fillet of Turbot with Slivers of Potato, Mushrooms and Truffle Oil* for the children.

'What's for supper?'

'*Braised Fillet of Turbot with Slivers of Potato, Mushrooms and Truffle Oil.*'

To which, with children there is only one answer: 'But I wanted fish fingers.'

I have a bit of a theory about dinner parties, a theory born of having held very few, since I spend most of my evenings cooking in the restaurant. Lack of knowledge is rarely a hindrance when it comes to pronouncing on anything! A dinner party should contain only one elaborate and stylish dish. The rest of the meal should be simple and composed of things with which your guests feel familiar. I almost feel that it is bad manners to impose too much cooking on your friends. This idea also underpins the menu at the restaurant: keep it simple and don't show off too much, because what counts is people's relaxed enjoyment. The food should almost be forgotten, just coming along effortlessly and reinforcing everyone's sense of well being, except for that one dish that everyone will remember so well.

Hopefully this is a chapter of memorable dishes. Certainly the *Spiny Lobster with Vanilla Sauce* (see p.140) would be, or the *Fillet of Bass on a Crisp Risotto Cake with Saffron Sauce* (see p.134). These are time consuming to prepare but terribly worthwhile. Others are equally elevated but really quite easy to make, such as *Fillets of Bass with Vanilla Butter Vinaigrette* (see p.137) and *Escalopes of Salmon with Champagne and Chive Sauce* (see p.150). This, then, is the chapter for really flying.

Poached Lobster with Butter and Basil (see p.132).

1 quantity of *Shellfish Nage*
   (see p.214), made using
   2.25 litres (4 pints)
   water and 300 ml
   (10 fl oz) wine
1 live lobster, weighing
   about 750 g (1½ lb), or
   2 small lobsters,
   weighing about 450 g
   (1 lb) each
1 carrot, sliced
1 baby turnip, sliced in half
2 celery sticks, sliced
1 small onion, sliced
100 g (4 oz) French beans,
   halved
100 g (4 oz) chilled
   unsalted butter, cut into
   small pieces
6 fresh basil leaves, very
   finely shredded, plus
   sprigs of basil to garnish
Salt

POACHED LOBSTER WITH BUTTER AND BASIL

The lobster is poached in a delicate shellfish nage, then some root vegetables are added. The poaching liquor is reduced right down and whisked with a little butter and a chiffonade of basil (very finely shredded basil). The reduction of the nage takes a long time, as you have to boil about 2.25 litres (4 pints) of liquid down to a mere cupful, but the fruits of your labour will be so very worthwhile that you will be amazed how much flavour there is in the shell of a smallish lobster. The finished sauce is truly wonderful. Do try it. I add some baby turnip to the bouillon for cooking this lobster. I love the taste of young turnips, so sweet and yet slightly bitter, and this flavour comes through in the final sauce as a subtle hint.

Put the nage into a pan just large enough to accommodate the lobster. Bring to a rapid boil, then add the lobster. Bring back to the boil and simmer for 12 minutes. Remove the lobster and set aside until cool enough to handle. Remove the meat from the lobster (see p.19), reserving the shell.

Add the carrot, turnip, celery, onion and the reserved lobster shells to the nage and boil rapidly until the liquid has reduced to about 150 ml (5 fl oz), but remove the two pieces of turnip after ten minutes, otherwise the flavour will overpower the final sauce.

Bring a small pan of salted water to the boil. Add the French beans and cook for about 3 minutes or until just tender. Drain and keep warm.

Strain the reduced stock into a small pan. Bring back to the boil and gradually whisk in the butter, a few pieces at a time. Check the seasoning, adding salt if necessary. Stir in the basil and leave over a very low heat for about 5 minutes to allow the flavour to infuse the sauce. Strain the sauce into a clean pan to remove the basil if you wish.

To serve, slice the lobster meat, re-heat gently and arrange it on 4 warmed plates. Pour the sauce around, then pile the French beans alongside the lobster and garnish with sprigs of basil.

GRILLED FILLETS OF DOVER SOLE WITH SAUTÉD POTATOES, CARAMELIZED APPLES AND CIDER SAUCE

Serves 4

900 g (2 lb) potatoes
2 tablespoons olive oil
75 g (3 oz) unsalted butter
150 ml (5 fl oz) dry cider
150 ml (5 fl oz) *Fish Stock*
   (see p.212)
8 Dover sole fillets,
   weighing about 75–100g
   (3–4 oz) each, skinned
3 Cox's Orange Pippins
   apples
¼ teaspoon caster sugar
1 tablespoon finely
   chopped fresh parsley
Salt and freshly ground
   black pepper

A simple dish inspired by one I ate in Brittany, where apples, cider and Dover sole are as plentiful as they are here in the West Country. You can use plenty of other types of fish for this, such as lemon sole, plaice, flounder, dabs, gurnard or even small cod (codling), hake or whiting.

Peel the potatoes, cut them in half lengthways and then cut each half into slices 5 mm (¼ in) thick. Cook in boiling salted water for about 8 minutes or until just tender, then drain and pat dry. Heat the olive oil and 25 g (1 oz) of the butter in a large frying pan. Add the potato slices, season well with salt and pepper and fry for about 7–8 minutes on each side, until they are pleasantly brown and sandy. Transfer to a baking tray and keep warm in a low oven.

Put the cider, fish stock and another 25 g (1 oz) of the butter in the frying pan, bring to the boil and boil for a few minutes, until reduced to a thick, well-flavoured sauce. Season with salt and pepper, pour into a small pan and keep warm.

Pre-heat the grill to high. Melt the remaining butter in the cleaned frying pan. Brush the Dover sole fillets with a little of the butter and lay them on the rack of the grill pan. Season with salt and pepper. Peel and core the apples, then cut each one into 8 wedges.

Grill the fish fillets for 3 minutes on one side only. Meanwhile, put the apples slices in the frying pan, sprinkle over the sugar and fry for about 1 minute on each side, until golden. Stir into the sautéd potatoes.

To serve, arrange the Dover sole fillets down the centre of a warmed oval serving dish and put the apples and potatoes around the edge. Bring the sauce back to the boil, stir in the parsley and pour it over the fish. Serve immediately.

1 quantity of *Shellfish Stock*
(see p.214)

½ teaspoon saffron strands

3 tablespoons *Olive Oil
Mayonnaise* (see p.217)

6 sea bass fillets, weighing
about 100 g (4 oz) each,
skin on

15 g (½ oz) unsalted butter,
melted

1 tablespoon olive oil

Salt and freshly ground
black pepper

Chopped fresh parsley, to
garnish

FOR THE RISOTTO

2 tablespoons olive oil

1 small onion, finely
chopped

1 garlic clove, very finely
chopped

225 g (8 oz) risotto rice
such as Arborio

85 ml (3 fl oz) dry white
wine

FILLET OF BASS ON A CRISP RISOTTO CAKE WITH SAFFRON SAUCE

All the flavours in this dish — the bass, the shellfish-flavoured risotto cake under it and the warm, mayonnaise-based saffron sauce — complement each other in a beguiling way. At the time of writing, this recipe has not had its premiere at the restaurant but I have a feeling it will go down rather well.

Make the *Shellfish Stock* (see p.214) if you haven't already done so, adding most of the saffron strands with the rest of the ingredients just before simmering. You should end up with about 1 litre (1¾ pints) — if you have any less, make it up with a little more fish stock.

For the risotto, heat the olive oil in a heavy-based pan. Add the onion and garlic and cook over a medium heat until soft and lightly browned. Add the rice and stir around for a couple of minutes, until well coated with the oil. Pour in the wine, bring to the boil and stir until the rice has absorbed all the liquid. Now add 900 ml (1½ pints) of the warm shellfish stock in 3 batches, stirring well until all the stock has been absorbed before adding the next amount. Season with salt and pepper. The risotto will take about 20 minutes to cook, by which time the rice should be tender and will have absorbed all the liquid. Since the risotto is to be moulded into cakes it should be allowed to become really quite thick.

Put six 9 cm (3½ in) pastry cutters or egg poaching rings on a baking sheet and line each one with a small sheet of cling film, leaving the edges overhanging. Divide the risotto between them, level the surface and cover with the overhanging cling film. Chill for at least 3 hours.

Pre-heat the grill to high. For the sauce, bring the last 150 ml (¼ pint) of shellfish stock to the boil and add the remaining saffron strands. Gradually whisk it into the mayonnaise, then pour it back into the pan and cook over a gentle heat for a couple of minutes, stirring constantly, until the sauce is thick enough to coat the back of a spoon. Do not let it get too hot or it will curdle. Keep warm while you finish the dish.

Cut each fillet of fish in half, brush both sides with a little of the melted butter and season with a little salt and pepper. Place skin-side up on the rack of the grill pan.

Heat the remaining melted butter and the oil in a large frying pan until quite hot. Unwrap the risotto cakes, put them in the pan and fry for 1½–2 minutes, until richly golden. Carefully turn them over, lower the heat to medium-high and fry for another 3–4 minutes, until they have heated right through. Meanwhile grill the fish for 2 minutes, skin-side up only.

To serve, put the risotto cakes on 6 warmed plates. Put 2 pieces of sea bass on top of each one, pour the sauce around and sprinkle lightly with chopped parsley.

Braised Fillet of Turbot with Slivers of Potato, Mushrooms and Truffle Oil

175 g (6 oz) waxy main-crop potatoes, such as Wilja

100 g (4 oz) unsalted butter

1 thin slice of cooked ham, weighing about 25 g (1 oz), cut into very fine dice

25 g (1 oz) shallots, finely chopped

85 ml (3 fl oz) dry vermouth, such as Noilly Prat or Martini

300 ml (10 fl oz) *Concentrated Chicken Stock* (see p.213)

100 g (4 oz) button mushrooms, thinly sliced

2 teaspoons lemon juice

1 tablespoon truffle oil

750 g (1½ lb) turbot fillet, skin on, cut into 8 pieces

1 tablespoon chopped fresh parsley

Salt and freshly ground black pepper

I originally devised this recipe using fresh black truffles but these are pretty impossible (and pretty expensive) to get, especially outside the restaurant business. However, the flavour of truffles is so good that it seemed a shame not to try and incorporate them somewhere. Then I found an Italian olive oil flavoured with white truffles. It is fantastic and quite easy to get in any good delicatessen. A little bottle is also fiendishly expensive but it goes a long way.

Peel and slice the potatoes as thinly as you can and then cut them across into thin matchsticks. Melt half the butter in a frying pan that is large enough to hold all the pieces of fish in one layer. Add the potatoes, ham and shallots and cook gently for 4–5 minutes. Add the vermouth and chicken stock and simmer for about 8 minutes, until the potatoes are almost, but not quite, cooked. You can prepare the dish to this stage some time in advance if you wish.

Stir the mushrooms, lemon juice, truffle oil and some salt and pepper into the pan and then rest the pieces of turbot on top, skin-side up. Cover and simmer for about 6 minutes or until the fish is cooked through. Lift the fish on to a plate and keep hot. Add the remaining butter to the pan and boil rapidly for 10 minutes or until the sauce has thickened and the potatoes are just beginning to break up.

To serve, peel the skin off the turbot and place the fish on 4 warmed plates. Stir the parsley into the sauce and spoon it on top of the fish.

Fillets of Bass with Vanilla Butter Vinaigrette

I cooked this dish for a friend of mine, Henry Gilbey, who is the most enthusiastic fisherman I have ever met. His whole life is geared towards fishing and yet he doesn't like fish. This is the dish I chose for him because it works so well together and all the flavours are pretty irresistible. A simple fillet of bass is cooked on a cast-iron ribbed pan to give that flavour, then served with a warm vinaigrette made with a good fish stock reduction, dry vermouth and vanilla. Maybe Henry was just being polite but he did say it was very good.

Clarify the butter by melting it gently in a small pan, then skimming off any froth and pouring off the clear liquid into another pan, leaving behind the butter solids which will have collected at the bottom.

Brush both sides of the sea bass fillets with a little of the clarified butter and season with salt and pepper.

For the vinaigrette, split the vanilla pod open lengthways, scrape out the seeds with a small teaspoon and then chop the pod very finely. Put the seeds and pod into a small pan with the Noilly Prat, vinegar and shallot, bring to the boil and boil for a few minutes until reduced to about 1 tablespoon. Add the fish stock and boil once more until reduced to about 3 tablespoons. Remove the shallot halves, then add the remaining clarified butter, plus the tomato, chervil, ¼ teaspoon of salt and 6 turns of the black pepper mill. Keep just warm over a very low heat.

Heat a lightly oiled cast-iron ribbed pan until very hot. Cook the fish fillets, skin-side down, for 1 minute, pressing down on top of each fillet in turn with the back of a fish slice to help mark them with the lines from the griddle. Turn over and cook for 30 seconds on the other side.

To serve, put the fish fillets on 4 warmed plates and spoon the vinaigrette to the side.

Serves 4

- 100 g (4 oz) unsalted butter
- 4 sea bass fillets, weighing about 100 g (4 oz) each, skinned
- ½ vanilla pod
- 50 ml (2 fl oz) Noilly Prat
- 2 teaspoons white wine vinegar
- 1 shallot, peeled and halved
- 150 ml (5 fl oz) *Fish Stock* (see p.212)
- 25 g (1 oz) peeled, seeded and diced tomato
- 1 tablespoon coarsely chopped fresh chervil
- Salt and freshly ground black pepper

100 g (4 oz) small lemon
    sole fillets, skinned
6 prepared scallops
    (see
    p.18)
4 sheets of filo pastry,
    about 30 x 40 cm
    (12 x 16 in)
25 g (1 oz) butter, melted
2 spring onions
2 tablespoons Japanese soy
    sauce
1 cm (½ in) piece of fresh
    root ginger, very finely
    chopped
1 tablespoon cold-pressed
    sesame oil
4 teaspoons *Mustard
    Mayonnaise* (see p.216)
1 teaspoon wasabi paste

MILLE FEUILLE OF SASHIMI WITH WASABI MAYONNAISE AND GINGER DRESSING

I had this dish in an excellent restaurant in Sydney called The Pier, which is in Rose Bay on the eastern side of the harbour. The chef there, Greg Doyle, is one of those exceptionally imaginative cooks who can just think up a new dish for virtually every service of lunch or dinner. I don't know whether this one ever appeared on the menu again there but it certainly should. It is such a sensible way of serving up the delicious raw fish flavours of sashimi in an elegant style. As with all my recipes calling for raw fish it is essential that the fish is extremely fresh, otherwise there is no point in doing this dish at all.

Cut the lemon sole fillets into small, thin slices by cutting at a slight angle across the top of each fillet as if you were slicing smoked salmon. Detach the coral from each scallop and, if large, cut in half lengthways. Cut each scallop horizontally into 4 thin slices. Cover the fish and set aside in the fridge.

Pre-heat the oven to 200°C/400°F/Gas 6.

Lay 2 sheets of filo pastry on a work surface and brush with melted butter. Cover each one with a second sheet and brush with more butter. Now cut out twelve 9 cm (3½ in) circles. Place on a lightly greased baking sheet and bake for about 5 minutes, until crisp and golden. Remove and leave to cool.

Cut the spring onions into 5 cm (2 in) lengths and then cut lengthways into very fine shreds.

To serve, place 4 filo pastry circles on 4 large plates. Cover each one with about 4 pieces of lemon sole and 3 pieces of scallop. Drizzle each layer of fish with a very small amount of the soy sauce and then sprinkle with a few of the spring onions. Place another pastry circle on top of each one, repeat the filling once more, then cover with the remaining pieces of pastry.

Mix the remaining soy sauce with the chopped ginger and sesame oil to make a dressing. Mix the mayonnaise with the wasabi paste. Using a teaspoon, spoon little drops of the dressing around each mille feuille and spoon some of the wasabi mayonnaise to one side. Serve immediately, otherwise the filo pastry will go soft.

1 live crayfish (spiny
    lobster), weighing about
    1.5–1.75 kg (3–4 lb), or
    2 live lobsters, weighing
    about 750 g–1 kg
    (1½–2¼ lb) each
½ vanilla pod
300 ml (10 fl oz) *Fish Stock*
    (see p.212)
2 tablespoons Noilly Prat
1 quantity of *Quick
    Hollandaise Sauce*
    (see p.215)
Salt and freshly ground
    black pepper

SPINY LOBSTER WITH VANILLA SAUCE

I make no apologies for using vanilla in two of my dishes, this and the sea bass recipe on p.137. The sauces are completely different but the flavour of vanilla is so good with seafood. The other great plus of using vanilla in a savoury sauce like this is that it has a particular affinity with Chardonnay or, more particularly, oaked Chardonnay. Wine writers often describe a good Chardonnay as having vanillary overtones. This comes from the flavour of the oak, and a dish like this, spiny lobster (often called crawfish or crayfish in Cornwall) with a sweet and aromatic sauce, cries out for a really good oaked Chardonnay. Try a white burgundy or, say, a Petaluma from Australia, a Cloudy Bay from New Zealand or one of the increasingly brilliant wines from South Africa such as Mulderbosch.

For the sauce, split the vanilla pod open lengthways and scrape out the seeds. Put the fish stock, vanilla pod and seeds and the Noilly Prat into a pan and boil rapidly until reduced to about 1½–2 tablespoons. Set aside.

Remove the meat from the lobster (see p.19). Lift out the tail meat in one piece and slice on a slant into 1 cm (½ in) pieces (see p.19).

Meanwhile make the hollandaise sauce (see p.215), adding the reduced hot fish stock with the melted butter. Season with salt and pepper.

To serve, heat the lobster gently and arrange the slices of tail meat on 4 warmed plates. Put a little pile of the warmed head meat to one side and a spoonful of the vanilla sauce to the other.

The Finest Seafood in a Small Ragout with a Deep Red Wine Sauce

This is unashamedly a real show-off dish. The quantities are small but the seafood is the best and the sauce contains an expensive amount of red wine, reduced by boiling to give the richest, deepest flavour imaginable. Some people are put off by the idea of fish in a red wine sauce but when wine and fish are joined as the dish is served and the red wine has been reduced down and sweetened with port, then finished with butter, the combination is irresistible.

Remove the meat from the lobster (see p.19), trying to remove the claw meat in as large pieces as possible. Slice the tail meat across into pieces 1 cm (½ in) thick. Lay the Dover sole fillets and the scallops on the lightly greased rack of the grill pan and season with a little salt and pepper and the paprika. This will give them a pleasing colour.

For the croûtons, cut four 5 cm (2 in) rounds from the bread. Heat the oil and butter in a frying pan and fry the croûtons for 1–2 minutes on each side, until golden. Drain on kitchen paper and keep warm.

For the sauce, put the fish stock, wine and port into a pan, bring to the boil and boil rapidly until reduced to about 120 ml (4 fl oz). Whisk in the butter a little at a time and keep warm over a low heat.

Pre-heat the grill to high. Grill the Dover sole and scallops for 2 minutes. Add the pieces of lobster meat to the rack and grill for a further minute.

To serve, pile up the seafood in the centre of 4 warmed plates, drizzle some of the sauce over the top and pour more around the edges. Lay a croûton on top of each pile.

Serves 4 as a first course

1 cooked lobster, weighing about 450 g (1 lb)
1 Dover sole, weighing about 350 g (12 oz), filleted and skinned (see pp.14–15)
4 prepared scallops (see p.18)
A pinch of paprika
Salt and freshly ground black pepper

FOR THE CROÛTONS
2 medium-thick slices of white bread
2 tablespoons sunflower oil
A small knob of unsalted butter

FOR THE RED WINE SAUCE
600 ml (1 pint) *Fish Stock* (see p.212)
600 ml (1 pint) red wine
120 ml (4 fl oz) port
75 g (3 oz) chilled unsalted butter, cut into small pieces

Serves 4 as a first course

1 quantity of *Egg Pasta Dough* (see p.218)
Freshly shaved Parmesan cheese, to serve

FOR THE CREAMED COD FILLING
75 g (3 oz) cod fillet
Salt
25 ml (1 fl oz) extra virgin olive oil, preferably lemon-flavoured
50 ml (2 fl oz) double cream
4 garlic cloves, sliced

FOR THE ROCKET PESTO
85 ml (3 fl oz) olive oil
25 g (1 oz) rocket leaves, tough stalks removed
1 garlic clove, roughly chopped
25 g (1 oz) Parmesan cheese, finely grated
15 g (½ oz) pine kernels
Salt and freshly ground black pepper

RAVIOLI OF CREAMED COD WITH ROCKET PESTO

Commercial salted and dried cod needs long soaking and has a distinctive flavour which is addictive once you are used to it. You can make your own salt cod for this which is easy to make and less assertively flavoured. Rocket is available everywhere now but for this dish to succeed it really needs to be a good, strong-leaved, peppery rocket, not the rather wishy-washy, limp stuff that is probably grown in hothouses out of season.

To make your own salt cod, put the cod in a plastic container and completely cover with a thick layer of salt. Refrigerate for 24 hours – the salt will turn to brine overnight.

The next day, remove the cod from the brine and soak it in cold water for 2 hours. If using commercial salt cod, soak in plently of cold water for 12 hours. Make the pasta (see p.218), leaving it to rest while you make the creamed cod filling.

Drain the salt cod, put it in a pan and cover with fresh water. Bring to the boil and simmer for 5 minutes. Lift out and, when cool enough to handle, flake the flesh, discarding the skin and bones.

Put the oil and cream into a small pan and bring to the boil. Put the flaked cod into a food processor with the garlic and the hot cream mixture and blend until smooth. Leave to cool.

For the rocket pesto, put all the ingredients into a food processor and blend until smooth. Scrape into a bowl and set aside.

Make the ravioli (see opposite). If you are not going to eat them immediately, drop them into a pan of boiling water and cook for just 1 minute. Drop into a bowl of cold water, then lift out and drain. Store in the fridge on oiled trays covered with cling film.

Otherwise, bring 1.75 litres (3 pints) of water to the boil with 1 tablespoon of salt. Add the ravioli and cook for 4 minutes (3 minutes if they have already been blanched). Drain well, then return the ravioli to the pan with the rocket pesto and toss together well. Spoon the ravioli into 4 large warmed pasta plates and serve sprinkled with a few shavings of fresh Parmesan.

Making Ravioli

1. Roll out the pasta dough on a lightly floured work surface into a 38 cm (15 in) square. Then **with** your fingertip, make small marks at 3 cm (1½ in) intervals in even rows over one half of the square.

2. Place a teaspoon of the creamed cod filling on each mark.

3. Brush lines of water between the piles of mixture and then **fold** over the other half of the square so that the edges meet.

4. Working from the centre of the folded side, outwards and downwards, **press firmly around each pile of mixture with your fingers** to push out any trapped air and seal in the filling.

5. Trim off the edges of the dough and **cut between the rows with a sharp knife or a fluted pasta wheel.**

½ quantity of *Egg Pasta Dough* (see p.218)

175 g (6 oz) cooked lobster tail, thinly sliced (see p.19)

Sprigs of fresh basil, to garnish

FOR THE TOMATO AND BASIL SAUCE

2 salad tomatoes, skinned, seeded and diced

6 fresh basil leaves, finely sliced

50 ml (2 fl oz) extra virgin olive oil

Salt and freshly ground black pepper

FOR THE CREAM SAUCE

150 ml (5 fl oz) *Fish Stock* (see p.212)

25 ml (1 fl oz) double cream

25 ml (1 fl oz) white wine

4 tablespoons *Olive Oil Mayonnaise* (see p.217)

OPEN RAVIOLI OF LOBSTER WITH TOMATO AND BASIL SAUCE

Here, cooked lobster is combined with some fresh basil, uncooked tomato and virgin olive oil, then loosely sandwiched between al dente *pasta squares to form an 'open ravioli'. The accompanying sauce is simply some mayonnaise whisked with a white wine and fish stock reduction. I must admit that this is one of those restaurant dishes designed to make a small amount of lobster go a long way but why not? The finished dish looks very professional and actually part of the art of a good cook is to present a small amount of expensive protein in an appetizing and imaginative way. You need to do plenty of advance preparation because the final assembly is a bit fiddly.*

Bring a large pan of salted water to the boil. Roll out the pasta dough on a lightly floured surface into a 15 x 30 cm (6 x 12 in) rectangle. Cut into eight 7.5 cm (3 in) squares.

For the tomato and basil sauce, put all the ingredients into a small pan and set aside.

Re-heat the slices of lobster meat. Meanwhile, drop the pasta squares into the boiling water and cook for 3–4 minutes or until *al dente*, then drain and lay out on a sheet of cling film. Put the tomato and basil sauce over a very low heat and leave just to warm through.

For the cream sauce, bring the fish stock, double cream and white wine to the boil and boil until reduced in volume by half. Put the mayonnaise into a bowl and gradually whisk the hot fish stock reduction into it. Season to taste with salt.

To serve, put a square of pasta in the centre of each of 4 warmed plates. Spoon a little of the cream sauce on to each one, divide the lobster meat between them and then spoon over half the tomato and basil sauce. Now cover with the remaining pasta squares and pour the remaining cream sauce over and around each ravioli. Finally spoon on the rest of the tomato and basil sauce. Serve immediately, garnished with sprigs of basil.

Pavé of Salmon with Easter Fennel and New Potatoes

Why Easter fennel, you may ask. There is a dead time between the depth of winter and the real arrival of spring. On the coast in February and March we get disconcertingly sharp easterly winds and the country seems covered in a layer of salt, with a grey bleakness about it and a smell of cold seas. Then you notice one or two bright green shoots of fennel with a sudden clean scent of aniseed, bringing a returning memory of summer and light, far more acute than some punnet of basil from the supermarket. I thought I'd celebrate that return of life in spring with a dish that uses fennel and new potatoes. The potatoes will have been grown under plastic and, though not of great flavour, are fresh tasting and confirmation of the skill of a local market gardener. They go well with local salmon, which reappears in the kitchen in March. Pavé is French for paving stone or slab, which perfectly suggests the shape of a thick fillet of salmon cut from the loin.

Season the salmon on both sides with salt and pepper. Clarify the butter by melting it over a low heat and then pouring off the liquid into a frying pan, leaving behind the milky solids that will have collected at the bottom.

Peel the potatoes, cut them into slices 5 mm (¼ in) thick and then cut the slices lengthways into matchsticks. Drop them into a pan of well-salted boiling water and simmer for 3–4 minutes, until just tender. Drain and keep warm.

Meanwhile, heat the clarified butter in the frying pan, add the salmon, skin-side down, and cook for 3–4 minutes, pressing down on the fish with the back of a fish slice to make sure that the skin browns evenly. Turn over and cook for another 1–1½ minutes.

Stir the olive oil, shallot, tomatoes, red wine vinegar, chopped fennel herb, salt and some pepper into the potatoes. Put the salmon skin-side up on 4 warmed plates and spoon the warm potatoes alongside.

Serves 4

4 thick pieces of salmon fillet, weighing about 175 g (6 oz) each, skin on (they should measure about 10 cm (4 in) square)

75 g (3 oz) unsalted butter

Salt and freshly ground black pepper

FOR THE POTATOES

450 g (1 lb) new potatoes

3 tablespoons extra virgin olive oil

1 shallot, very finely chopped

2 large plum tomatoes, skinned, seeded and chopped

1 tablespoon red wine vinegar

3 tablespoons chopped fresh fennel herb

½ teaspoon salt

**4 red mullet, weighing
about 225 g (8 oz) each,
filleted**

**Extra virgin olive oil for
brushing**

**Salt and freshly ground
black pepper**

**FOR THE TOMATO AND
BASIL DRESSING**

**85 ml (3 fl oz) extra virgin
olive oil**

**Finely grated zest and
juice of ¼ lemon**

**½ red finger chilli, seeded
and very finely chopped**

**1 salad tomato, skinned,
seeded and diced**

**12 fresh basil leaves, finely
shredded**

½ teaspoon salt

**FOR THE SPICED FISH
SAUSAGE**

**225 g (8 oz) conger eel
fillet**

40 ml (1½ fl oz) olive oil

1 tablespoon beaten egg

1 anchovy fillet

¼ teaspoon salt

**7 turns of the black pepper
mill**

**1 small garlic clove,
chopped**

1 teaspoon harissa paste

½ teaspoon lemon juice

**40g (1½ oz) tinned
pimento or roasted red
pepper, finely chopped**

CHARGRILLED RED MULLET WITH SPICED FISH SAUSAGE AND TOMATO AND BASIL DRESSING

*I cook a lot of fish fillets on a cast-iron ribbed pan to give that
attractive branded look. Here, grilled red mullet is served with a simple
tomato and basil dressing and, more unusually, some sliced fish sausage
made of conger eel and flavoured with harissa. You should be able to buy
this fiery North African chilli paste in tins from good delicatessens and
some large supermarkets.*

For the spiced fish sausage, put everything except the pimento or red pepper
in a food processor and blend until smooth. Stir in the pimento or red pepper,
then spoon the mixture in a thick line on to a large sheet of food-grade cling
film. Fold over the edge of the cling film nearest to you, roll the mixture over
once or twice until well encased in the cling film and then use your hands to
shape it into a sausage 5 cm (2 in) thick. Firmly twist the ends of the cling film
to make a watertight package. Bring some water to the boil in a large, deep
frying pan, reduce to a simmer and add the fish sausage. Poach for 10 minutes,
then transfer to a bowl of cold water and leave to cool for 2 minutes. You can
make this some time before the final cooking. Keep it wrapped in the fridge.
Remove the cling film and cut on the diagonal into 12 slices 5 mm (¼ in) thick.

Place a cast-iron ribbed pan over a high heat. Brush the slices of fish sausage
with a little oil, season with salt and pepper and grill for 1 minute on just one
side. Set aside on a plate and keep warm.

Reheat the pan until very hot. Brush the red mullet fillets with oil, season
and grill for 1 minute on each side.

To make the dressing, whisk the oil with the lemon zest and juice, then stir in
the chilli, tomato, shredded basil and salt. Warm through over a low heat.

To serve, put the fish fillets on 4 warmed plates and arrange the fish sausage
to one side. Spoon a little of the dressing around the edge of the plate.

600 ml (1 pint) *Fish Stock*
(see p.212), made from
the turbot bones

900 g (2lb) piece of
turbot, filleted and
skinned (see pp.14–15)

50 g (2 oz) carrot

50 g (2 oz) celeriac

50 g (2 oz) white of leek

75 g (3 oz) butter

50 ml (2 fl oz) Vouvray or
other medium dry
white wine

50 g (2 oz) button
mushrooms, thinly
sliced

8 large or 12 queen
scallops prepared
(see p.18)

10 fresh basil leaves, thinly
shredded

150 ml (5 fl oz) double
cream

Salt and freshly ground
white pepper

Lemon juice

Sprigs of fresh basil, to
garnish

RAGOUT OF TURBOT AND SCALLOPS WITH VOUVRAY, BUTTER AND BASIL

The essential point of this dish is not to exceed the cooking times by a second so that the seafood is beautifully succulent. Don't feel you have to buy Vouvray for this dish — any medium dry white wine will suffice but Vouvray is the best.

Pour the fish stock into a pan and boil rapidly until reduced to 150 ml (5 fl oz).

Cut the turbot fillet across into slices 2 cm (¾ inch) thick. Cut the carrot, celeriac and leek into 2.5 cm (1 in) pieces and then cut each piece into thin slices. Heat the butter and half the Vouvray in a wide, heavy-based pan large enough to hold the slices of turbot in one layer. Add the carrot, celeriac and leek strips, cover and cook gently for 5 minutes, until just tender. Stir in the mushrooms and a little seasoning.

Lay the slices of turbot on top of the vegetables, spoon over the rest of the Vouvray and the reduced fish stock and season lightly. Cover and cook over a gentle heat for 3 minutes. Add the scallops to the pan, cover and cook for a further 1–2 minutes, until both the turbot and scallops are only just cooked.

Carefully lift the turbot and scallops out of the pan on to a warmed plate and keep warm. Add the basil to the vegetables in the pan with the cream. Bring to the boil and cook for 1–2 minutes until the sauce has thickened slightly. Season with salt and pepper and add a little freshly squeezed lemon juice to taste.

Spoon the vegetables on to 4 warmed plates. Arrange the turbot and scallops on top and serve garnished with sprigs of fresh basil.

LOBSTER À L'AMÉRICAINE

Serves 4

I like to keep good things simple and the best way, to me, of eating lobster is to serve it simply boiled and split in half with new potatoes and some melted butter. However, there are one or two more complicated lobster dishes that I do approve of and this is one of them. Many people add cream in the recipe for Lobster à l'Américaine, but to me it's gilding the lily. The advantage with this recipe, rather than a more simple approach, is that you use all the intense flavour in the shell to make the tomato, white wine and tarragon sauce.

Cut the live lobsters in half lengthways. Pull each tail section away from the head section and cut each section of tail into 4–5 pieces. Break the claw sections apart and crack each section so that the meat can be extracted easily later (see p.19). The easiest way to do this is with the thickest part of a large knife.

Put the olive oil into a heavy-based pan, big enough to hold all the pieces of lobster. Sweat the onion and garlic in the olive oil until they are beginning to soften, then add all the pieces of lobster. Turn up the heat a little and turn the lobster pieces over until they are beginning to colour red. Add the cognac and let the alcohol boil off. Add the tomatoes, chopped tarragon, white wine, sugar and fish stock. Cover. Leave the lobsters to cook through for about 8 minutes. Remove the lobster pieces and keep warm. Return the pan to the heat and reduce the sauce by half.

When the sauce has reduced, return the lobster pieces to the sauce, heat through, and transfer to an attractive serving dish.

2 live lobsters, each weighing about 750–900 g (1½–2 lb)

85 ml (3 fl oz) olive oil

50 g (2 oz) onion, finely chopped

1 tablespoon cognac

2 garlic cloves, finely chopped

750 g (1½ lb) fresh tomatoes, skinned, seeded and chopped

1 tablespoon roughly chopped tarragon

85 ml (3 fl oz) dry white wine

1 teaspoon sugar

600 ml (1 pint) *Fish Stock* (see p.212)

750 g (1½ lb) salmon fillet, taken from a good-sized salmon
2 tablespoons sunflower oil
Salt

FOR THE CHAMPAGNE AND CHIVE SAUCE
25 g (1 oz) unsalted butter
1 small shallot, finely chopped
120 ml (4 fl oz) champagne plus 1 tablespoon
600 ml (1 pint) *Fish Stock* (see p.212)
½ teaspoon caster sugar
120 ml (4 fl oz) double cream
1 tablespoon chopped fresh chives

ESCALOPES OF SALMON WITH CHAMPAGNE AND CHIVE SAUCE

What a shame. You're going to have to open a whole bottle of champagne to make this dish. Now what are you going to do with the rest of the champagne!

For the sauce, melt 10 g (¼ oz) of the butter in a saucepan, add the shallot and cook, without colouring, until softened. Add the 120 ml (4 fl oz) of champagne and boil for 2 minutes, then add the stock and sugar. Boil rapidly until reduced by three-quarters. Add half the cream, bring to the boil and reduce until the sauce is thick enough to coat the back of a spoon.

Meanwhile, prepare the salmon escalopes. Remove any bones from the fillet with tweezers or by trapping them between the point of a small, sharp knife and your thumb. Then, with a large filleting knife or a carving knife, cut the salmon into 12 slices about 5 mm (¼ in) thick, holding the knife at a 45-degree angle to the fillet and cutting at a slant down towards the skin. This will give you wider slices. Brush each escalope with a little of the oil, season lightly with salt and then put them on a lightly oiled baking tray.

Pre-heat the grill to high. For the sauce, whisk the remaining cream with the tablespoon of champagne and 2 teaspoons of the chopped chives until it forms soft peaks. Set aside.

To finish the dish, grill the salmon escalopes for about 1 minute, then put them on 4 warmed plates. Bring the reduced sauce back to the boil, whisk in the remaining butter, then the whipped cream mixture and pour around the salmon. Sprinkle with the remaining chives and serve immediately, while the sauce is still foaming.

16 small clams, such as
    carpetshell or
    cherrystone clams

20 cockles

4 pieces of turbot fillet,
    weighing about 175 g
    (6 oz) each, skin on

2 shallots, finely chopped

85 ml (3 fl oz) Chardonnay
    wine, preferably
    Australian

300 ml (10 fl oz) *Fish Stock*
    (see p.212)

175 g (6 oz) chilled
    unsalted butter, cut into
    small pieces

2 tablespoons chopped
    fresh flatleaf parsley

Salt

FILLET OF TURBOT WITH CLAMS, COCKLES AND CHARDONNAY

The clams and cockles are steamed open in a rich Chardonnay, then a butter sauce is made with the cooking liquor and plenty of flatleaf parsley. I thought up this dish as an attractive way of using the small clams called butterfish which live at one end of the estuary and the small cockles that live at the other, combining them in a main course with that magnificent fish, the turbot. The steamed turbot fillets are served covered in the parsley and butter sauce with cockles and clams both in and out of the shell, the idea being to use some of the shells as a garnish. If you can't get small live clams and cockles, however, use small mussels instead. We quite often do the dish with mussels in the restaurant.

Scrub the clams and cockles with a stiff brush to remove any sand or dirt, then wash in plenty of cold water and set aside.

If you don't have a steamer big enough for cooking the turbot, take a very large saucepan into which a dinner plate will fit and put some sort of trivet in the bottom, such as a small upturned bowl. Add about 5 cm (2 in) of water and bring to the boil. Season the turbot fillets lightly with salt, then put them on the plate, rest it on the trivet, cover and steam for about 10 minutes.

Meanwhile, put the shallots, Chardonnay, clams and cockles into a pan, cover and cook over a high heat, shaking the pan every now and then, for 2–3 minutes, until the clams have opened. Discard any that remain closed. Pour the shellfish through a colander set over a shallow pan, keeping back the last tablespoon of so of liquid as this will contain some grit. Shell half the clams and cockles. Add the fish stock to the cooking liquor in the pan and boil rapidly until reduced to about 6 tablespoons. Whisk in the butter, a piece at the time. Return all the shellfish to the sauce with the parsley.

To serve, put the turbot fillets on to 4 warmed plates and pour the sauce right over them. Rearrange the shells so that they look attractive and then serve with, naturally, a bottle of Australian Chardonnay.

SEA BASS BAKED IN A SALT CRUST WITH A LEMON SAUCE AND POTATO, TOMATO AND BASIL CONFIT

This method of baking in a salt crust ensures perfectly cooked, moist fish. It is served with a simple mayonnaise flavoured with lemon, white wine and fennel seeds and also a great potato dish which I got from the South of France. You can cook any of the bream family, red mullet, John Dory and even gurnard in the same way.

Pre-heat the oven to 200°C/400°F/Gas 6.

For the sauce, put the fish stock, fennel seeds, sliced lemon and white wine into a pan and boil rapidly until the liquid has reduced to about 4 tablespoons. Strain into a small bowl and leave to cool. Put the whole egg, egg yolk, reduced stock mixture and some salt and pepper in a liquidizer. With the motor running, gradually pour in the oil until you have a thick mayonnaise. Transfer to a bowl and season to taste.

For the potato confit, heat the olive oil in a pan, add the onion and garlic and cook for 5 minutes, until softened and lightly browned. Add the potatoes, tomato and basil and cook gently for 25 minutes or until the potatoes are tender. Season with salt and pepper and keep warm.

For the fish, mix the salt with the egg whites and spread a layer of this mixture in a roasting tin. Put the sea bass on top and then completely cover with the remaining salt mixture, making sure that there are no gaps (but don't worry if the tail is still exposed). Bake in the oven for 30 minutes.

To serve, crack the salt crust by giving it a sharp tap with the back of a knife, lift it away from the top of the fish and then carefully transfer the whole fish to a serving plate, leaving behind the rest of the salt crust. Pull away the skin from the top of the fish and gently lift the flesh away from the bones. Lift the bones off the remaining fish and discard, then remove the remaining fillets. Put the fish on 4 warmed plates, spoon a little of the sauce to the side and serve with the potato, tomato and basil confit.

Serves 4

1.75 g (4 lb) table salt or
    coarse sea salt
2 egg whites
I sea bass, weighing about
    1.5 kg (3 lb), gutted but
    not scaled (see p.11)

FOR THE LEMON SAUCE
600 ml (1 pint) *Fish Stock*
    (see p.212)
I tablespoon fennel seeds
I small lemon, sliced
120 ml (4 fl oz) white wine
I egg
I egg yolk
300 ml (10 fl oz) olive oil
Salt and freshly ground
    black pepper

**FOR THE POTATO,
TOMATO AND BASIL
CONFIT**
50 ml (2 fl oz) olive oil
I small onion, finely
    chopped
I garlic clove, finely
    chopped
450 g (1 lb) waxy new
    potatoes, peeled and
    cut into quarters
I beefsteak tomato or
    2 large plum tomatoes,
    skinned and chopped
2 tablespoons finely
    shredded fresh basil

QUICK AND SIMPLE FISH

Most people don't have time to cook elaborate dishes these days so fish, as it does not need lengthy cooking, is ideal. Often it tastes all the better for simple treatment, and lends itself well to quick cooking methods such as stir-frying and grilling, which appear many times in this chapter.

Funnily enough, in my first book I said people ought to spend a bit more time cooking and, although I have conceded to the pressure of modern life in this chapter, I still feel the same way. Cooking is therapeutic. It calms you down and puts you back in touch with the things that really matter.

I thought it might be apt to quote part of a poem which I read recently called 'Ratatouille', on the subject of the need for people to get back into the kitchen.

See p.98 for a good recipe using ratatouille.

Men who forget
Lovingly chopped-up cloves of *ail*, who scorn
The job of slicing two good peppers thinly,
Then two large onions and six aubergines –
Those long, impassioned and imperial purples –
Which, with six courgettes, you sift with salt
And cover with a plate for one round hour;
Or men who do not care to know about
The eight ripe *pommes d'amour* their wives
　　have need of,
Preparing ratatouille, who give no thought to
The cup of olive oil that's heated in

Their heaviest pan, or onions, fried with garlic
For five observant minutes, before they add
Aubergines, courgettes, peppers, tomatoes;
Or men who give no thought to what their wives
Are thinking as they stand beside their stoves
When seasoning is sprinkled on, before
A bouquet garni is dropped in – these men
Invade Afghanistan, boycott the Games
Call off their fixtures and prepare for war.

Douglas Dunn (*Saint Kilda's Parliament*, 1981)

Basque-style Stuffed Crab (Shangurro) (see p.170).

**4 hake steaks, weighing
about 175 g (6 oz) each**
25 g (1 oz) butter, melted
**Salt and freshly ground
black pepper**

FOR THE CHAMP
**900 g (2 lb) floury
potatoes, peeled and
cut into chunks**
50 g (2 oz) butter
300 ml (10 fl oz) milk
**6 spring onions, thinly
sliced**

**FOR THE BLACK BEAN
BUTTER**
**300 ml (10 fl oz) *Fish Stock*
(see p.212)**
**1½ tablespoons black bean
sauce**
½ tablespoon lemon juice
50 g (2 oz) unsalted butter
**1 tomato, skinned, seeded
and diced**
**1 tablespoon chopped
fresh leaf celery**

GRILLED HAKE STEAKS WITH CHAMP AND BLACK BEAN BUTTER

This is a very popular dish at our bistro. If you can't get the celery herb specified in the recipe, use the leaves from a head of celery instead. I grow a lot of leaf celery in my herb garden which is very closely related to ordinary celery but with a much stronger flavour. This dish is a bit of an eclectic mix of East – the black bean sauce – and West – the champ, an Irish recipe for mashed potato with plenty of spring onions. There is butter in the sauce as well, and tomato, and it's very easy to make. Really, the most time-consuming part of the whole recipe is the mashed potato.

For the champ cook the potatoes in boiling salted water until tender, then drain. Return to the pan and mash until smooth. Beat in the butter, milk, spring onions and salt and pepper to taste. Keep hot.

Meanwhile, for the sauce, put the fish stock, black bean sauce, lemon juice and butter into a wide pan and boil over a high heat for about 12 minutes, until reduced and thickened to the consistency of single cream. Set aside and keep warm.

Pre-heat the grill to high. Brush both sides of the fish steaks with the melted butter and season well with salt and pepper. Place on the oiled rack of the grill pan and grill for 3 minutes on each side. Bring the sauce back to the boil, take off the heat and stir in the diced tomato, juices from the grill pan and celery herb. Season to taste with a little salt if necessary.

To serve, put the hake steaks on 4 warmed plates with the champ, then spoon the sauce around the fish.

CARPETSHELL CLAMS WITH AÏOLI

I came across this dish in the Camargue region of the South of France, where it is made with tiny clams called tellines. *These are virtually impossible to find in Britain but* palourdes, *or carpetshells as they are known here, are getting easier and easier to obtain. However, if you can't get any live clams for this dish do try it with small mussels instead. You simply steam open the shellfish with a little white wine, then stir in some aïoli, a garlic mayonnaise. And that's it. Plenty of French bread. Pure delight.*

To make the aïoli, mix the mayonnaise with the garlic and set aside.

Scrub the clams with a stiff brush to remove any sand or dirt, then wash in plenty of cold water. Put the clams in a large pan with the white wine, then cover and cook over a high heat, shaking the pan occasionally, for 2–3 minutes, until they have opened. Discard any clams that remain closed. Take the pan off the heat and stir in the garlic mayonnaise and the parsley. Serve hot or cold, with lots of crusty French bread.

Serves 4

½ **quantity of** *Olive Oil Mayonnaise* **(see p.217)**

5 **garlic cloves, very finely chopped**

900 g (2 lb) **carpetshell clams**

50 ml (2 fl oz) **dry white wine**

1 **tablespoon finely chopped fresh parsley**

A HASH OF FRESH SALMON WITH PARSLEY AND CHIVES

This dish is just fried potatoes, onion and salmon – an ideal way of using up leftover salmon or, indeed, any other leftover fish. It is based on corned beef hash and just as good, in my view. Put in plenty of parsley to lift the colour.

Cook the potatoes in boiling salted water for 6 minutes or until tender, then drain well. Break the salmon into pieces roughly the same size as the potatoes and season well with salt and pepper. Melt 40 g (1 ½ oz) of the butter in a frying pan large enough to take the salmon and potatoes in one layer. Add the onion and fry gently for 2–3 minutes, until softened but not browned. Add the potatoes and fry for 7–10 minutes, turning now and then, until lightly browned. Now add the salmon and the rest of the butter and fry for 1–2 minutes or until the salmon has heated through, turning the mixture over gently so as not to break up the salmon too much. Season with salt and cayenne pepper and serve sprinkled with the parsley and chives or spring onion tops.

Serves 4

900 g (2 lb) **floury potatoes such as Maris Piper, peeled and cut into 2.5 cm (1 in) chunks**

450 g (1 lb) **cooked salmon fillet**

50 g (2 oz) **butter**

1 **large onion, chopped**

A pinch of cayenne pepper

2 **tablespoons chopped fresh parsley**

1 **tablespoon chopped fresh chives or green spring onion tops**

Salt and freshly ground black pepper

Serves 4

3 courgettes

50 ml (2 fl oz) olive oil

750 g (1½ lb) prepared
    squid (see p.16), cut into
    thin rings

2 garlic cloves, finely
    chopped

1 red chilli, seeded and
    finely chopped

3 plum tomatoes, skinned,
    seeded and chopped

2 tablespoons chopped
    fresh parsley

Salt and freshly ground
    black pepper

SAUTÉD SQUID WITH GARLIC, PARSLEY, TOMATO AND COURGETTES

Another dish from the South of France, which I ate in a restaurant in Marseilles called Le Lunch. A great name, I thought, and it harks back to the 1920s when the British first started going to the Mediterranean. This is a very simple dish. The squid is fried with garlic, parsley, chilli, tomatoes and some small pieces of courgette, which add a crisp textural note. When I had it in France, it was made with cuttlefish which tastes almost nicer than squid, but it is a little hard to get hold of here.

Cut the courgettes lengthways into quarters and then across into slices 1 cm (½ in) thick. Heat the olive oil in a large frying pan, add the squid and fry over a high heat, stirring, for 2 minutes, until lightly browned. Lower the heat, add the garlic, chilli and courgettes and cook gently for 2 minutes. Add the tomatoes, parsley and seasoning, toss together and serve with crusty bread.

Serves 4

225 g (8oz) shelled whelks

3 tablespoons sunflower oil

3 garlic cloves, very finely
    chopped

5 cm (2 in) piece of fresh
    root ginger, very finely
    chopped

1 large red finger chilli,
    seeded and sliced

100 g (4 oz) button
    mushrooms, thinly sliced

50 g (2 oz) mustard
    greens or pak choi,
    coarsely shredded

50 g (2 oz) beansprouts

2 tablespoons oyster sauce

½ tablespoon soy sauce

2 tablespoons dry sherry

CHINESE WHELKS WITH BEANSPROUTS AND BUTTON MUSHROOMS

Traditionally, whelks are served with malt vinegar, freshly ground white pepper and lots of fresh brown bread and butter. But actually, they're incredibly good thinly sliced and stirred into a Chinese stir-fry.

Thinly slice the whelks and set aside.

    Heat the oil in a wok or large deep frying pan. Add the garlic, ginger and chilli and stir-fry over a high heat for 30 seconds. Add the sliced whelks and stir-fry for 1 minute. Add the mushrooms and stir-fry for 30 seconds, then add the Chinese leaf and the beansprouts and stir-fry for another 30 seconds, until the leaves have just wilted into the bottom of the pan. Add the oyster sauce, soy sauce and sherry and cook for another 1 minute. Serve immediately with some steamed rice or noodles.

Sautéd Squid with Garlic, Parsley, Tomato and Courgettes.

1 kg (2 ¼ lb) piece of ling,
cut from just behind the
cavity

**FOR THE COURT
BOUILLON**
1.75 litres (3 pints) water
3 tablespoons salt
85 ml (3 fl oz) cider
vinegar
1 teaspoon caster sugar
10 black peppercorns,
lightly crushed
3 fresh bay leaves, finely
shredded
1 onion, sliced
¼ teaspoon dried chilli
flakes

FOR THE SAUCE MESSINE
1 quantity of *Hollandaise
Sauce (see p.215)*
1 teaspoon French
mustard
2 shallots, very finely
chopped
50 ml (2 fl oz) double
cream
1 teaspoon finely chopped
fresh tarragon
1 teaspoon finely chopped
fresh chervil
1 teaspoon finely chopped
fresh chives

POACHED LING SERVED WITH SAUCE MESSINE

I think that ling is a much underrated fish. It is always dismissed into the same sort of category as pollack but I think it has a good flavour and, more importantly, an excellent firm texture, particularly the smaller fish. Nevertheless, being one of the cod family it is a bit bland, so I have used a well-flavoured court bouillon to cook it in here and accompanied it with a butter sauce with lots of herbs and a little finely chopped shallot, which I think you will find partners the fish extremely well. If you wish to use a more upmarket fish, salmon would be a very good choice.

Put all the ingredients for the court bouillon in a large saucepan, bring to the boil and simmer for 10 minutes. Add the piece of ling, cover and simmer very gently for 10 minutes. Don't worry if it seems a little undercooked at this stage; it will be fine. Set aside for 5 minutes in the court bouillon.

Meanwhile, make the hollandaise sauce (see p.215). Put the mustard, shallots and cream in a small pan and bring to the boil. Stir into the hollandaise sauce with the chopped herbs, then set aside in a bowl of warm water.

Lift the ling out of the court-bouillon and leave to cool slightly. Then cut through the skin along both edges of the joint and carefully peel it off. You will now see a natural break in the flesh, about half-way down. Divide the fish into 2 fillets by cutting down along this line, then turn the knife and ease one fillet off, keeping the knife close to the bones. Remove the other fillet in the same way. Turn the ling over and repeat on the other side.

Serve the ling with the sauce, accompanied by boiled waxy potatoes such as Pink Fir Apple, Belle de Fontenay or Charlotte.

MUSSELS WITH A CREAM AND WHITE WINE SABAYON

In the days before cheap flights I used to drive everywhere on the continent with a group of friends in a series of ancient VW vans. Every time the ferry docked at Calais, we went to the nearby town of Gravelines and ordered immense bowls of this superb mussel dish. This first taste of France would always fill us with excited anticipation, because in those days you couldn't possibly imagine eating a dish like this on the other side of the Channel.

Put the onion, bay leaf and wine into a large saucepan. Bring up to the boil and leave to simmer for 5 minutes. Add the mussels to the pan, cover and cook over a high heat for 3-4 minutes until the mussels have opened. Discard any that remain closed. Lift the mussels into a large serving dish with a slotted spoon, cover and keep hot.

Whisk the egg yolks and cream together in a large bowl. Strain the mussel cooking liquor into the bowl, rest it over a pan of just simmering water and continue to whisk briskly until the mixture is light and frothy. Make sure not to let the sauce get too hot or the eggs will curdle. Whisk in the butter, a small piece at a time. Remove the bowl from the heat and season to taste with the lemon juice, salt and pepper. Pour the sauce over the mussels, sprinkle with the chopped parsley and serve.

Serves 4

½ onion, sliced

1 small bay leaf

150 ml (¼ pint) dry white
  wine

1.75 g (4 lb) mussels,
  cleaned (see p.17)

3 medium egg yolks

150 ml (5 fl oz) double
  cream

100 g (4 oz) unsalted
  butter

Squeeze fresh lemon juice

Salt and pepper

2 tablespoons chopped
  fresh parsley

**4 small red mullet,
weighing about 150 g
(5 oz) each, filleted
(see p.13)**

450 g (1 lb) spaghettini

4 tablespoons olive oil

**2 garlic cloves, finely
chopped**

**1 red finger chilli, seeded
and finely chopped**

**4 plum tomatoes, skinned,
seeded and chopped**

**20 g (¾ oz) fresh flatleaf
parsley, finely chopped**

**Salt and freshly ground
black pepper**

**Extra virgin olive oil, to
serve**

Sautéd Red Mullet with Parsley, Garlic and Spaghettini

The quantities in this recipe make four hearty servings but I always think that a good pile of pasta is what everybody really likes. I've never seen a recipe for this dish anywhere in Britain but my good friend and the director of my television series, David Pritchard, rang me up from Italy, where he was filming with the mushroom expert Antonio Carluccio, to say how excited he was to have just eaten this fantastic fish pasta. As he explained, the great thing about it is that the well-flavoured skin of the red mullet goes slightly grainy when it is fried and seems to coat the spaghettini with the sweet taste of seafood.

Cut the mullet fillets across into strips 2 cm (¾ in) wide. Bring 3.4 litres (6 pints) of water to the boil in a large pan with 2 tablespoons of salt. Add the pasta, bring back to the boil and cook for 5 minutes or until *al dente*.

Meanwhile, heat the olive oil in a large frying pan. Fry the strips of red mullet, skin-side down, for 3 minutes. Turn them over, fry for 1 minute and then season with salt and pepper.

Drain the pasta well and tip it into a large warmed serving bowl. Add the garlic and red chilli to the frying pan with the red mullet and fry for 30 seconds. Add the tomatoes and fry for a further 30 seconds. Tip everything into the bowl with the pasta, scraping up all the little bits that may have stuck to the bottom of the pan, then add 3 tablespoons of the parsley and gently toss everything together so that the fish just begins to break up. Serve immediately, drizzled with extra virgin olive oil and sprinkled with the remaining parsley.

MUSSELS WITH BLACK BEANS, GARLIC AND GINGER

Serves 4

1 teaspoon salted black beans

¼ teaspoon sugar

3 spring onions

2 tablespoons groundnut oil

4 garlic cloves, finely chopped

15 g (½ oz) fresh root ginger, finely chopped

1.4 kg (3 lb) mussels, cleaned (see p.17)

1 tablespoon dark soy sauce

2 tablespoons Chinese rice wine or dry sherry

3 tablespoons *Chicken Stock* (see p.213)

1 tablespoon chopped fresh coriander

In her excellent Classic Chinese Cookbook, *Yan-Kit So comments that black beans and clams go together for the Chinese as horseradish and roast beef do for us. This dish is based on her recipe for clams in black bean sauce.*

Rinse the black beans and mash them with the sugar. Thinly slice the spring onions, keeping the white part separate from the green.

Heat the groundnut oil in a wok or a large, deep frying pan until smoking hot. Add the garlic, ginger and black beans and stir-fry until the smell of hot ginger and garlic rises. Stir in the white of the spring onions and stir-fry for a few seconds. Add the mussels, soy sauce, rice wine or sherry and stock. Cover and cook for about 3 minutes, until the mussels open. Discard any that remain closed. Add the coriander and green part of the spring onions, toss together and serve.

WHELK FRITTERS

Serves 4

8–10 cooked whelks

2 medium eggs, separated

2 plum tomatoes, skinned seeded and chopped

50 g (2oz) onion, very finely chopped

2 cloves garlic, very finely chopped

2 tablespoons chopped fresh parsley

40 g (1 ½ oz) Matzo meal or fresh breadcrumbs

Sunflower oil for frying

Salt and freshly ground black pepper

I've got a lot of time for whelks. This recipe is adapted from one using giant clams and you can in fact use large clams in place of whelks.

Remove the cooked whelks from their shells (you will need about 50 g (2 oz)) and roughly chop. Put the egg yolks into a bowl and lightly break up with a fork. Stir in the chopped whelks, tomatoes, onion, garlic, parsley, Matzo meal or breadcrumbs and some salt and pepper to taste.

In another bowl whisk the egg whites into soft peaks and then gently fold them into the main fritter mixture.

Pour a good layer of sunflower oil into a large heavy-based frying pan and leave over a high heat until very hot. Lower the temperature a little, then drop 4 large spoonfuls of the batter into the pan and fry for about 1 ½ minutes on each side, until golden brown. Lift out on to kitchen paper and keep hot while you cook the rest. You should end up with about 12 fritters. Serve immediately.

Stir-fried Chicken and Monkfish with Prawns, Cucumber and Waterchestnuts

I have purposely kept the soy sauce and other oriental flavourings quite muted in this dish. Sometimes I think these stir-fries are too salty and spicy and you miss the taste of the fish, meat and vegetables. So this one is light and full of fresh flavours.

Cut the cucumber into 5 cm (2 in) lengths, cut these into slices 1 cm (½ in) thick and then cut into matchsticks. Cut each waterchestnut into 3. Cut the spring onions into 5 cm (2 in) lengths and then lengthways into fine shreds.

Put a wok or a large, deep frying pan over a high heat and, when hot, add the sunflower and sesame oils. Add the garlic and ginger and stir-fry for 30 seconds. Add the chicken and stir-fry for 3 minutes. Add the monkfish and stir-fry for about 1 minute, until just firm. Add the prawns and lemon zest and stir-fry for another minute. Add the soy sauce and dry sherry and stir-fry for 1 minute, until the liquid is slightly reduced. Add the cucumber and waterchestnuts and toss for 30 seconds. Add the spring onions, season with salt and pepper and toss together quickly. Serve straight away.

Serves 4

½ cucumber

200 g (7 oz) can of waterchestnuts, drained

1 bunch of spring onions

2 tablespoons sunflower oil

1 teaspoon sesame oil

3 garlic cloves, very finely chopped

2.5 cm (1 in) piece of fresh root ginger, very finely chopped

175 g (6 oz) boneless skinless chicken thighs or breasts, cut into short, chunky strips

175 g (6 oz) monkfish fillet, cut into short, chunky strips

225 g (8 oz) raw, headless, prawns, peeled and de-veined (see p.18)

1 strip of lemon zest, very finely shredded

2 tablespoons dark soy sauce

1 tablespoon dry sherry

Salt and freshly ground black pepper (Sichuan pepper if possible)

Serves 4

16 small, very thin slices of
  smoked pancetta or
  8 thin rashers of
  rindless smoked streaky
  bacon, halved
2 tablespoons sunflower oil
40 g (1 ½ oz) unsalted
  butter
25 g (1 oz) plain flour
½ teaspoon salt
10 turns of the white
  pepper mill
8 plaice fillets, weighing
  about 75–100 g (3–4 oz)
  each, skinned
Juice of ¼ lemon
2 teaspoons chopped fresh
  fines herbes, i.e. parsley,
  chervil, chives and
  tarragon

FILLETS OF PLAICE WITH PANCETTA AND BEURRE NOISETTE

This incredibly simple dish relies on presentation for its effect. The fillets of fish are arranged down the centre of a nice oval serving dish, interleaved with thin slices of fried pancetta or, if you can't get it, extremely thinly sliced bacon. It looks wonderful when surrounded with beurre noisette, *which is simply butter heated until brown and nutty-smelling, then sharpened with lemon juice. Next time you're in France and wandering through a market, do make sure you buy one of those long, narrow, elegant, white oval fish dishes for presenting food like this. Owing to the demise of silver service in restaurants, it is all too rare to see dishes served up in a formal manner from the kitchen but if it's done well it is extremely effective. I suspect that, as everything in restaurant cooking appears to be of a cyclical nature, the era of presenting beautiful large platters of food at the table will return.*

Pre-heat the grill to high. Grill the slices of pancetta or streaky bacon for 1–1½ minutes on each side, until crisp. Set aside and keep warm.

Heat the oil and 15 g (½ oz) of the butter in a large frying pan. Season the flour with the salt and white pepper and spread it over a large plate. Cut each plaice fillet across in half and then dip the pieces in the seasoned flour. Fry for 2 minutes on each side, until lightly golden, then arrange them down the centre of a warmed oval serving platter, interleaving them with the slices of grilled pancetta or bacon.

Discard the frying oil and add the remaining butter and allow it to melt over a moderate heat. When the butter starts to smell nutty and turn light brown, quickly add the lemon juice and herbs and then pour it right over the fish and bacon. Serve straight away.

Serves 4

15 g (½ oz) dried ceps

720 ml (24 fl oz) water

2 Dover sole, weighing
about 400 g (14 oz)
each, filleted and
skinned (see pp.14–15)

85 ml (3 fl oz) dry white
wine

1 medium onion, sliced

150 ml (5 fl oz) double
cream

25 g (1 oz) butter, cut into
pieces

350 g (12 oz) egg
tagliatelle

Salt and freshly ground
black pepper

DOVER SOLE AND CEPS WITH TAGLIATELLE IN A CREAM SAUCE

You can use any pasta for this but thin, flat ribbons such as tagliatelle seem to go particularly well. The dish is made with dried ceps; if you can get fresh, of course, that's even better. All you need to do is make a quick stock with the fish trimmings, boil the pasta, then make a simple cream sauce with the stock, cep soaking liquid and some pieces of Dover sole.

Soak the dried ceps in 120 ml (4 fl oz) of the water for 10 minutes. Cut the fish fillets diagonally into strips 2.5 cm (1 in) wide and set aside. Put the fish bones into a pan with the wine, onion and the remaining water, bring to the boil and simmer for 15 minutes. Strain this stock into a clean pan, bring to the boil and add the cream, butter pieces and the ceps with their soaking liquid. Boil rapidly until reduced by about three quarters to a sauce that is thick enough to coat the back of a spoon (about the consistency of single cream).

Cook the tagliatelle in a large pan of boiling salted water for about 4 minutes, until *al dente*, then drain.

Put the pieces of Dover sole in the sauce and poach gently for about 2 minutes, then season with salt and pepper. Tip the pasta into a large warmed serving bowl. Add the sauce, toss together lightly and serve immediately.

Serves 4

10 good-sized scallops

6 small heads of chicory

100 g (4 oz) unsalted
butter

120 ml (4 fl oz) *Fish Stock*
(see p.212) or *Chicken
Stock* (see p.213)

Juice of ½ lemon

1 teaspoon chopped fresh
parsley

Salt and freshly ground
white pepper

SAUTÉD SCALLOPS WITH CARAMELIZED CHICORY

The sweetness of scallops goes well with the slight bitterness of chicory, particularly when the chicory is lightly browned and slightly crisp around the edges.

Detach the corals from the scallops, remove the white ligament from the side of each scallop meat and then slice the meat horizontally in half.

Remove the outer leaves of the chicory if they are damaged. Trim the base if it is brown but don't cut off too much or the leaves will detach themselves from the base. Cut them lengthways through the base into 3 thin slices.

Melt 25 g (1 oz) of the butter in a large frying pan. As soon as it starts to turn brown and smell slightly nutty, add the scallop slices and corals and cook briefly for about 30 seconds on each side. Remove from the pan and keep warm. Add a little more butter to the pan if necessary and fry the chicory slices in batches for about 1 minute on each side, until lightly browned. Transfer to another plate and keep warm while you cook the rest.

Add the stock and remaining butter to the pan, bring to the boil and boil until the sauce is thick enough to coat the back of a spoon. Add the lemon juice, season with a little salt and pepper and stir in the chopped parsley.

To serve, put the chicory on 4 warmed plates, top with the scallops and then spoon over the sauce.

GRILLED WHOLE DOVER SOLE WITH SEA SALT AND LIME

The sauce with this sole goes very well with all fresh fish. Its pure simplicity makes it a winner at my restaurant.

De-scale the soles and cut off the fins. Dry the fish with kitchen paper.

To make the sauce put the fish stock and fish sauce in a small pan. Grate the rind of 1 lime and add to the pan with its juice.

Pre-heat the grill until it's very hot. Then brush the fish with vegetable oil and sprinkle the dark side with sea salt. Place on the oiled rack of the grill pan and cook for about 10 minutes. Remove the fish from the grill and sprinkle with more sea salt.

Place each fish on a warmed plate, then finish the sauce. Bring the ingredients in the pan to the boil and add the butter. Whisk until it has all melted, then add the chopped red onion and the parsley. Simmer for 30 seconds, then pour the sauce around the fish and garnish with the remaining limes cut into wedges and sprigs of parsley.

Serves 4

4 Dover soles, each weighing about 400–450 g (14 oz–1 lb), skin on
Vegetable oil, for brushing
Sea salt

FOR THE SAUCE
300 ml (10 fl oz) *Fish Stock* (see p.212)
1½ teaspoons Thai fish sauce (*nam pla*)
3 limes
15 g (½ oz) unsalted butter
¼ small red onion, finely diced
1 bunch fresh flatleaf parsley, roughly chopped, a few sprigs reserved for a garnish

2 large cooked brown crabs, or approximately 450 g (1 lb) white crab meat and 100 g (4 oz) brown crab meat

3 tablespoons olive oil

2 onions, finely chopped

8 small garlic cloves, finely chopped

225 g (8 oz) plum tomatoes, skinned, seeded and chopped

50 ml (2 fl oz) dry white wine

1 teaspoon caster sugar

¼ teaspoon dried chilli flakes

3 tablespoons chopped fresh parsley

50 g (2 oz) fresh white breadcrumbs

15 g (½ oz) butter, melted

1 garlic clove, very finely chopped

Salt and freshly ground black pepper

Basque-style Stuffed Crab (Shangurro)

I like using shells as natural containers for seafood. Mussels, scallops, clams and crabs all look much more appetizing to me presented in this way. The great charm of shangurro, *which comes from the Basque coast of Northern Spain is that in San Sebastian, Santander and Bilbao it is normally served using the back shell of a spider crab as a gratin dish for the combination of spider crab meat, tomato, garlic, chilli, olive oil, parsley and breadcrumbs. I must admit, however, that if you have time to pick out four spider crabs, you would hardly call this a quick and simple dish. It is so good, however, it is worth using brown crab meat and gratin dishes rather than shells.*

Pre-heat the oven to 200°C/400°F/Gas 6.

If using cooked crabs, remove the meat from the shell (see pp.20–21). Wash out the back shells and then break away the edge along the visible natural line to give a flat open shell. Set aside.

Heat the oil in a heavy-based frying pan, then add the onions and all except 1 chopped garlic clove. Fry over a gentle heat for 2 minutes, until softened. Increase the heat, add the tomatoes, wine, sugar, chilli flakes and some salt and pepper and simmer for about 4 minutes, until the mixture has reduced to a thick sauce. Stir in 2 tablespoons of the parsley and the flaked crab meat and spoon the mixture into the crab shells, if using, or individual gratin dishes. If using crab shells, rest them in a shallow ovenproof dish. Mix the breadcrumbs with the melted butter and the rest of the parsley and garlic, sprinkle this mixture over the crab and bake in the oven for 10 minutes or until the topping is crisp and golden.

Pan-fried Whiting with Lime Butter and Salsify

I wrote this recipe in Australia using their version of whiting called sand whiting which is actually rather better tasting than ours. But small, perfectly fresh whiting are well worth eating. However, if you should ever get the chance to buy some small hake instead, called pin hake, then you're in for a treat. You can get hold of the vegetable salsify from all good greengrocers. I hope you like the lime butter.

For the lime butter, beat all the ingredients together, spoon onto a large sheet of food-grade clingfilm and shape into a 2.5 cm (1 in) wide roll. Chill in the freezer or fridge until firm. For the salad dressing mix the olive oil and lime juice with some salt and pepper and set to one side.

Scale and trim the fish (see p.11). Melt the butter in a small pan, spoon off the scum from the surface and then pour the clarified butter into a large heavy-based frying pan, leaving behind the milky-white liquid.

Coat the fish in the seasoned flour. Add the oil to the butter in the frying pan and, when hot, add two of the fish and fry for 4-5 minutes on each side until crisp and golden. Remove and keep warm whilst you cook the other two fish.

Cut the lime butter into 12 thin slices. Lift the fish onto 4 warmed plates and place 3 slices of butter down the centre of each fish whilst you cook the other two fish. Meanwhile, fry the salsify gently in the butter until soft, then turn up the heat to brown a little, season with salt and pepper, add the lime juice and parsley and keep warm. Serve the salsify beside the fish.

Serves 4

- 4 x 450 g (1 lb) whiting or pin hake
- 25 g (1 oz) unsalted butter
- 25 g (1 oz) plain flour seasoned with salt and freshly ground black pepper
- 1 tablespoon sunflower oil

FOR THE LIME BUTTER
- 50 g (2 oz) unsalted butter, softened
- Finely grated zest 1 lime
- 2 teaspoons chopped fresh thyme
- ½ teaspoon finely grated fresh root ginger
- Salt and freshly ground white pepper

FOR THE SALSIFY
- 1 lb salsify, peeled and cut in half then cut in half lengthways
- 1 oz unsalted butter
- Salt and ground black pepper
- 2 teaspoons fresh lime juice
- 1 tablespoon chopped fresh parsley

6 spring onions

Salt

50 g (2 oz) watercress or
  rocket, washed and
  larger stalks removed

2 tablespoons sunflower oil

16 prepared scallops or 24
  queens (see p.18)

2 garlic cloves, very finely
  chopped

2.5 cm (1 in) piece of fresh
  root ginger, very finely
  chopped

2 tablespoons Thai fish
  sauce (*nam pla*)

2 tablespoons oyster sauce

120 ml (4 fl oz) water

SEARED QUEENS WITH GARLIC, GINGER AND GREENS

I cooked this dish of queen scallops for the Padstow Carnival Queen last year. The 'Queen' turned out to be George Masters, who doesn't exactly fit the bill for a carnival queen as he usually works behind the bar in the London Inn, but there you go, that's Padstow. George was highly delighted with my spicy dish – to which I added some mustard greens and cress from my garden, which is what you get if you allow those little punnets of salad cress to grow on. We sat on the roof of the restaurant drinking champagne, eating the queens with George dressed up in his taffeta finery including a bouffant wig and high-heeled shoes. The whole thing seemed a bit like something out of a Fellini film.

Cut the spring onions in half and then cut each half lengthways into very fine shreds. Set aside.

Bring a large pan of salted water to the boil. Add the watercress or rocket and cook for just 2 minutes. Drain, divide equally between 16 cleaned scallop shells or 4 soup plates and keep hot.

Heat a large, heavy-based frying pan until very hot. Add 1 tablespoon of the oil and the scallops in a single layer and fry over a high heat for about 2 minutes, turning once, until they are richly caramelized on both sides but only just cooked in the centre. This is very important to the flavour and appearance of the finished dish.

Lift out the scallops and divide equally between the scallop shells or bowls. Add the garlic, ginger and the remaining oil to the pan and stir-fry for about 30 seconds. Add the Thai fish sauce, oyster sauce and water, bring to the boil and then quickly spoon this sauce over the scallops. Sprinkle with the shredded spring onions and serve immediately.

WARM CRAB PANCAKES WITH LEMON GRASS AND CORIANDER

Serves 4

You will need a 10 cm (4 in) frying pan for these delicate little pancakes, which are filled with white crab meat and lots of Thai flavourings, all kept very mild. They are warmed through in the oven and served with a light sauce of sesame oil, Thai fish sauce, lime juice and coriander. Serve, I would suggest, with an ice-cold bottle of Alsace Pinot Blanc.

For the pancakes, sift the flour and salt into a bowl, make a slight dip in the centre and add the egg. Gradually whisk in the milk and then the melted butter to make a smooth batter.

Pre-heat the oven to 200°C/400°F/Gas 6.

Heat a 10 cm (4 in) frying pan. Brush with a little melted butter, pour in a little of the batter and swirl it around so that it coats the base of the pan. Cook for about 1 minute, flipping the pancake over as soon as it has browned underneath. Repeat this process to make 8 pancakes.

Mix together all the ingredients for the filling and divide between the pancakes. Roll them up and lay side by side, seam-side down, in a lightly buttered ovenproof dish. Cover loosely with foil and warm through in the oven for 8–10 minutes.

Just before the pancakes are ready, put all the ingredients for the sauce into a small pan and whisk over a high heat until it comes to the boil. To serve, put the pancakes on 4 plates and spoon a little of the sauce over and around them. Garnish with sprigs of coriander.

FOR THE PANCAKES

50 g (2 oz) plain flour

¼ teaspoon salt

½ beaten egg

150 ml (5 fl oz) milk

10 g (¼ oz) unsalted butter, melted, plus extra for frying

FOR THE FILLING

5 cm (2 in) piece of lemon grass, finely chopped

100 g (4 oz) white crab meat

½ green chilli, seeded and very finely chopped

Finely grated zest of ½ lime

1 teaspoon freshly squeezed lime juice

1 teaspoon Thai fish sauce (*nam pla*)

2 teaspoons chopped fresh coriander, plus a few sprigs to garnish

25 g (1 oz) iceberg lettuce, very finely shredded

FOR THE SAUCE

150 ml (5 fl oz) water

1 tablespoon sesame oil

1 teaspoon Thai fish sauce (*nam pla*)

Juice of ½ lime

15 g (½ oz) unsalted butter

A pinch of salt

1 teaspoon chopped fresh coriander

HAND-HELD AND PARTY FOOD

This chapter contains the sort of dishes you can eat in your hand and also the little items you might pick up and nibble at a cocktail party. Several of the recipes were inspired by the type of food that is sold by street vendors. I have a great affection for street food. After all, what is a Cornish pasty if not that sort of cheap, convenient and nourishing hand-held food? There is a recipe for *Crab Pasties with Leek and Saffron* here (see p.177) which perhaps takes hand-held food into the realms of *haute cuisine* but I still think it should be eaten in the hand. I think there's something a bit second rate about eating a pasty with a knife and fork.

My other source of inspiration was bars. The fishermen of Spain are not particularly well liked in Cornwall because there is a theory that they are taking all our fish, particularly undersized ones, and should never have been allowed to fish the rich waters between Cornwall and Ireland, known as the Irish Box. I've always had a slight ambivalence about this because, while I support our local fishermen, I have a sneaking regard for the way the Spanish cook fish and their immense enthusiasm for it. So I went on a long weekend break to Madrid, partly because I wanted to see the Goya paintings but also to check out Spanish seafood. I've long been told that if you want to eat the best seafood in Spain you should go not to the coast, where it is normally very good, but to Madrid where it is excellent. So for about five days and nights we visited lots of restaurants and did the rounds of the tapas bars. It was an exhilarating experience and the fish cookery was just as I would have expected: simple, relying on the freshest ingredients, and showing a deep respect for the raw materials – a respect that I sometimes think we lack in this country. In one restaurant the couple at the next table ordered a spider crab and that's what they got: just one large spider crab between two. I remarked to my wife Jill that I wouldn't be surprised if it had come from Cornwall. Wouldn't it be nice if you could sell something like that in Britain – just plain, freshly boiled spider crab, and have people eating it with such enthusiasm and leaving absolutely nothing afterwards.

All the tapas in this chapter – the *empanadas* and the two mussel dishes – were the result of that trip to Madrid.

225 g (8 oz) new potatoes,
    sliced
50 ml (2 fl oz) olive oil
I leek, thinly sliced
2 garlic cloves, finely
    chopped
50 g (2 oz) *chorizo* sausage,
    finely chopped
25 g (I oz) sun-dried
    tomatoes in oil, drained
    and thinly sliced
I tablespoon white wine
Leaves from 2 sprigs of
    fresh thyme
A small pinch of saffron
    strands
A pinch of cayenne pepper
450 g (I lb) conger eel
    fillet, skinned
Salt and freshly ground
    black pepper
Beaten egg, to glaze

FOR THE OLIVE OIL
PASTRY
225g (8oz) plain flour
I teaspoon salt
I egg, beaten
100 ml (3 ½ fl oz) olive oil
3–4 tablespoons tepid
    water

EMPANADAS WITH CONGER EEL, SUN-DRIED TOMATO AND CHORIZO SAUSAGE

These large, oblong pies made with olive oil pastry are sliced and served as tapas in Spain. They make ideal drinks party food. Serve with glasses of ice-cold Aguila or San Miguel beer or with manzanilla sherry. In tapas bars beer is served in small glasses so that you've drunk it before it has a chance to get at all warm. They do the same in Queensland, too.
I have suggested conger eel for the filling but you can use any thick fillets of white fish such as cod, coley, pollack or ling.

For the pastry, sift the flour and salt into a bowl. Make a well in the centre and add the egg, olive oil and 3 tablespoons of warm water. Gradually work the flour into the liquid ingredients, adding more water if necessary. Gather the dough into a ball, turn out on to a lightly floured surface and knead briefly until smooth. Wrap in cling film and leave to rest at room temperature for I hour.

Meanwhile, cook the potato slices in boiling salted water for about 4–5 minutes, until only just tender. Heat the olive oil in a pan, add the leek and garlic and fry for 2 minutes, until softened. Add the chorizo sausage and fry for 2 minutes, then stir in the cooked potatoes, sun-dried tomatoes, white wine, thyme, saffron, cayenne and a little salt and pepper. Set aside to cool.

Pre-heat the oven to 200°C/400°F/Gas 6.

Cut the pastry in half and roll each piece out into a 30 x 23 cm (12 x 9 in) rectangle. Place each one on a lightly oiled baking tray and spoon the filling lengthways along one half of each piece of pastry. Cut the piece of conger eel lengthways into 2 thick strips. Slice each one across thinly and put on top of the filling, overlapping the slices slightly. Season with salt and black pepper.

Brush the edges of the pastry with a little water. Fold the pastry over the filling so that the edges meet, then pinch and twist over the edge to make a good seal. Brush with beaten egg and bake in the oven for 20–25 minutes, until golden. Remove from the oven and set aside to cool slightly. Then cut across on the diagonal into slices 2.5 cm (I in) thick and serve.

CRAB PASTIES WITH LEEK AND SAFFRON

We make these pasties at our bakery and they are enormously popular. I wrote the recipe with, essentially, a Cornish theme in mind: local vegetables, local brown crabs and saffron, which has long been connected with the county in the form of saffron cake. At one time saffron was grown in Cornwall just as in Essex.

Pre-heat the oven to 200°C/400°F/Gas 6.

Divide the pastry into 6 pieces. Roll out each piece on a lightly floured surface and cut into a 19 cm (7 ½ in) circle.

For the filling, soak the saffron in the hot water for 5 minutes. Put the white and brown crab meat, leeks, breadcrumbs, salt and pepper into a bowl and stir together until well mixed. Crush the saffron a little into the water to release the colour and flavour, then stir it into the melted butter. Now stir this into the rest of the filling ingredients.

Divide the filling mixture between the pastry circles. Brush the edge of one half with a little water, bring both sides together over the top of the filling and pinch together well to seal. Crimp the edge of each pasty decoratively between your fingers, transfer to a lightly greased baking sheet and bake for 35 minutes, until golden brown. Serve hot or cold.

Makes 6

900 g (2 lb) chilled fresh
    puff pastry
¼ teaspoon saffron strands
2 teaspoons hot water
350 g (12 oz) white crab
    meat
75 g (3 oz) brown crab
    meat
225 g (8 oz) leeks, thinly
    sliced
50 g (2 oz) fresh white
    breadcrumbs
1 teaspoon salt
10 turns of the white
    pepper mill
25 g (1 oz) butter, melted

FISH TACOS FROM BAJA CALIFORNIA

2 sea bream, sea bass or
    red mullet, weighing
    about 350 g (12 oz)
    each, filleted (see p.13)

8 soft flour tortillas

225 g (8 oz) iceberg
    lettuce, finely shredded

300 ml (10 fl oz) soured
    cream

Salt and freshly ground
    black pepper

Sunflower oil for deep-
    frying

FOR THE BATTER

225 g (8 oz) plain flour

2 eggs

200 ml (7 fl oz) water

FOR THE SALSA

1 medium red onion, finely
    chopped

5 tomatoes, skinned,
    seeded and finely
    chopped

3–4 red chillies, seeded and
    finely chopped

1 teaspoon sugar

Juice of 1 lime

4 tablespoons chopped
    fresh coriander

Perhaps the most thoroughly irresistible dish in this chapter. I've never been to Baja California in Mexico but I got the idea for this recipe from the television presenter and food journalist, Hugh Fearnley-Whittingstall, who lent me a book on the Baja because I'm very keen on surfing and the waves there are fantastic. He told me about this great dish consisting of a tortilla filled with deep-fried fish, coriander, chilli, tomato, a little soured cream and some salad. I knocked it all up according to how it sounded to me and it's brilliant. One day I'll make the trip to Ensenada with my big old Malibu and ride the odd small wave that may just happen down there.

First make the salsa by mixing together all the ingredients with a pinch of salt. Set aside.

Cut the fish fillets across into strips 1 cm (½ in) wide and season with plenty of salt and pepper. For the batter, put the flour, eggs, water and a pinch of salt into a liquidizer and blend until smooth.

Pour the sunflower oil into a pan until it is about one-third full and heat to 190°C/375°F or until a small piece of white bread dropped into the oil browns and rises to the surface in 1 minute. Warm the tortillas in a low oven or a microwave.

Dip the strips of fish into the batter and then drop them into the hot oil and fry for 4 minutes, until crisp and golden. Lift out with a slotted spoon and drain briefly on kitchen paper.

To serve, put some lettuce down the centre of each tortilla, top with the fried fish, then spoon over some salsa and soured cream. Fold in the sides, roll up as tightly as you can and serve straight away, with some cold Mexican beer.

Serves 4–6

900 g (2 lb) mussels,
cleaned (see p.17)

50 ml (2 fl oz) dry white
wine

4 tablespoons extra virgin
olive oil

100 g (4 oz) onions, very
finely chopped

2 garlic cloves, very finely
chopped

1 red finger chilli, seeded
and very finely chopped

250 ml (8 fl oz) tomato
passata or sieved
canned chopped
tomatoes

12 sun-dried tomatoes in
oil, drained and very
finely chopped

Leaves from 4 sprigs of
fresh thyme, finely
chopped, plus a few
whole leaves to garnish

4 thin slices of Serrano
ham

MUSSELS WITH TOMATO AND SERRANO HAM

The mussels are steamed open with a little white wine and lots of fresh chilli, then served on the half shell with a rich tomato sauce and thin strips of Serrano ham. If you can't get Serrano ham, just use Parma ham instead. Serve with a glass of chilled manzanilla or fino sherry.

Put the mussels into a large pan with the wine. Cover and cook over a high heat for about 3–4 minutes, shaking the pan every now and then, until the mussels have opened. Discard any that remain closed. Remove the top half of each shell, leaving the mussel in the other half.

Heat the olive oil in a small pan. Add the onions and garlic and fry for a few minutes, until softened but not browned. Add the chillies, passata, sun-dried tomatoes, thyme and the mussel cooking liquor. Bring to the boil and simmer for 7–10 minutes, until reduced to a thick sauce.

Cut the Serrano ham into very small, fine strips and stir into the sauce. Spoon about 1 teaspoon of the sauce over each mussel, sprinkle with a few thyme leaves and serve.

MONKFISH SATÉS WITH A SPICY PEANUT SAUCE

If you travel to Singapore you must go to the park in Orchard Road, where you can eat Chinese, Indian, Indonesian or Malay food from stalls all in the same place and all really cheap. It's a bit like an Asian food fair and almost worth a trip to Singapore just to visit it. All the food is very good but the barbecued satés are exceptional. The operators crouch next to their charcoal barbecues endlessly fanning the flames and producing a tireless succession of chicken or fish satés with the hot but sweet peanut sauce which I know will never taste quite so good anywhere else. This recipe is based on my memory of those uniquely satisfying satés.

Put the monkfish in a bowl with all the marinade ingredients and mix together well. Set aside for 20 minutes. Cover the bamboo skewers with cold water and leave to soak. This stops them burning under the grill.

For the spicy peanut sauce, heat the oil in a pan, add the shallots or onion, garlic, chilli and cayenne pepper and fry for 7 minutes, until soft and lightly golden. Coarsely grind the roasted peanuts in a coffee grinder, then stir them into the fried onion mixture with all the remaining sauce ingredients. Simmer gently for 4–5 minutes until thickened. Keep warm while you cook the fish.

Pre-heat the grill to high.

Thread the fish on to the bamboo skewers and put them on the lightly oiled rack of the grill pan. Cook for about 8 minutes, turning them over half-way through. Serve with the spicy peanut sauce.

Serves 4

450 g (1 lb) prepared
    monkfish fillet (see p.15),
    cut into 2 cm (¾ in) pieces
16 x 15 cm (6 in) bamboo
    skewers

FOR THE MARINADE

3 large garlic cloves, very
    finely chopped
2.5 cm (1 in) piece of fresh
    root ginger, finely chopped
½ teaspoon turmeric powder
3 tablespoons Thai fish sauce
    (*nam pla*)
1 tablespoon freshly
    squeezed lime juice
1 teaspoon palm sugar or
    muscovado sugar
½ teaspoon cayenne pepper
2 tablespoons vegetable oil

**FOR THE SPICY PEANUT
SAUCE**

2 tablespoons sunflower oil
2 shallots or 25 g (1 oz)
    onion, finely chopped
2 garlic cloves, chopped
1 red finger chilli, seeded and
    chopped
½ teaspoon cayenne pepper
40 g (1 ½ oz) roasted peanuts
40 g (1 ½ oz) crunchy peanut
    butter
4 teaspoons freshly squeezed
    lime juice
1 tablespoon palm sugar or
    muscovado sugar
½ teaspoon salt
175 ml (6 fl oz) coconut milk

900 g (2 lb) mussels,
cleaned (see p.17)

50 ml (2 fl oz) dry white
wine

600 ml (1 pint) *Fish Stock*
(see p.212)

¼ teaspoon saffron strands

75 g (3 oz) inner sticks of
celery, finely diced

3 tomatoes, skinned,
seeded and finely diced

175 g (6 oz) chilled
unsalted butter, cut into
small pieces

Juice of ¼ lemon

Salt and freshly ground
black pepper

MUSSELS WITH TOMATO, CELERY AND SAFFRON BUTTER

Like the recipe on p.180, this uses mussel shells as a natural container for serving at a drinks party, without need of knives, forks or plates. The mussels are served on the half shell with a rich saffron butter sauce, some finely chopped celery that has been lightly cooked so it is still a little crunchy, and some finely diced good, sweet tomatoes.

Put the mussels into a large pan with 1 tablespoon of the wine. Cover and cook over a high heat for about 3–4 minutes, shaking the pan every now and then, until the mussels have opened. Discard any that remain closed. Remove from the heat, strain off the juice and stir 2 tablespoons of it into the fish stock. Discard the remainder.

Bring the stock, the remaining wine and the saffron to the boil and boil rapidly until reduced to about 4 tablespoons.

Meanwhile, bring a small pan of salted water to the boil, add the celery and cook for 1 minute. Drain and refresh under cold running water, then set aside.

Pre-heat the oven to 140°C/275°F/Gas 1.

Remove the top half of each mussel shell, leaving the mussel in the other half. Lay them side by side in a shallow ovenproof serving dish. Put the diced celery and tomato on top of the mussels and season with a little salt and black pepper. You can do this up to an hour beforehand if you wish, but don't refrigerate the cooked mussels as they never taste the same again. Cover with cling film, however, to stop them drying out.

When you are ready to serve, remove the cling film and cover the mussels with aluminium foil. Warm through in the oven for just a few minutes. Meanwhile, bring the reduced fish stock back to the boil and then whisk in the butter a few pieces at a time, adding more as the butter amalgamates. I prefer to make these mounted butter sauces over a brisk heat, adding the butter and whisking all the time. The action of boiling stock with the butter causes a natural liaison. If the sauce separates, simply add a little more water, bring it back to the boil and it will cohere again. Stir in the lemon juice and season with salt and pepper to taste. Remove the mussels from the oven, uncover, and spoon a little of the sauce over each one. Serve immediately.

1 ciabatta loaf

3 garlic cloves, peeled

85 ml (3 fl oz) olive oil

50 g (2 oz) tin of anchovy
fillets or salt pilchard
fillets, very finely
chopped

75 g (3 oz) red onion, finely
chopped

6 plum tomatoes, skinned,
seeded and finely
chopped

3 tablespoons coarsely
chopped fresh flatleaf
parsley

20 turns of the black
pepper mill

Sprigs of fresh flatleaf
parsley, to garnish
(optional)

BRUSCHETTA OF ANCHOVIES WITH TOMATO AND RED ONIONS

I got this recipe from a friend of mine in Newlyn, Nick Howell, who runs the only pilchard salting and pressing sheds left in Cornwall. If it weren't for the enthusiasm of the Italians for this old method of preserving the most famous of Cornish fish there would be none left, but they still import them from Cornwall. Nick Howell is trying to reintroduce chilled salt pilchard fillet in Britain and if he succeeds maybe you will be able to prepare this piquant and savoury bruschetta with pilchard, as he does, rather than anchovy. It's not everyone's cup of tea, being raw, earthy and salty, but I love it, particularly when made with pilchards.

Pre-heat the grill to high. Slice the ciabatta in half horizontally and toast the cut side only for about 2 minutes, until lightly golden. Rub with one of the peeled cloves of garlic. Drizzle each half with 1 tablespoon of the olive oil and slice diagonally into quarters.

Finely chop the remaining garlic. Gently mix with the anchovies or pilchards, red onion, tomatoes, parsley, remaining oil, and black pepper. Spoon a little of the mixture on to each piece of bread, garnish with sprigs of parsley, if liked, and serve straight away, before the bread becomes soft again.

DEEP-FRIED SHREDDED FISH WRAPPED IN LETTUCE WITH CHILLI, PRAWNS AND CORIANDER

Serves 4

2 sea bream, red snapper, gurnard, grey mullet or mackerel, weighing about 350 g (12 oz) each filleted (see p.13)
6 cooked tiger prawns or *crevettes*, thinly sliced
2 red finger chillies, seeded and very finely chopped
3 tablespoons chopped fresh coriander
Juice of 2 limes
3 tablespoons Thai fish sauce (*nam pla*)
16–20 medium-sized cos lettuce leaves, washed and stalks trimmed off
Sunflower oil for deep-frying

A great combination of textures and flavours, this works marginally better with oily fish, which has a more pronounced flavour, but it is also a good way of using cold leftover fish and slightly less than perfectly fresh fish. For cocktail pieces, simply make them all up at once, tie in place with long chives and serve immediately before the lettuce leaves go too limp.

Bring 600 ml (1 pint) water and 1 tablespoon of salt to the boil in a frying pan. Reduce to a simmer, add the fish fillets and poach for 3 minutes, turning them over half way through. Lift out with a slotted spoon on to plenty of kitchen paper and leave to go cold. Remove any skin and bones and finely shred the flesh using 2 forks. Blot the excess moisture from the fish with more kitchen paper – this is important because if it is too wet it will cause the oil to foam up and possibly overflow.

Put the sliced prawns, red chillies, chopped coriander, lime juice, fish sauce and lettuce leaves into separate bowls and place in the centre of the table.

Pour the oil into a large pan so that it is about one-third full and heat to 190°C/375°F or until a small cube of white bread dropped into the oil browns and rises to the surface in 1 minute. Place the flaked fish in the hot oil and deep-fry for 2 minutes. Lift out with a slotted spoon and drain briefly on kitchen paper, then transfer to a bowl and take to the table. Instruct your guests to take a lettuce leaf and place a small amount of fish, prawns, chilli and coriander towards the fatter end. Sprinkle with a little lime juice and fish sauce, roll up and eat straight away.

WARM OYSTERS WITH BLACK BEANS, GINGER AND CORIANDER

Serves 4

20 Pacific oysters

2.5 cm (1 in) piece of fresh root ginger, very finely chopped

7.5 cm (3 in) piece of cucumber

1 tablespoon chopped fresh coriander

1 teaspoon chopped fresh chives

1 tablespoon salted black beans or black bean sauce

1 garlic clove, very finely chopped

1 tablespoon dark soy sauce

2 tablespoons dry sherry

4 tablespoons cold-pressed sesame oil

The oysters are opened, leaving about half the liquor that surrounds the oyster meats in the shell, and then grilled until just set. The liquor gives a delightful salty tang to the sauce but do discard half of it otherwise the sauce will be too salty. If you can get the fermented and salted black beans available in Chinese food shops you will be glad I suggested trying, because they keep for ages and are a great addition to so many stir-fry dishes. However, these oysters are also very well worth preparing with black bean sauce; try and get the type with whole black beans in it rather than the smooth one.

Pre-heat the grill to high. Open the oysters (see p.17), pour away half the liquor surrounding the meats and nestle the oysters in the grill pan so that they can't roll over during cooking. Sprinkle each one with the chopped ginger and set aside.

Cut the cucumber into 2.5 cm (1 in) pieces, then thinly slice each piece and cut lengthways into matchstick-width shreds. Mix with the coriander and chives and set aside.

If using salted black beans, rinse them and then chop them up a little. Put the salted black beans or black bean sauce in a small pan with the garlic, soy sauce, sherry and sesame oil. Leave over a very low heat to warm through.

Grill the oysters for 3 minutes. Arrange on 4 warmed plates and sprinkle a little of the cucumber mixture over each one. Spoon over a little of the sauce and serve immediately.

100 g (4 oz) prepared
   squid (see p.16)

175 g (6 oz) pork escalope

6 spring onions

2 tablespoons toasted
   sesame oil

2 garlic cloves, finely
   chopped

1 cm (½ in) piece of fresh
   root ginger, finely
   chopped

100 g (4 oz) bean sprouts

50 g (2 oz) shiitake
   mushrooms, thinly
   sliced

175 g (6 oz) white crab
   meat

1 tablespoon dark soy
   sauce

A pinch of caster sugar

1 teaspoon salt

Freshly ground Sichuan
   pepper

2 tablespoons plain flour

12 large spring roll
   wrappers

Sunflower oil for deep-
   frying

SPRING ROLLS WITH SQUID, CRAB, BEAN SPROUTS AND SHIITAKE MUSHROOMS

The filling for these spring rolls is stir-fried briefly, then rolled up in spring roll wrappers and deep-fried. The wrappers are easy to get hold of in oriental food shops but you can use filo pastry instead. This is not an authentic recipe but spring rolls are such a good idea and generally I find the fillings a bit dull — often little more than cabbage, bean sprouts and soy sauce. I think seafood and oriental mushrooms work rather well but you could also try shredded green summer cabbage, pork, shredded cooked skate with soy sauce, a pinch or two of star anise and a little finely diced red chilli. Alternatively use the crab, leek and saffron filling for the pasties on p.177.

Slit the squid pouch open along one side and cut it into thin strips about 10 cm (4 in) long. Cut the pork escalope into similar-sized pieces. Cut the spring onions into 7.5 cm (3 in) lengths and then cut lengthways into fine shreds.

Heat the sesame oil in a wok or a large deep frying pan. Add the garlic and ginger and stir-fry for a few seconds. Add the squid and pork and stir-fry over a high heat for 3 minutes. Add the bean sprouts and mushrooms and stir-fry for 30 seconds only. Tip into a bowl and gently stir in the spring onions, crab meat, soy sauce, sugar, salt and Sichuan pepper.

Mix the flour with 2 tablespoons of cold water to make a paste. Fill the spring roll wrappers (see opposite).

Pour the oil into a large pan so that it is about one-third full and heat to 190°C/375°F or until a small piece of white bread dropped into the oil browns and rises to the surface in 1 minute. Deep-fry the spring rolls, 4 at a time, for 5–6 minutes, until crisp and golden. They tend to float in the oil so a good trick is to rest a frying basket or sieve on top of them to keep them submerged during cooking.

Mix together all the ingredients for the dipping sauce and pour into small saucers or bowls. Serve with the hot spring rolls.

Making Spring Rolls

1. Put a spring roll wrapper on a work surface with one corner facing you. (Keep the other wrappers covered with a slightly damp cloth to prevent them drying out.) **Put 3 heaped teaspoons of the filling in a line about 5 cm (2 in) in from the corner.**

2. Fold the corner of the spring roll wrapper over the line of filling and give it a little roll, making sure that the filling stays in place.

3. Fold in first one side of the wrapper and then the other, so that they overlap in the centre and the filling is completely enclosed.

4. Roll up the spring roll tightly, holding in the sides as you do so. Seal the end with a little of the flour and water paste.

Make the remaining spring rolls in the same way, keeping them covered with a damp cloth.

FOR THE DIPPING SAUCE

2 tablespoons dark soy sauce

1 tablespoon sweet chilli sauce

1 tablespoon cold water

2.5 cm (1 in) piece of fresh root ginger, finely grated

1 garlic clove, very finely chopped

1 small red finger chilli, seeded and very finely chopped

1 tablespoon chopped fresh coriander

FOOD TO FINISH WITH

At long last I've been able to include pudding recipes in one of my books. Although I write about fish, when you think about it I've got recipes for first courses and main courses, so why not some puddings, too? All the recipes in this chapter come from the restaurant and have been particularly successful. We've always tried to keep our puddings simple, like everything else. So, not for us those rather elaborate and extravagant concoctions you get in starred restaurants in Britain and France, with about seven different little piles of this and that all artfully arranged on one plate. I prefer simple tarts, classic English puddings, and fruit and cream combinations. I suppose the most original dish in this chapter is the *Crème Brûlée Ice-cream*, which I can honestly say was my invention, albeit one that arose from a mistake (see p.196 for the full story). Extraordinarily enough, two or three years after the pudding first appeared on the menu, with an explanation of how it came about, somebody from Canada came to the restaurant and said they had seen exactly the same remarks about the very same pudding on a menu in a restaurant in Canada. Whether somebody had copied us, or whether the *doppelgänger* theory really does apply and there are exact replicas – my restaurant on the other side of the world – I don't know.

The trick with creating a good pudding menu is to balance wholesome and substantial puddings and tarts with light fruit, cream and ice confections. Throw in the obligatory and ever-popular chocolate dessert and maybe some cheese and fruit combinations and you're there. I hope you like them.

Pine Kernel and Ricotta Tart (see p.201).

1 quantity of *Basic Sweet
   Pastry* (see p.220)
175 g (6 oz) Agen prunes
   or other good-quality
   moist pitted prunes
2 eggs
65 ml (2½ fl oz) double
   cream
4 tablespoons vanilla sugar
   (see **Note** below), or use
   caster sugar and a few
   drops of vanilla extract
3 tablespoons ground
   almonds
2 tablespoons Armagnac
   or cognac
2 tablespoons cold water
25 g (1 oz) butter, melted
Icing sugar, for dusting

PRUNE TART WITH ARMAGNAC

*I just don't remember where this recipe came from but it was designed to
use those fantastic prunes from Agen, in the Southwest of France, which are
so moist and heavy. It really does depend on having a good juicy prune,
and if you can't get any Agen ones the Californians are now producing
something pretty similar. Prunes are the sort of thing that when I was a boy
you had with rice pudding at school and nobody thought much of. But how
wrong we were.*

Roll out the pastry thinly on a lightly floured surface and use to line a lightly
greased 21 cm (8½ in) loose-bottomed flan tin, 2.5 cm (1 in) deep. Prick the
base with a fork and chill for 20 minutes.

   Pre-heat the oven to 200°C/400°F/Gas 6.

   Line the pastry case with a sheet of crumpled greaseproof paper, then cover
the base with a generous layer of baking beans. Bake blind for 15 minutes.
Remove the paper and beans and return the pastry to the oven for a further
3–4 minutes. Set aside while you make the filling.

   Arrange the prunes in a single layer over the base of the pastry case. Put the
eggs, cream, sugar, almonds, Armagnac or cognac and water into a bowl and
whisk together until smooth. Stir in the melted butter. Pour the batter over the
prunes and bake in the oven for 25–30 minutes, until set and lightly golden.
Remove from the oven and leave to cool slightly, then dust with icing sugar and
serve with a little unwhipped double cream.

Note: To make vanilla sugar, slit a vanilla pod open and put it in a jar of caster
sugar. Leave for 1 week before use.

POACHED PEACHES WITH FRESH FRUIT AND BASIL ICE-CREAM

The idea for this came from Michel Guérard's restaurant at Eugénie-les-Bains in France. He serves an identical dish but with an ice-cream made from verbena, a lemon-scented leaf rather like lemon balm. I haven't been able to get hold of verbena and neither have I been able to grow it very successfully. Then I went to Franco Taruschio's restaurant, The Walnut Tree Inn at Abergavenny in Wales — a place of such joy, good humour and great food. I had basil ice-cream there and thought, that's the one for this dish. I've since found that Joyce Molyneux of The Carved Angel in Dartmouth also has a recipe for it and I think that Franco may have got it from her. So you see how we all share recipes and borrow and nip and tuck!

First make the ice-cream. Put the milk, cream, vanilla pod and half the basil leaves into a pan and bring slowly to the boil over a gentle heat. Set aside for 5 minutes to allow the flavour of the basil to infuse the milk.

Meanwhile, beat the egg yolks and sugar together until pale and creamy. Strain the hot milk mixture on to the egg yolks and mix together well. Return to the pan and cook over a gentle heat, stirring all the time, until the mixture is thick enough to coat the back of the spoon. Do not let the custard boil or it will curdle. Remove from the heat and leave to cool.

Freeze the ice-cream in an ice-cream maker if you have one. If not, strain the mixture into a plastic container and freeze for 2 hours or until almost set, then scrape it into a food processor and blend until smooth. Finely shred the remaining basil and stir it into the ice-cream. Return it to the freezer and leave for 3 hours or until firm.

Meanwhile, bring the stock syrup to the boil. Make a small, shallow cross in the top of each peach, lower them into the hot syrup and simmer for 3–4 minutes or until just tender. Lift the peaches out of the syrup and peel off the skin. When the syrup has cooled, return the peaches to it, cover and chill until needed.

To serve, put the peaches in 8 chilled dessert bowls, add one or two scoops of ice-cream to one side of each peach and a few summer berries to the other. Decorate with sprigs of fresh basil and serve immediately.

Serves 8

1 quantity of *Stock Syrup* (see p.220)
8 firm, ripe peaches
100 g (4 oz) mixed fresh summer berries, such as raspberries, strawberries, blueberries, redcurrants etc.

FOR THE BASIL ICE-CREAM
300 ml (10 fl oz) milk
300 ml (10 fl oz) double cream
½ vanilla pod
15 g (½ oz) fresh basil leaves
5 egg yolks
175 g (6 oz) caster sugar
Sprigs of fresh basil, to decorate

1 quantity of *Stock Syrup*
(see p.220)

3 firm, ripe dessert pears,
peeled, quartered and
cored

300 ml (10 fl oz) milk

3 eggs, separated

65 g (2½ oz) caster sugar

1 tablespoon powdered
gelatine

2½ tablespoons Poire
William, kirsch or
brandy

300 ml (10 fl oz) double
cream

Sprigs of fresh mint, to
decorate (optional)

**FOR THE PASSION FRUIT
COULIS**

150 ml (5 fl oz) freshly
squeezed orange juice

Juice of 1 small lemon

4 ripe passion fruit

1 teaspoon arrowroot

PEAR BAVAROIS WITH A FRESH PASSION FRUIT COULIS

I got this recipe from a restaurant quite near Rheims in France. It is one of those places where you don't really expect to get much of interest in your 95-franc meal but that's the great thing about eating out in France: you often come across just one dish that is really worth having. I'm always looking for puddings out of the summer season that don't rely on rather tasteless imported soft fruit from warmer countries and this fits the bill exactly. At the restaurant we turn the bavarois out of its mould, dust it thickly with icing sugar and caramelize it with a blowtorch, which gives the whole thing a new dimension of texture and visual appeal. As a matter of fact, no kitchen should be without a blowtorch. Surely you've got one lurking around in the tool shed somewhere! It's ideal for making quick tops for crème brûlées or even for glazing a fruit tart that has been dusted with icing sugar. However, if you don't have a blowtorch, don't worry; just cover the bavarois with the passion fruit sauce. I always leave the seeds in passion fruit sauces like this because I love their crunchy texture and acidic taste.

Bring the stock syrup to the boil, add the quartered pears and simmer until just tender. Lift the pears out with a slotted spoon and leave to cool, then chop them into small pieces. Reserve the syrup for the coulis (and for later use – it will keep in the fridge).

Put the milk in a pan and bring just to the boil. Put the egg yolks into a bowl with the caster sugar and beat together until pale and creamy. Gradually beat in the hot milk, then return the mixture to the pan and cook over a low heat, stirring all the time, until it is thick enough to coat the back of the spoon. Do not let the custard boil or it will curdle. Pour into a bowl, press a sheet of cling film on the surface and leave to cool. Meanwhile, line the base of eight 200 ml (7 fl oz) ramekins or similar-sized moulds with greaseproof paper.

Put 3 tablespoons of cold water in a small pan and sprinkle the gelatine over it. Set aside for 5 minutes, then heat gently until clear. Stir into the cooled custard with the chopped pears and the Poire William, kirsch or brandy.

Lightly whip the cream until it forms soft peaks. Now rest the bowl of custard in a larger bowl filled with iced water and stir gently until the mixture begins to show signs of thickening and setting. Remove from the cold water and fold in the whipped cream. Whisk the egg whites into soft peaks and gently fold them in. Spoon the mixture into the prepared moulds, cover loosely with cling film and chill for 3 hours or until set.

For the passion fruit coulis, strain the orange and lemon juice into a small pan. Add 300 ml (10 fl oz) of the reserved stock syrup, bring to the boil and boil rapidly until reduced to 175 ml (6 fl oz). Halve the passion fruit and scoop the pulp out into the pan. Mix the arrowroot with 1 teaspoon of cold water. Bring the coulis back to the boil, then stir in the arrowroot and simmer for 1 minute. Pour into a bowl, leave to cool and then chill.

To serve, unmould the bavarois on to 8 plates and spoon the passion fruit coulis over and around them. Decorate with sprigs of mint, if liked.

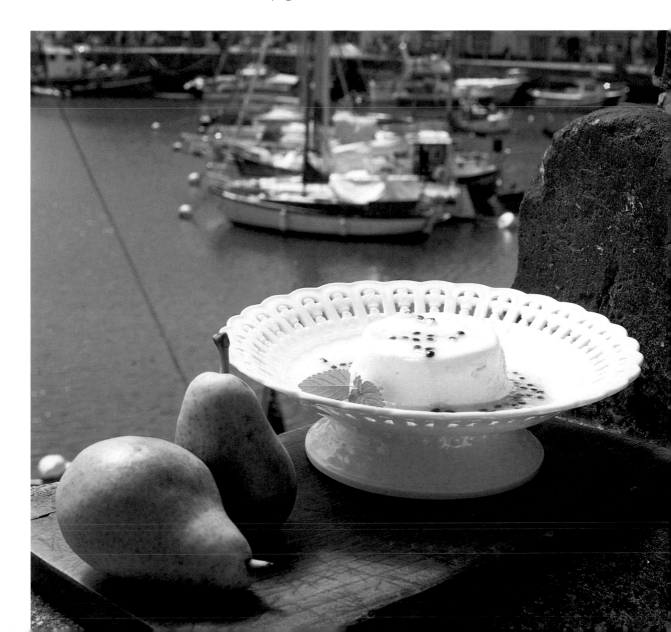

Serves 8

200 ml (7 fl oz) milk

**375 ml (13 fl oz) double
cream**

1 teaspoon vanilla extract

5 egg yolks

120 g (4½ oz) caster sugar

CRÈME BRÛLÉE ICE-CREAM

*This ice-cream was invented quite by accident when Christine Hope, who is
now our head baker, curdled a rich custard intended for a crème brûlée and
asked me whether she should throw it away and start again. 'No,' I said, 'it
would be a waste. Sprinkle it with sugar, burn the top as you would
normally under a grill and then bung it in the ice-cream machine and
we'll see what happens.' And what happened was that it turned into the
most superbly flavoured and textured ice-cream because the caramel broke
up into exquisite little crunchy pieces. We normally serve it with pears
poached in port and cinnamon, or just a pile of fresh berries and maybe a
little fruit coulis and a sprig of mint.*

Put the milk, cream and vanilla extract into a pan and bring slowly to the boil.
Meanwhile beat the egg yolks with 50 g (2 oz) of the caster sugar until pale
and creamy. Gradually beat in the hot milk and cream, then return the mixture
to the pan and cook over a gentle heat until it is thick enough to coat the back
of the spoon. Do not let it boil or it will curdle.

Pour the custard into a shallow ovenproof dish – it should be about 2.5 cm
(1 in) deep and come near the top of the dish. Leave to cool, then cover and
chill for 6 hours or until set.

Pre-heat the grill to its highest setting. Remove the custard from the fridge
and sprinkle with the remaining caster sugar. Put it under the grill for about 5
minutes, until the sugar has caramelized. Alternatively, if you have a blowtorch
you can achieve the same results by playing the flame across the top of the
sugar. Remove and leave to cool, then break up the caramel topping here and
there with the handle of a kitchen knife and stir the pieces into the creamy
mixture below. Transfer to an ice-cream maker or a plastic container and freeze
for 3 hours or until firm.

Hot Bread Pudding with Armagnac Sauce

Like so many apparently mundane nursery puddings, this is really good when made with the best ingredients. I've specified three different types of bread only to give the idea that a mixture should be used. Bread pudding is a great way of using up stale bread. Although originally it was the most economical of Northern puddings and also eaten as a cake, it's recently been elevated to restaurant status, particularly when served with a rich Armagnac custard like this.

Cut the bread into 2.5 cm (1 in) cubes, put them into a large bowl and cover with cold water. Leave to soak for 15 minutes.

Pre-heat the oven to 160°C/325°F/Gas 3.

Tip the soaked bread into a colander. Take a handful at a time and squeeze out all the excess water. Put the bread back into the bowl and add the dried fruit, spices, orange and lemon zest, eggs, butter and 100 g (4 oz) of the demerara sugar. Mix together well and then put the mixture into a greased and lined 20 x 25 cm (8 x 10 in) cake tin, 3 cm (1½ in) deep. Sprinkle with the remaining demerara sugar and bake for 1 hour.

Meanwhile, for the sauce, bring the milk and cream just to the boil in a small pan. Whisk the egg yolks and sugar together in a small bowl until pale and creamy. Gradually beat in the hot milk, then return the mixture to the pan and cook over a gentle heat, stirring all the time, until it is thick enough to coat the back of the spoon. Do not let it boil or it will curdle. Stir the Armagnac into the sauce.

Cut the bread pudding into squares and serve with the Armagnac sauce.

Serves 8

150 g (5 oz) day-old white bread
200 g (7 oz) day-old Walnut Bread (see p.219)
200 g (7 oz) day-old Granary bread
75 g (3 oz) sultanas
75 g (3 oz) currants
½ teaspoon freshly grated nutmeg
¾ teaspoon ground cinnamon
Finely grated zest of ½ orange
Finely grated zest of ½ lemon
2 small eggs, beaten
90 g (3 ½ oz) unsalted butter, softened
175 g (6 oz) demerara sugar

FOR THE ARMAGNAC SAUCE

175 ml (6 fl oz) milk
175 ml (6 fl oz) double cream
2 large egg yolks
40 g (1½ oz) caster sugar
2 tablespoons Armagnac or cognac

150 g (5 oz) unsalted
    butter
900 ml (1½ pints) milk
75 g (3 oz) caster sugar
1 vanilla pod
4 large eggs, beaten
½ teaspoon ground
    cinnamon

FOR THE BRIOCHE

15 g (½ oz) fresh yeast
3 tablespoons warm water
4 tablespoons caster sugar
3 tablespoons tepid milk
450 g (1 lb) strong plain
    flour
1 teaspoon salt
4 eggs
100 g (4 oz) unsalted
    butter, melted and
    cooled
Beaten egg, to glaze

**FOR THE CARAMEL
APPLES**

100 g (4 oz) unsalted
    butter
8 dessert apples such as
    Cox's Orange Pippins,
    peeled, cored and
    thickly sliced
150 g (5 oz) caster sugar
150 ml (5 fl oz) double
    cream
2 tablespoons Calvados

PAIN PERDU WITH CINNAMON SUGAR AND CARAMEL APPLES

I suppose you could call pain perdu *France's answer to bread and butter pudding. You dip some slices of bread in sweet milk and beaten egg and fry them in butter to give a set, slightly crispy outside and a soft centre. If you then sprinkle the* pain perdu *with a little sugar spiced with cinnamon and serve it with some caramelized apple slices and caramel sauce — you're in heaven. This recipe is a luxurious version made with home-made brioche but you could use a good-quality bought brioche or any good white bread.*

For the brioche, put the yeast, water, 2 tablespoons of the sugar, the milk and 1 tablespoon of the flour in a bowl and whisk together until smooth. Cover with a damp tea towel and leave in a warm place for about 1 hour, until the mixture has become frothy. Sift the rest of the flour and sugar and the salt into a large mixing bowl, make a well in the centre and add the yeast mixture, eggs and melted butter. Gradually mix the flour into the wet ingredients to make a sticky dough. Beat it with your hand for 2–3 minutes, then cover with a damp tea towel and leave in a warm place for 1–2 hours, until doubled in size.

Pre-heat the oven to 200°C/400°F/Gas 6.

Knock the air out of the dough, turn it out on to a floured surface and knead for a couple of minutes until smooth. Put it in a buttered 900 g (2 lb) loaf tin, cover and leave in a warm place until the mixture has risen to the top of the tin. Glaze the top with beaten egg and bake for 30–35 minutes, until the loaf is golden brown on top and sounds hollow when tapped on the base. Remove from the tin and leave to cool on a wire rack.

For the caramel apples, clarify the butter by melting it over a low heat, then pouring off the clear butter into a bowl, leaving behind the milky solids that will have collected at the bottom. Pour a little of the clarified butter into a large frying pan, add a layer of apple slices and fry for about 3 minutes, turning them over half way through, until they are just soft. Lift out with a slotted spoon and cook the remaining apples in the same way.

Add the rest of the clarified butter to the pan with the sugar and leave over a very low heat, stirring occasionally. It will look very dry and grainy to start with but eventually the sugar will melt and turn into a toffee-coloured mixture. Take the pan off the heat and add the cream and Calvados. Return the pan to a low heat and cook, stirring, until all the pieces of hardened toffee have melted. Return the apples to the pan and keep warm.

For the *pain perdu*, clarify the butter as for the apples and set aside. Put the milk, 50 g (2 oz) of the caster sugar and the vanilla pod into a pan and leave over a gentle heat until almost boiling. Take off the heat and leave to cool. Remove the vanilla pod and pour the milk into a wide, shallow dish. Pour the beaten eggs into another shallow dish. Cut the brioche into slices 1 cm (½ in) thick (you will need 8 slices) and then cut each slice in half diagonally. Mix the rest of the caster sugar with the cinnamon and set aside.

Heat a little of the clarified butter in a large non-stick frying pan. Put a couple of slices of brioche in the milk, leave for 30 seconds, then turn them over and leave for another 30 seconds – the bread should have absorbed the milk but not gone soggy. Now dip the soaked brioche into the beaten egg, put in the frying pan and fry over a medium heat for 1 minute on each side, until golden. Lift out on to a serving plate and keep warm in a low oven while you cook the rest.

Sprinkle the *pain perdu* lightly with the cinnamon sugar and serve immediately with the caramel apples.

BAKED CHOCOLATE MOUSSE WITH CORNISH CLOTTED CREAM

Serves 6–8

150 g (5 oz) good-quality
    plain chocolate
150 g (5 oz) softened
    unsalted butter, plus
    extra for greasing
150 g (5 oz) caster sugar
3 eggs, separated
Icing sugar, for dusting
Clotted cream, preferably
    Cornish, to serve

It's funny how often people describe extremely dark, rich chocolate cakes as wicked or sinful. Yet there is something indefinably seductive about really good chocolate desserts and this one must top the bill for the most sensual chocolate gâteau in the world. Most so-called chocolate gâteaux leave me cold, and they should more appropriately be described as chocolate cakes to serve for afternoon tea. But this one is so dark and moist and delicate.

Pre-heat the oven to 160°C/325°F/Gas 3. Grease a 20 cm (8 in) springform cake tin with a little butter and then line the base with greaseproof paper.

Melt the chocolate in a bowl set over a pan of barely simmering water, making sure the bowl isn't touching the water. Leave to cool.

Beat the butter and sugar together until pale and fluffy. Beat in the egg yolks, one at a time, then fold in the melted chocolate.

In another bowl whisk the egg whites until they stand in soft peaks. Stir 2 large spoonfuls into the chocolate mixture to loosen it slightly and then gently fold in the remainder. Put the mixture into the tin and bake for 1 hour or until a crust has formed on top and there is no movement if you shake the tin gently. The cake will rise up dramatically during cooking but will sink once you take it out of the oven. Leave to cool on a wire rack, then remove it from the tin.

Serve the cake dusted lightly with icing sugar and accompanied by scoops of clotted cream.

LEMON MERINGUE TART

Serves 6

1 quantity of *Basic Sweet
    Pastry* (see p.220)
3 large eggs
250 g (9 oz) caster sugar
150 ml (5 fl oz) double
    cream
4 tablespoons lemon juice
Finely grated zest of
    1 large lemon
2 egg whites

Much as I've always liked lemon meringue pie, I find that most recipes call for a rather bland cornflour mixture to make the lemon filling. If you use a proper lemon tart filling in a deep pastry shell the result is so much better.

Roll out the pastry on a lightly floured surface and use to line a lightly greased 20 cm (8 in) loose-bottomed flan tin, 4 cm (1½ in) deep. Prick the base with a fork and chill for 20 minutes. Pre-heat the oven to 200°C/400°F/Gas 6.

Line the pastry case with a sheet of crumpled greaseproof paper, cover the base with baking beans and bake for 15 minutes. Remove the paper and beans and return the pastry case to the oven for 3–4 minutes. Remove from the oven and set aside. Reduce the oven temperature to 150°C/300°F/Gas 2.

For the filling, lightly stir together the eggs, 150 g (5 oz) of the sugar and the cream. Gradually stir in the lemon juice, then strain into a jug and stir in the zest. Pour the mixture into the pastry case and bake for 50 minutes, until set. Remove from the oven and leave to cool. Raise the oven temperature to 180°C/350°F/Gas 4.

Whisk the egg whites into stiff peaks. Very gradually beat in the remaining sugar to produce a stiff, glossy meringue. Spread it over the cooled tart, making sure it makes a good seal with the pastry edge. Swirl the top with the tip of a knife and bake for 15 minutes, until lightly browned. Serve the tart warm or cold.

PINE KERNEL AND RICOTTA TART

The filling of this delicious tart is considerably enhanced by the inclusion of a little lemon zest. It's an Italian recipe, a sort of light baked cheesecake.

Roll out half the pastry thinly on a lightly floured surface and use to line a lightly greased 21 cm (8½ in) loose-bottomed flan tin, 2.5 cm (1 in) deep. Prick the base with a fork and chill for 20 minutes.

Pre-heat the oven to 200°C/400°F/Gas 6.

Line the pastry case with a sheet of crumpled greaseproof paper, cover the base with baking beans and bake blind for 15 minutes. Remove the paper and beans and bake for a further 3–4 minutes. Remove from the oven and set aside.

For the filling, toast the pine kernels in the oven for about 6 minutes, until golden, then leave to cool. Lower the oven temperature to 160°C/325°F/Gas 3.

Beat together the ricotta, egg yolks, lemon zest and sugar until smooth. Stir in the cream and pine kernels. Pour the filling into the pastry case. Roll out the remaining pastry and cut it into strips 5 mm (¼ in) wide. Lay some of them over the tart about 2.5 cm (1 in) apart, then lay the remaining strips crosswise on top to make a lattice. Seal the ends with a little water and then bake the tart for 1 hour or until set and lightly golden. Dust with icing sugar and serve with unwhipped double cream. It can be eaten hot but is exceptionally good cold, too.

Serves 6

2 quantities of *Basic Sweet Pastry* (see p.220), each made with grated zest of ½ lemon

50 g (2 oz) pine kernels

350 g (12 oz) ricotta cheese

3 egg yolks

Finely grated zest of 1 small lemon

100 g (4 oz) caster sugar

50 ml (2 fl oz) double cream

Icing sugar, for dusting

Serves 6

1 vanilla pod

300 ml (10 fl oz) double
    cream

300 ml (10 fl oz) milk

6 tablespoons caster sugar

2 teaspoons powdered
    gelatine

**FOR THE STEWED
RHUBARB**

350 g (12 oz) young
    rhubarb

225 g (8 oz) granulated
    sugar

250 ml (8 fl oz) water

1 orange

1 lemon

300 ml (10 fl oz) red wine

50 ml (2 fl oz) port

1 tablespoon dark
    muscovado sugar

7.5 cm (3 in) piece of
    cinnamon stick

1 clove

PANNA COTTA WITH STEWED RHUBARB

This Italian light set cream can be served with rhubarb in winter and, in summer, with whatever fresh berries you like but I always favour raspberries – particularly puréed and very lightly sweetened to make a coulis. A great thing about panna cotta *is that it is set with only a tiny amount of gelatine, and in this particular recipe the cream only just holds its shape. For the television series accompanying this book, we filmed the making of this dish during a splendid day where I instructed a dozen or so chefs on a four-course menu I had written for a special dinner for 100 guests at Blenheim Palace that evening. I demonstrated the dishes and then we all prepared them together. However, disaster loomed when it looked extremely doubtful whether the tiny amount of gelatine I had allowed for the 100 portions of* panna cotta *would, in fact, set the cream. In the end I reluctantly decided that we would have to tip the mixture out into a big bowl and add more gelatine, which would firm it up more than I wanted. Just as we were about to do that, Paul Ripley, our head chef, came in bearing a plate of* panna cotta *that had just set in the softest, most melting way. At some stage in any 'away match', as I like to call it, things start to go wrong and you think it is all going to collapse. It just takes a little moment like that to make you think, 'Oh yes, it's going to be all right after all.' And it was. The star turn, in spite of all the brilliant fish, was the* panna cotta, *which everybody said tasted so fresh.*

For the *panna cotta*, split open the vanilla pod and scrape out the seeds. Put both the pod and seeds into a small pan with the cream, milk and sugar and simmer gently for 5 minutes, then remove from the heat. Meanwhile, put 2 tablespoons of cold water in a small pan and sprinkle the gelatine over it. Set aside for 5 minutes, then heat gently until clear.

Remove the vanilla pod from the cream and stir in the dissolved gelatine. Pour into 6 dariole moulds or 6 cm (2½ in) ramekins, cover and chill for 3 hours or until set.

Peel the rhubarb if it is woody but if it is very young this shouldn't be necessary. Cut it into 2.5 cm (1 in) lengths. Put the sugar and water into a pan and leave over a low heat until the sugar has completely dissolved. Bring to the boil and boil for 2 minutes. Pour half this syrup into another pan and stir in half the prepared rhubarb. Simmer it for 1–2 minutes, until only just tender – it should still be slightly firm. Cover and leave to cool.

Pare the zest off a quarter of the orange and a quarter of the lemon, being careful not to remove any of the bitter white pith underneath. Squeeze out the juice of both the orange and the lemon and add to the remaining syrup with the pared zests, red wine, port, dark muscovado sugar, cinnamon and clove. Bring to the boil and boil until the liquid has reduced to 150 ml (5 fl oz). Strain into another pan, stir in the remaining rhubarb and simmer gently for 2–3 minutes, until just tender. It should be a little more cooked through than the first batch but not falling apart. Transfer to a bowl and leave to cool. (Remember the rhubarb will continue to cook in the syrup after it has been removed from the heat.)

To serve, unmould the *panna cotta* on to 6 serving plates and arrange a pile of each type of rhubarb to the side, along with a little of the syrup.

900 g (2 lb) puff pastry

12 fresh figs

4 teaspoons granulated
  sugar

3 tablespoons redcurrant
  jelly

**FOR THE YOGHURT
SOURED CREAM**

300 ml (10 fl oz) double
  cream

65 ml (2½ fl oz) natural
  yoghurt

LIGHT FIG TARTS WITH YOGHURT SOURED CREAM

These are simply some sliced fresh figs baked on puff pastry rounds, then glazed and served with what I call yoghurt soured cream. I developed this type of soured cream in the days before we could buy crème fraîche in Britain but actually I almost prefer it. You just mix some yoghurt and double cream together, leave it in a warm place overnight, then put it in muslin and let it drain. The result is a superb, slightly acidic cream which makes the perfect accompaniment to the fig tarts. You need to start making the cream a good 24 hours before you wish to serve it.

For the yoghurt soured cream, bring the cream to the boil in a small pan and then set aside to cool. Stir in the yogurt, cover the pan with a cloth and leave in a warm place (about 21°C/70°F) overnight – an airing cupboard is ideal.

The next morning, spoon the cream into a muslin-lined sieve and rest it over a bowl. Cover and leave in the fridge for 12 hours to drain.

Pre-heat the oven to 220°C/425°F/Gas 7.

Divide the pastry into 8, roll out each piece thinly on a lightly floured surface and cut into a 15 cm (6 in) oval. Put them well spaced apart on 2 lightly greased baking trays.

Cut each fig across into 4–5 slices and arrange them slightly overlapping on the pastry ovals, leaving a 1 cm (½ in) border. Sprinkle each tart with ½ teaspoon of granulated sugar and bake for about 12 minutes, until the pastry is puffed up and golden and the sugar has lightly caramelized.

Meanwhile, put the redcurrant jelly into a pan with 2 teaspoons of water and leave over a gentle heat until melted. Set aside to cool slightly but do not let it set.

Remove the tarts from the oven and brush the fruit with the redcurrant glaze. Slide each tart on to a warmed plate and serve with the yoghurt soured cream.

SAFFRON ICE-CREAM WITH BRANDY SNAPS

The recipe is for quite a lot of ice-cream. I thought of cutting it down and, of course, you can halve everything if you feel so inclined but we find, with a family of children, that the ice-cream has a habit of disappearing from the freezer in the most mysterious circumstances.

For the ice-cream, grind the saffron to a powder in a pestle and mortar or with the end of a rolling pin in a small bowl. Put the milk, cream and ground saffron into a pan and bring slowly to the boil over a gentle heat. Meanwhile, beat the egg yolks and caster sugar together until pale and creamy. Pour on the hot milk, mix well and return to the pan. Cook over a gentle heat, stirring all the time, until the mixture is thick enough to coat the back of the spoon. Do not let it boil or it will curdle. Strain the mixture, then leave to cool. Freeze in an ice-cream maker if you have one. Alternatively, pour it into a plastic container and freeze for 2–3 hours, until almost set, then scrape it into a food processor and process until smooth. Pour back into the container and freeze for another 3 hours or until firm.

Pre-heat the oven to 180°C/350°F/Gas 4.

For the brandy snaps, melt the butter in a pan, add all the remaining ingredients and beat until smooth. Drop 4 teaspoons of the mixture about 15 cm (6 in) apart on a non-stick baking tray and bake for 11–12 minutes, until richly golden. Leave to cool and set a little – about 1 minute – then use a palette knife to lift them off the tray and drape them over a rolling pin for an open shape (or wrap them round a wooden spoon or sharpening steel for a cigar shape). Press down lightly to curve them and leave until cold. Repeat with the remaining mixture; you should have about 16 brandy snaps in total.

To serve, scoop the ice-cream into chilled dessert glasses and push 2 brandy snaps into the top of each one. Serve immediately.

Serves 8

½ teaspoon saffron strands
300 ml (10 fl oz) milk
300 ml (10 fl oz) double cream
4 egg yolks
100 g (4 oz) caster sugar

FOR THE BRANDY SNAPS
60 g (2¼ oz) butter
50 g (2 oz) plain flour
½ teaspoon powdered ginger
100 g (4 oz) caster sugar
50 g (2 oz) golden syrup

2 quantities of *Basic Sweet*
Pastry **(see p.220)**
100 g (4 oz) good-quality
plain chocolate
2 eggs
20 g (¾ oz) caster sugar
150 ml (5 fl oz) double
cream

FOR THE COMPOTE OF
DRIED FRUITS
175 g (6 oz) mixed dried
fruit, such as apples,
pears, peaches, prunes,
apricots and figs
65 ml (2½ fl oz) white wine
100 g (4 oz) granulated
sugar
5 cloves
5 cm (2 in) piece of
cinamon stick
1 strip of pared orange
zest
1 strip of pared lemon zest
Juice of ½ lemon

HOT CHOCOLATE TARTS WITH A COMPOTE OF DRIED FRUITS

These little individual chocolate tarts puff up into a wonderful light extravagance when baked. They are served with dried fruit that has been poached in a syrup spiced with cloves, cinnamon and orange and lemon zest. This is the sort of winter pudding that makes you feel the colder months, when soft, ripe summer fruits are not available, have some tremendous compensations after all. Remember you need to soak the dried fruit the night before.

First make the dried fruit compote. Cover the dried fruit with plenty of cold water and leave to soak overnight. The next day, drain the fruit, reserving the soaking liquid. Cut any large pieces of fruit in half. Put 300 ml (10 fl oz) of the soaking liquid into a pan with the rest of the compote ingredients (except the fruit). Bring to the boil and simmer for 10 minutes. Add the fruit and simmer for 15 minutes. Leave to cool and then chill until needed.

Pre-heat the oven to 200°C/400°F/Gas 6.

Cut the pastry into 8 and roll out each piece thinly on a lightly floured surface. Use to line eight 10 cm (4 in) loose-bottomed tartlet tins and chill for 20 minutes.

Line the pastry cases with pieces of crumpled greaseproof paper, cover the bases with a generous layer of baking beans and bake blind for 15 minutes, Remove the paper and beans and return the pastry cases to the oven for 2–3 minutes. Remove from the oven and set aside. Lower the oven temperature to 190°C/375°F/Gas 5.

Melt the chocolate in a bowl set over a pan of barely simmering water, making sure the bowl doesn't touch the water. Leave the chocolate to cool.

Lightly whisk the eggs and sugar together, then stir in the melted chocolate and the double cream. Pour the mixture into the tartlet cases and bake for about 15 minutes, until set. Serve the warm chocolate tarts with the chilled fruit compote.

300 ml (10 fl oz) water

175 g (6 oz) stoned dates,
    coarsely chopped

I teaspoon bicarbonate of
    soda

I teaspoon vanilla extract

50 g (2 oz) butter

175 g (6 oz) caster sugar

2 eggs

225 g (8 oz) plain flour

I teaspoon baking powder

150 ml (5 fl oz) clotted
    cream or whipped
    double cream, to serve

FOR THE SAUCE

300 ml (10 fl oz) double
    cream

225 g (8 oz) dark
    muscovado sugar

100 g (4 oz) butter

STICKY TOFFEE PUDDING

This is the famous and original sticky pudding from Sharrow Bay, that delightful hotel in Ullswater in the Lake District. Francis Coulson and Brian Sack are two of the country's best exponents of British food. Whenever I go there I am filled with a real enthusiasm for the food of this country and the whole experience of staying there fills me with optimisim, as all good hotels and restaurants should. Francis Coulson invented this sweet, perhaps the most well loved of all our puddings.

Pre-heat the oven to 180°C/350°F/Gas 4.

Put the water, dates, bicarbonate of soda and vanilla extract into a pan and bring to the boil. Meanwhile, cream the butter and sugar together until pale and fluffy. Beat in the eggs one at a time, adding a tablespoon of the flour with the second egg if the mixture looks as if it is about to curdle. Sift the remaining flour with the baking powder and gently fold in.

Bring the date mixture back to the boil. Slowly beat the liquid into the creamed mixture to make a smooth batter, then stir in the dates. Pour into a greased and lined 20 x 25 cm (8 x 10 in) cake tin, 3 cm (1½ in) deep, and bake for 30 minutes or until a skewer inserted in the centre of the pudding comes away clean.

For the sauce, put the cream, sugar and butter into a pan and leave over a low heat until the sugar has melted.

To serve, cut the pudding into 8 pieces and put them on warmed serving plates. Bring the sauce to the boil, pour it over the pudding and serve with clotted cream or whipped double cream.

CRÉMETS DE SAUMUR WITH FRESH RASPBERRIES

This recipe comes from Elizabeth David's French Provincial Cooking *and differs from the more familiar* coeurs à la crème *in that no cream cheese is used. We serve these* crémets *sprinkled with lemon sugar (made by drying pared lemon zest and then powdering it with caster sugar in a liquidizer) and fresh berries and accompanied by a simple coulis. You can buy moulds for draining cream quite easily. Alternatively you can just drain the cream mixture in a muslin bag and serve it from a bowl.*

Line 4 *coeur à la crème* moulds with clean muslin, leaving some overlapping the sides. Whip 300 ml (10 fl oz) of the cream with the sugar into soft peaks. Whisk the egg whites into soft peaks and then gently fold them into the cream. Spoon the mixture into the lined moulds and lightly level the tops. Cover with the overhanging pieces of muslin and place in the fridge with a plate on the shelf underneath to catch the liquid. Leave for about 12 hours or overnight.

Unmould the creams on to plates and pour the remaining cream around them. Add some raspberries to each plate and sprinkle with a little sugar.

Serves 4

350 ml (12 fl oz) double cream
1 teaspoon caster sugar, plus extra to serve
2 egg whites
50–75 g (2–3 oz) fresh raspberries

FRUIT AND CHEESE COMBINATIONS

I often find in restaurants that, after a fairly filling meal, all I want is something light and not necessarily too sweet. It is rare to find something that fits the bill. In Italy, menus often give you the option of fresh fruit served with cheese – say, Parmesan or pecorino. I like to order a glass of Vin Santo, that sweet, slightly earthy dessert wine, to go with this. The perfect finish to a meal.

So how about some fresh peaches, preferably those white ones with an ephemeral fragrance, served with slivers of Parmesan? Or maybe some slices of the large pears that you get in the autumn in Italy, beautifully tender and moist, with some dolcelatte just spooned out on to the plate. Or perhaps a little pile of mascarpone cheese and some fresh, sweet figs to eat with it. Some nutty farmhouse Cheddar such as Montgomery's would go well with a sweet Cox's Orange Pippin apple. Or you could try that excellent Scottish cheese, Lanark Blue, with a pile of tayberries. Not a recipe but just a few suggestions.

BASICS

I used to play rugby in the front row of the scrum and though one naturally assumes that wherever you play in a team sport is the most important position, I do think that games of rugby are won or lost in the front two rows of the scrum. This is a perfect analogy with cooking. Many dishes are won or lost through good or bad basics, particularly stock. And to make a good stock, to prepare bones and vegetables and simmer everything gently to produce a clear and well-flavoured liquid, that's real cooking. I mean by real cooking, the care and attention to the background details in a dish. Many recipes today involve the last minute cooking of good ingredients and don't involve long slow cooking or elaborate sauces and long laboured garnishes. Most of the dishes in this book are like that because those are the sort of dishes we all like to eat now but when a dish calls for a stock or one of the other basic recipes in this chapter it needs to be made properly. I suppose my style of cooking would be described as simple, straightforward, those sort of words, but it's not quite as simple as that! 'In my salad days when I was green in judgement' I used to think that the only way to succeed as a restaurant chef was to pile ingredients on ingredients. I once had a dish on the menu which had three fish cooked in three different ways with three different sauces. Now I like a mininum of ingredients but everything has to be just right.

It's really well worth taking care with these basics, what after all is better in this world than a freshly boiled crab with a fluffy mayonnaise or a slab of turbot with a rich, lemony hollandaise. The curry pastes too will be better than anything you can buy in a bottle. Again, a lot of work will go into assembling the ingredients, but it will be well worth it.

FISH STOCK

Makes 1.2 litres (2 pints)

1 kg (2¼ lb) fish bones,
    such as lemon sole, brill
    and plaice
2.25 litres (4 pints) water
100 g (4 oz) onions,
    chopped
100 g (4 oz) celery,
    chopped
100 g (4 oz) carrots,
    chopped
25 g (1 oz) button
    mushrooms, sliced
1 teaspoon chopped fresh
    thyme

Unlike meat stocks, fish stock should only be simmered for 20 minutes to extract all the flavour from the bones. A longer simmering time will make it taste bitter and a bit gluey. You can use any fish for stock except oily ones such as herring and mackerel, although in an emergency I have used these without the heads, which is where all the oil is.

Put the fish bones and water in a pan, bring just to the boil and simmer very gently for 20 minutes. Strain through a sieve lined with muslin into a clean pan, add the vegetables and thyme and bring back to the boil. Simmer for 35 minutes, until reduced to about 1.2 litres (2 pints). Strain once more. The stock is now ready to use or store.

ROASTED FISH STOCK

Makes 1.2 litres (2 pints)

25 g (1 oz) butter
1 kg (2¼ lb) fish bones, such
    as lemon sole, brill and
    plaice
100 g (4 oz) onions,
    chopped
100 g (4 oz) celery,
    chopped
100 g (4 oz) carrots,
    chopped
1 teaspoon chopped fresh
    thyme
2.25 litres (4 pints) water

This robust stock has a slightly caramelized flavour from the roasted vegetables. It can be used in any dish where a strong flavour is required.

Pre-heat the oven to 200°C/400°F/Gas 6.

Melt the butter in a large roasting tin. Add the fish bones, vegetables and thyme and turn them over a few times until they are well coated in the butter. Roast in the oven for 30 minutes, then transfer the mixture to a saucepan, add the water and bring just to the boil. Simmer for 20 minutes and then strain through a sieve lined with muslin into a clean pan. Bring back to the boil and boil until reduced to about 1.2 litres (2 pints). The stock is now ready to use or store.

Chicken Stock

Makes 1.75 litres (3 pints)

This light, clear chicken stock crops up quite frequently in my recipes where the particular flavour of a fish-based stock is not important but the clean and fragrant body of a good, clean chicken stock will count for a great deal. A good stock is often what makes a dish like a paella or risotto memorable. I have enjoyed those dishes with very little else in them other than rice and a good stock. I use chicken stock in fish dishes when I want plenty of savoury body for a well-flavoured sauce, such as the robust red wine sauce with cod and lentils on p.121.

This chicken stock should be made with fresh carcasses or winglets. Much as I like stocks made from the leftovers of a roast chicken for vegetable soups and to enrich gravy, the dishes in this book need something a bit more refined.

**Bones from a 1.5 kg
(3–3½ lb) chicken or 450 g
(1lb) chicken winglets
2 tablespoons vegetable oil
1 large carrot, chopped
2 celery sticks, sliced
2 leeks, sliced
2 fresh or dried bay leaves
2 sprigs of fresh thyme
2.25 litres (4 pints) water**

Put all the ingredients into a large pan and bring just to the boil, skimming any scum from the surface as it appears. Leave to simmer very gently for 2 hours – it is important not to let it boil as this will force the fat from even the leanest chicken and make the stock cloudy. Regularly skim off any fat that does collect on top of the stock.

Strain through a sieve lined with muslin and leave to cool, then chill. Remove the film of fat from the surface. The stock is now ready to use or store.

Concentrated Chicken Stock For a really good concentrated chicken stock, simmer the strained stock until reduced in volume by half.

Light Asian Chicken Stock

Makes 1.75 litres (3 pints)

Use this for any dish with Asian flavours.

**2 chicken carcasses
2 spring onions
1 garlic clove, unpeeled
2 slices of fresh root
ginger, unpeeled
1 star anise (optional)**

Put the chicken carcasses into a large pan and cover with cold water. Slowly bring to the boil, skimming any scum from the surface. Trim the green tops off the spring onions and split the spring onions in half lengthways. Lightly crush the garlic, leaving the skin on. Add the spring onions, garlic, ginger and star anise, if using, to the pan and simmer very gently for 1½ hours, skimming off any fat as it collects on the surface. Strain and leave to cool. The stock is now ready to use or store.

1 leek, thinly sliced

2 celery sticks, sliced

1 onion, thinly sliced

1 fennel bulb, thinly sliced

Pared zest and flesh of
  ½ lemon

Pared zest and flesh of
  ½ orange

2 fresh bay leaves

15 black peppercorns,
  cracked

1.75 litres (3 pints) water

150 ml (5 fl oz) dry white
  wine

Makes 1 litre (1¾ pints)
stock or 150 ml (5 fl oz)
reduction

50 g (2 oz) carrot, chopped

50 g (2 oz) onion, chopped

50 g (2 oz) celery, chopped

15 g (½ oz) unsalted butter

350 g (12 oz) unshelled
  North Atlantic prawns,
  small crabs or shrimps

1 tablespoon cognac

2 tablespoons white wine

1 teaspoon chopped fresh
  tarragon

75 g (3 oz) tomato, roughly
  chopped

1.2 litres (2 pints) *Fish
  Stock* (see p.212)

A pinch of cayenne pepper

SHELLFISH NAGE

A nage is a well-flavoured court bouillon used for poaching shellfish. The court bouillon can then be reduced and butter whisked in to make a simple, fresh sauce, as in the recipe for Poached Lobster with Butter and Basil *(see p.132)*

Put all the ingredients except the white wine into a large pan, bring to the boil and simmer for 25 minutes. Add the white wine and simmer for a further 5 minutes, then strain. The nage is now ready to use.

SHELLFISH STOCK AND SHELLFISH REDUCTION

To make the shellfish stock, fry the carrot, onion and celery in the butter for 2–3 minutes. Add the prawns, crabs or shrimps and the cognac and fry for 2 minutes. Add the remaining ingredients and simmer for 40 minutes, then strain through a sieve lined with muslin. The stock is now ready to use or store.

   To make the shellfish reduction, liquidize the stock before straining. Pass it through a conical strainer and then through a very fine-meshed or muslin-lined sieve, squeezing out as much of the liquid as possible. Return the strained liquid to a clean pan, bring to the boil and boil until reduced to about 150 ml (5 fl oz). It is now ready to use or store.

HOLLANDAISE SAUCE

Serves 4

225 g (8 oz) unsalted
    butter
2 tablespoons water
2 egg yolks
Juice of 1 lemon
A good pinch of cayenne
    pepper
½ teaspoon salt

*I like my hollandaise sauce to be quite lemony. The sauce is so rich it does
need some acidity to balance it.*

Clarify the butter by melting it over a low heat, then skimming off any froth from
the surface. Pour off the clear butter into another pan, leaving behind the white
solids that will have collected at the bottom. Keep the clarified butter warm.

Put the water and egg yolks in a stainless steel or glass bowl set over a pan
of simmering water, making sure the base of the bowl is not touching the
water. Whisk until voluminous and creamy. Remove the bowl from the pan and
gradually whisk in the warm clarified butter, building up an emulsion. Add the
lemon juice, the cayenne pepper and salt. If the sauce splits, warm a clean pan,
add 1 tablespoon of water and graduallly whisk in the curdled sauce.
Hollandaise is best used immediately but you can hold it for up to 2 hours if
you keep it covered in a warm place, such as over a pan of warm water.

QUICK HOLLANDAISE SAUCE
Use the same ingredients for the recipe above but put egg yolks, lemon juice
and water into a liquidizer. Turn on and pour in the hot clarified butter. Season
with cayenne pepper and salt.

GREEN CURRY PASTE

Makes 75g (3oz)

2–4 green chillies
1 medium onion
2 lemon grass stalks
2.5 cm (1 in) piece of fresh
    galangal or root ginger
25 g (1 oz) fresh coriander
3 garlic cloves, peeled
1 teaspoon ground coriander
1 teaspoon ground cumin
2 pared strips of lime zest,
1 teaspoon *blachan*
1 teaspoon salt
2 tablespoons water

*This paste is made green with lots of fresh green chillies and fresh coriander.
As with the red curry paste below, although there are plenty of commercial
pastes available now, freshly made curry pastes and masalas are much more
fragrant and take me right back to those bustling streets in Bangkok.*

Roughly chop the chillies, onion, lemon grass and galangal or ginger. Put all the
ingredients in a good processor and blend until smooth.

OLIVE OIL DRESSING

Makes 85 ml (3 fl oz)

85 ml (3 fl oz) extra virgin
   olive oil
½ tablespoon white
   wine vinegar
½ teaspoon salt

Put all the ingredients in a bowl and whisk them together. Toss with salad just before serving.

MUSTARD DRESSING

Makes 120 ml (4 fl oz)

85 ml (3 fl oz) sunflower oil
1 tablespoon white
   wine vinegar
½ teaspoon salt
½ shallot, finely chopped
½ small garlic clove,
   finely chopped
1 teaspoon English
   mustard

Either whisk all the ingredients together in a small bowl or put them in a screw-top jar and shake well to combine.

MUSTARD MAYONNAISE

Makes 300 ml (10 fl oz)

1 tablespoon English
   mustard
1 egg
1 tablespoon white
   wine vinegar
¾ teaspoon salt
A few turns of the white
   pepper mill
300 ml (10 fl oz)
   sunflower oil

This is good with dressed crab, cooked prawns and boiled whelks. See the recipe for Olive Oil Mayonnaise (opposite) if you prefer to make your mayonnaise by hand.

Put the mustard, egg, vinegar, salt and pepper into a liquidizer. Turn on the machine and then gradually add the oil through the hole in the lid until you have a thick emulsion. The mayonnaise will keep for about a week in the fridge.

OLIVE OIL MAYONNAISE

This recipe includes instructions for making mayonnaise in the liquidizer and by hand. It is lighter made mechanically because the process uses a whole egg, and it's very quick, but I still prefer making it by hand since I like to do as much as possible in the kitchen by hand.

To make the mayonnaise in a machine, you need to use a whole egg. Put the egg, vinegar and salt into a liquidizer. Turn on the machine and then gradually add the oil through the hole in the lid until you have a thick emulsion.

To make the mayonnaise by hand, use 2 egg yolks. Make sure all the ingredients are at room temperature before beginning. Put the egg yolks, vinegar and salt into a mixing bowl, then place the bowl on a tea towel to stop it slipping. Using a wire whisk, beat the oil into the egg mixture a few drops at a time until you have incorporated it all. Once you have carefully added about the same volume of oil as the original mixture of egg yolks and vinegar, you can add the oil more quickly.

The mayonnaise will keep for about a week in the fridge.

Makes 300 ml (10 fl oz)

1 egg or 2 egg yolks
2 teaspoons white wine
  vinegar
½ teaspoon salt
300 ml (10 fl oz) olive oil

LEMON MAYONNAISE

See the recipe for Olive Oil Mayonnaise *(above) if you prefer to make your mayonnaise by hand.*

Put the lemon juice, egg, lemon zest and salt into a liquidizer. Turn on the machine and then gradually add the oil through the hole in the lid until you have a thick emulsion. The mayonnaise will keep for about a week in the fridge.

Makes 300 ml (10 fl oz)

1 tablespoon lemon juice
1 egg
Finely grated zest of
  1 small lemon
½ teaspoon salt
150 ml (5 fl oz) sunflower
  oil
150 ml (5 fl oz) olive oil

TAPENADE

Makes 150 g (5 oz)

150 g (5 oz) pitted black
olives
8 anchovy fillets
2 tablespoons capers
1 lemon juice
2 tablespoons cognac
½ teaspoon mustard
Olive oil

Tapenade is a purée of black olives with anchovies and capers. It is available in all supermarkets now but if you want to make your own, this is the recipe I use.

Mix all the ingredients together and purée.

EGG PASTA DOUGH

Makes 100 g (4 oz)

100 g (4 oz) plain flour
A large pinch of salt
¼ teaspoon olive oil
1 egg
2 egg yolks

This makes a rich, deep-yellow pasta dough which is ideal for making ravioli, since the extra egg helps them hold together during poaching. If you want a general-purpose pasta dough that is not so rich, just use 1 egg in the recipe. It will provide enough liquid to produce a stiff dough suitable for rolling through a pasta machine. If rolling by hand, you may need to add a little extra water. The drier the dough is when you are making pasta, the less it will stick together when shaped.

Put all the ingredients into a bowl and mix together into a ball. Turn out on to a lightly floured surface and knead for about 10 minutes, until smooth and elastic. Wrap in cling film and leave to rest for 10–15 minutes before using. This dough will not keep for more than a couple of days wrapped in the fridge.

BAKED RICE

Serves 4

350 g (12 oz) long-grain
rice, such as Thai
jasmine or basmati
A small knob of butter
½ teaspoon salt
700 ml (24 fl oz) boiling
water

This way of preparing rice prevents it becoming overcooked or waterlogged. Properly cooked rice is a good accompaniment to almost any fish dish in the Hot and Spicy chapter.

Pre-heat the oven to 200°C/400°F/Gas 6.

Wash the rice in cold water until the water runs clear. Melt the butter in a flameproof casserole dish, add the rice, salt and water and bring to the boil. Cover with a tight-fitting lid or foil, and bake in the oven for 15 minutes.

WALNUT BREAD

This is quick to make because it requires no bulk proving.

Mix the flour, salt and sugar together in a large bowl. Put the yeast in a small bowl and gradually stir in 150 ml (5 fl oz) of the water. Add the yeast mixture to the remaining water and then gradually stir it into the flour with the melted butter to make a soft dough.

Turn the dough out on to a lightly floured surface and knead for 3 minutes, then knead in the walnuts. (The dough only has a short kneading time because the flour is low in gluten. Strong flours need longer to 'develop' the gluten, i.e. to make it as elastic as possible to trap air.) Cut the dough in half and form into 2 fat sausage shapes. Put them in 2 buttered 450 g (1 lb) loaf tins. Tie each tin into a large plastic bag and leave in a warm place for 45 minutes–1 hour or until doubled in size.

Pre-heat the oven to 230°C/450°F/Gas 8.

Sprinkle the sesame seeds over the loaves. Bake in the centre of the oven for 25–30 minutes, then remove the loaves from the tins and return them to the oven for a further 5 minutes to crisp the crust. Leave to cool on a wire rack.

Makes two 450 g (1 lb) loaves

600 g (1 lb 6 oz) wholewheat flour
2 teaspoons salt
1 tablespoon light soft brown sugar
15 g (½ oz) fresh yeast
450 ml (15 fl oz) hand-hot water
20 g (¾ oz) butter, melted
40 g (1½ oz) walnut pieces
2 teaspoons sesame seeds

RED CURRY PASTE

This is a curry paste made red with lots of fresh red chillies and paprika. As well as being the base for the Thai Red Seafood *on p. 70, it's also very good for using in meat and vegetable curries.*

Blend all the ingredients in a food processor until smooth. If necessary, add a little water to help it purée more easily.

Makes 75g (3oz)

5 large red finger chillies, roughly chopped
1 teaspoon salt
1 teaspoon chopped fresh galangal or root ginger
1 tablespoon lemon grass
3 tablespoons chopped garlic
3 tablespoons roughly chopped shallots
1 teaspoon ground coriander
1 teaspoon ground cumin
1 teaspoon *blachan* (optional)
2 teaspoons paprika
½ teaspoon turmeric powder
1 tablespoon sunflower oil

Basic Sweet Pastry

Sufficient to line a
21–23 cm (8 ½–9 in) flan tin

100 g (4 oz) plain flour
65 g (2½ oz) chilled butter,
  cut into pieces
25 g (1 oz) caster sugar
½ tablespoon beaten egg
1 tablespoon cold water

Put the flour and butter in a food processor and blend until the mixture looks like fine breadcrumbs. Add the sugar and blend for a few seconds. Mix the beaten egg with the cold water. Turn on the machine and pour the egg through the feed tube – after a couple of seconds the mixture will start to stick together in small lumps. Switch off the machine, tip the dough into a bowl and bring together gently into a ball. Chill for 30 minutes before use.

Stock Syrup

Makes 600 ml (1 pint)

600 ml (1 pint) water
350 g (12 oz) granulated
  sugar
Pared zest of 2 lemons
Pared zest of 2 small
  oranges
1 vanilla pod

This is useful for poaching fruit and can also be used in fruit salads and sorbets.

Put all the ingredients into a pan and leave over a low heat until the sugar has completely dissolved. Bring to the boil, then remove from the heat and set aside for 30 minutes to allow the flavours to infuse. Lift out the zest and vanilla pod (you can rinse the vanilla pod, dry it and save it for later use). The syrup can be used immediately or stored in the fridge for up to 2 weeks.

Preserved Lemons

10 lemons
275 g (10 oz) salt
1.2 litres (2 pints) water

These can be used finely chopped in salads, dressings and sauces.

Cut the lemons almost into quarters, leaving them joined at one end. Sprinkle a little salt into the centre of each, then arrange them, tightly packed, in a plastic or glass container. Bring the water and the rest of the salt to the boil in a large pan. Boil until the salt has dissolved, then remove from the heat and leave to cool. Pour the brine over the lemons, weigh them down with some sort of non-metallic weight and leave for 3–4 weeks before using. They will keep indefinitely.

Listing of American, Australian and New Zealand Fish

The following list gives local names, where necessary, or suggests a similar fish as an alternative.

British Isles	USA	Australia and NZ
Anchovies	Anchovies	Anchovies
Brill	Petrale sole, brill sole	Sole, flounder, brill
Cod	Cod, Pacific cod	Blue cod
Coley	Haddock	Hoki
Conger eel	Conger eel	Blue grenadier, ribbon fish
Dover sole	English sole, gray sole	Sole, flounder
Flounder	Flounder	Flounder
Garfish	Skipper	Garfish
Grey mullet	Mullet, striped bass	Mullet
Gurnard	Searobin	Gurnard
Haddock	Haddock	Blue cod, hoki
Hake	Hake, silver hake	Hake, gemfish
Huss	Spurdog	Flake
John Dory	John Dory, Oreo Dory	John Dory
Lemon sole	English sole, flounder	Sole, flounder
Ling	Cusk, cobia	Ling
Mackerel	Atlantic mackerel	Mackerel, Spanish mackerel
Megrim sole	Flounder	Flounder
Monkfish	Monkfish, anglerfish	Monkfish, stargazer
Red bream	Red snapper	Snapper
Red mullet	Goatfish	Red mullet, barbounia
Salmon	Salmon	Atlantic salmon
Sardines	Sardines	Sardines, pilchards
Sea bass	Sea bass	Jewfish
Sea bream	Bream	Bream
Sea trout	Steelhead trout	Ocean trout
Shark	Shark	Shark, flake
Skate	Skate	Skate
Snapper	Snapper	Snapper
Squid	Squid, calamari	Squid, calamari
Swordfish	Swordfish	Swordfish, broadbill
Tuna	Tuna	Tuna
Turbot	Flounder	Sole, John Dory, flounder

Shellfish

British Isles	USA	Australia and NZ
Brown crab	Dungeness crab	Blue swimming crab
Clams	Hardshell clams	Clams
	Littleneck clams	Littleneck clams, pipi
	Cherrystone clams	Clams
Cockles	Cockles	Pipi, cockles
Crayfish, crawfish	Crayfish, spiny lobster	Yabbies, marron
Lobster	Lobster	Rock lobster
Mussels	Blue Mussels	Mussels
Oysters	Oysters	Oysters
Prawns	Shrimp	Prawn
Scallop	Sea scallop, bay scallop	Sea scallop, bay scallop
Spider crab	Spider crab, snow crab	Blue swimming crab, salad crab
Spiny lobster	Spiny lobster, crawfish	Crayfish, spiny lobster

Alternative Fish

This is a list of all the fish and shellfish in the book, giving an alternative to use if you can't get hold of the one in the recipe. The alternatives are not necessarily the most similar fish biologically but rather ones that work almost, if not equally, as well.

Conger eel: Shark, swordfish or tuna
Huss: Tope or shark
Mackerel: Herring
Sardines: Sprats
Salmon: Large sea trout
Sea trout: Salmon or trout
John Dory: Turbot or brill
Ocean perch: Snapper or grey mullet
Sea bream: Bass or snapper
Grey mullet: Bass or gurnard
Red mullet: Any of the bream family or sea bass
Sea bass: Grey mullet or red mullet
Cod: Haddock
Garfish: Grey mullet, gurnard, Dover sole
Gurnard: Sea bass or weever fish
Monkfish: Chargrilled recipes – swordfish; others – turbot or John Dory

Haddock: Cod or hake
Hake: Haddock or cod
Ling: Monkfish
Shark: Tuna, swordfish or conger eel
Tuna: Swordfish or monkfish
Dover sole: Witch sole, sand sole; fillets of Dover sole – megrim sole, lemon sole, witch sole
Lemon sole: Megrim sole, witch sole, plaice
Plaice: Lemon sole, dabs, witch sole, flounder
Turbot: Brill, John Dory
Skate: Angel shark, porbeagle shark
Squid: Cuttlefish
Brown crab: Spider crab
Spider crab: Brown crab
Scallops: Slices of monkfish
Prawns: Another species of prawn
Clams: Cockles or mussels
Oysters: Mussels or clams
Lobster: Spiny lobster
Spiny lobster: Lobster

Index